TAROT and the MILLENNIUM

REVIEW COPY, NOT FOR SALE

TAROT and the MILLENNIUM:
The Story of Who's On the Cards and Why
by: Timothy Betts, Ph.D.

Internet: http://tarot-cards.com
Pub date: July 98 (shipping now)
ISBN 0-9641020-5-6 $24.95 US (softcover)

The author

TAROT and the MILLENNIUM

The Story of Who's On the Cards and Why

Timothy Betts, Ph.D.

New Perspective Media
1998

Published by New Perspective Media, 7 Plumtree Road, Rancho Palos Verdes, CA 90275-5911

First Edition. ISBN 0-9641020-5-6

Publisher's Cataloging-in-Publication
(*Provided by Quality Books, Inc.*)

Betts, Timothy, 1945-
Tarot and the millennium : the story of who's on the cards and why / Timothy Betts. -- 1st ed.
p. cm.
Includes bibliographical references and index.
Preassigned LCCN: 98-91311
ISBN: 0-9641020-5-6

1. Tarot. I. Title.

BF1879.T2B488 1998 133.3'2424
QBI98-371

Printed in the United States of America.

M 9 8 7 6 5 4 3 2 1

For Keith and Craig

6. Tarot and the Millennium

WHAT IS IT THAT HATH BEEN? THE SAME THING THAT SHALL BE. What is it that hath been done? the same that shall be done.

Nothing under the sun is new, neither is any man able to say, 'Behold this is new': for it hath already gone before in the ages that were before us.

THERE IS NO REMEMBRANCE OF FORMER THINGS: nor indeed of those things which hereafter are to come shall there be any remembrance...

— *Ecclesiastes* 1:9-11

Grateful acknowledgement is made to the following for permission to reproduce materials used in this book:

The Beinecke Rare Book and Manuscript Library, Yale University. Cary ITA sheet 3S (*New Haven deck*) and ITA 109 (*Visconti-Modrone deck*).

Henry René D'Allemagne, *Les Cartes à Jouer du XIVe au XXe Siècle*, Paris. (*Tarot of Marseilles, d'Este* and *Charles VI decks*).

Michael Dummett, *The Game of Tarot from Ferrara to Salt Lake City*. By permission of Gerald Duckworth & Co. Ltd.

Francesco Gabrieli, *Arab Historians of the Crusades – Selected and Translated from the Arabic Sources*. Edited/translated by E. J. Costello. Copyright © 1969 Routledge & Kegan Paul Ltd.

The National Gallery of Art, Washington. Italian 15th Century Playing Cards: detail (*Washington deck*), Rosenwald Collection, © Board of Trustees, National Gallery of Art, Washington.

The Pierpont Morgan Library, New York. M. 630 (*Visconti-Sforza deck*).

The Szépmüvészeti Múzeum, Budapest. Playing card, Inv. Nr.:5044 & 5045 (*Budapest deck*).

Contents

Chapter One

Chance or Design?

Invited, some years ago, to call upon an acquaintance of our friends, Madame the Countess of H., who had come from Germany or Switzerland, we found her busy playing a game with some other people.

"We're playing a game you surely don't know," she said.

"Perhaps, what is it?" I asked.

"The game of Tarot," she replied.

"I had occasion to see it when I was very young, but I know nothing about it," I said.

"It is a rhapsody of the most bizarre, most absurd figures," she said. And selecting an example, she carefully choose one loaded with figures with no relation to its name, saying, "This is the World."

I glanced at it, and immediately recognized the allegory. Everyone stopped playing and came to see this wonderful card and appreciate what they'd never noticed before. Each person showed me another card, and within a quarter of an hour the deck was examined, explained and proclaimed to be Egyptian. And since none of this was a product of our imagination, but the result of informed and knowledgeable accounts of the game in harmony with everything known

> about Egyptian ideas, we promised ourselves to share it with the public one day; persuaded they would be pleased with a discovery and offering of this kind, an Egyptian book which has survived barbarism, the ravages of time, accidental and deliberate fires, and ignorance - the most disastrous of all.[1]
>
> — *Du Jeu des Tarots*

ANTOINE COURT DE GÉBELIN, SCHOLAR OF ANCIENT MYTHOLOGIES and an acquaintance of Benjamin Franklin, published this account of Tarot in 1781 – inaugurating its scientific study. De Gébelin was seeking a primitive tongue, the parent of all modern languages, which would unify and explain the world's mythologies. His investigations on Tarot, reported in a single chapter of his eight volume opus *The Primitive World: Analyzed and Compared with the Modern One* (*Monde Primitif: analsé et comparé avec le monde moderne*), was only part of this larger project. Nevertheless, it's what he's remembered for today; chiefly because his theories have been appropriated by occultists ever since. It's difficult to say how de Gébelin himself would feel about this. For immediately after his "Game of Tarot" (*Du Jeu des Tarots*) chapter follows "Studies on Tarot: and Divination Using Tarot Cards" (*Recherches Sur Les Tarots: et sur la divination par les cartes des tarots*) by an anonymous author, *Monsieur* C. de M.*** – inaugurating their occult study. Thus, the scientific mind clandestinely found room for the supernatural. Perhaps he took all this seriously, perhaps not.

Cartomancy, or divination using cards, was in vogue in the Paris of de Gébelin's day. He was well aware of how much a Tarot-cartomancy connection could increase subscriptions to his book. On the other hand, he wasn't about to sully his scholarly reputation for money. Neither should we let the second article blind us to the scientific value of the first. De Gébelin made two major claims about Tarot: first, Tarot cards have meanings, and second, their symbolism identifies them as Egyptian.

It's popular to point out that de Gébelin worked 20 years before Napoleon's Egyptian campaign and the beginnings of modern Egyptology, and 40 years before Champollion deciphered hieroglyphics, thereby dismissing him out of hand. But this overlooks the fact that modern research proves him right. Tarot symbolism does have Egyptian and Babylonian antecedents. So he can't be disposed of so easily.

Some would like to, since the scholarly, scientific study of Tarot he began has borne so little fruit. Only a handful of authors have managed to add anything substantial to the questions he addressed. In comparison, the occult side of the subject has burgeoned.

Occult interpretations of Tarot reached the English speaking world by the end of the nineteenth century when the now famous Order of the Golden Dawn attracted attention as influential writers began incorporating its doctrines into their novels and poems. W. B. Yeats belonged to the Golden Dawn. Both Charles William's mystical novel *The Greater Trumps* and T. S. Eliot's poem *The Waste Land* incorporate some of its tenets. In 1918 an edition of the *Pictorial Key to the Tarot* by one of the Golden Dawn's members, Arthur Edward Waite, landed on America's shores and the rest is history.

In response, academics have attempted to gain the high ground with their own hypothesis of Tarot's origins:

> "We shall not gain any enlightenment if we study the iconography of the Tarot pack. ...it is highly improbable that, by this means, we shall learn anything relevant to the game played with Tarot cards, or, therefore to the primary purpose for which the pack was originally devised....
>
> In the mid-fifteenth century, indices of any kind were unknown: card players were used to identifying each card – court card or numeral card – from the whole design, not from one special ingredient of it. It was therefore necessary to choose, for the picture cards, a series of very definite subjects, that could be easily distinguished, and with each of which could be associated a name that could be used to refer to the card.
>
> The subjects on the Tarot triumphs – the Sun, the Devil, Death, the Virtues, the Wheel of Fortune, Love, the Pope and all the rest – served just this purpose. By and large, they were standard subjects of medieval and Renaissance

> iconography, to be met with in many other contexts; they were precisely the sort of subjects which any fifteenth-century Italian, faced with the problem of devising a sequence of twenty-one picture cards, would have been likely to select.
>
> We can derive some entertainment from asking why that particular selection was made, and whether there is any symbolic meaning to the order in which they were placed; and we may or may not come up with a plausible or illuminating answer. (If we do not, that may not indicate that we have failed to solve the riddle; there may be no riddle to solve.)"
>
> – *The Game of Tarot*

In reality, this is just as strong an assertion – without proof – as de Gébelin's. It claims that Tarot has *no* meaning whatsoever, and that historical records point to its origin in fifteenth-century Italian noble's courts. This is what I call the "chance" hypothesis, and de Gébelin's, one of many possible "design" hypotheses of Tarot's origins. Is iconography a relevant or legitimate subject of study? Are we wasting our time looking for meaning where none exists? No one has proven the chance hypothesis wrong. On the other hand, it's difficult to prove correct. So it must take its place along side the many other conjectures about Tarot until something comes along to supplant them all.

A Medieval Story

THIS BOOK PURPORTS TO BE THAT SOMETHING. IT AGREES WITH DE GÉBELIN that Tarot has meaning and the design hypothesis is correct – but disagrees that it's Egyptian. The symbolism on Tarot cards has been reused on a number of occasions since ancient times. It's not unusual in such borrowings for symbols themselves to remain unchanged while their meanings are reinterpreted. Thus, the same Dolphin that adorned Nero's palace in ancient Rome was transformed into an icon of Christ as friend, savior, and guide of souls. De Gébelin neglected to check for these other possibilities and missed a stunning discovery.

I believe that Tarot represents a medieval retelling of the story of Christ's Second Coming and the ensuing Millennium. Tarot is not about the hoary past, it's about the future and the end of history! This is, and is not, surprising. On the one hand, the Second Coming has been one of the most familiar themes in western civilization for almost 2,000 years. If you knew absolutely nothing about Tarot and had to guess it's meaning, this would be a good bet. On the other hand, cards like The Fool, Emperor, and Lovers seem to have nothing to do with the Second Coming – at least not to our eyes. A preliminary answer to this objection is that thinking has changed considerably in the almost 600 years since Tarot was created. We're more naive about the last times now. We find it difficult to interpret the cards correctly for three reasons: first, late medieval and early Renaissance people postulated elaborate scenarios for the last times that only a handful of scholars are familiar with today; second, many medieval meanings of familiar symbols were forgotten in the Renaissance; and third, entire categories or modes of medieval thought are held in little repute today.

As an example of what I mean by scenarios, these fifteen signs of the last times were once common knowledge:

"Day one. The sea will rise forty cubits higher than the mountains, and will rear up like a solid wall.

Day two. It will sink so far down that it will be barely visible.

Day three. Monsters of the deep will appear on the surface of the sea, and their roaring will rise to the heavens. And no one but God will understand it.

Day four. The sea and all the waters will catch fire.

Day five. The trees and the planets will exude a bloody dew. All birds of the air will come together, each of its kind, and they will neither eat nor drink, for fear of the strict Judge.

Day six. Cities and all that is built will collapse, and fiery bolts of lightning will appear from sundown to sunrise.

Day seven. Stones will rub one against the other, and break into four pieces.

Day eight. An earthquake will shake the whole earth, laying low man and beast.

> Day nine. The earth will be leveled; mountains and hills will be reduced to dust.
>
> Day ten. Men will come out of the caverns in which they fled, and will wander around like madmen, unable to converse with one another.
>
> Day eleven. Skeletons of the dead will come forth from their tombs. And all the tombs will open from sunrise to sunset so that all the dead may come forth.
>
> Day twelve. The stars will fall.
>
> Day thirteen. All living beings will die, to rise again with the dead.
>
> Day fourteen. The heavens and the earth will be consumed by fire.
>
> Day fifteen. There will be a new heaven and a new earth, and all will rise again.
>
> – *The Golden Legend*

These omens appear in the opening chapter of one of the most popular works of the Middle Ages, and were illustrated in some of the first mass produced books for popular consumption. How many of us know of them today?

And how many are familiar with the lion as a symbol for resurrection? It was once believed that:

> "When the Lioness gives birth,
> Her cub drops to the earth, stillborn;
> Showing no signs of life.
> Until, three days later, the father
> Kisses and licks it out of love;
> And in that way, breathes life into it.
> No other remedy could save it.
>
> So it was with Jesus Christ
>
> . . .
>
> When our Savior was entombed,
> He only remained three days.
> And on the third day, his Father

> Raised him up and breathed life into him.
> Just as the Lion,
> Breathes life into its little cub." [2]

This is why a lion is pictured near the tomb of the risen Christ on the stained-glass window of the cathedral at Bourges, France. As today, the lion was also a symbol of strength and power then. But the first meaning was lost in the Renaissance when artists insisted on portraying objects as they appeared, or later during the Protestant Reformation, when the Bible became the ultimate arbitrator for symbolism.

Finally, the Middle Ages recognized modes of logic we reject today. I use the word logic; their own term was intelligences, insights, perceptions, or understandings (*intellectus*). They believed people could comprehend and be convinced of truth argued in ways which appear bewildering, if not superstitious, to us today. We, for example, are comfortable interpreting the Bible in both a historical and moral sense. To these, the Middle Ages added two additional modes, encapsulated in the mnemonic:

> "HISTORY teaches deeds; ALLEGORY, faith;
> MORALITY, how to act; and ANAGOGY what lies ahead." [3]

Allegory and anagogy have been largely passed over by modern thought. The former established elaborate correspondences called Types between persons and events of the Old Testament foreshadowing Christ and the promises of the New Testament. The latter is poorly translated by "what lies ahead, what to expect, or what to look forward to." It denoted a mystical or spiritual interpretation, hidden from the senses. Important symbols could be simultaneously comprehended under each mode, leading to four different interpretations:

> "...one and the same JERUSALEM can be taken in four senses: historically as the CITY OF THE JEWS; allegorically as CHURCH OF CHRIST, anagogically as the HEAVENLY CITY OF GOD 'which is the mother of us all,' and morally, as the SOUL OF MAN."
>
> – *Conference Fourteen*

Some of these interpretations might seem as every bit as bizarre as ones offered for Tarot, except that they've been documented in religious writings and studied extensively by scholars. This fact proves to be the key to unlocking Tarot's secrets.

Because the Second Coming story is so well documented, a wealth of relevant materials exist from history, religion, literature and art which can be applied to understanding Tarot. We know, for instance, who the historical figures on the Tarot cards are and what they did and said – sometimes in their own words. We can identify the groups whose beliefs are portrayed on the cards and follow them in history for over 200 years. And we can identify the specific authors who formulated these ideas well enough to name John of Rupescissa as the "intellectual father" of Tarot. Finally, we can even say why some cards look the way they do. At least I think so.

Contemporary Writings Prove It So

MY AIM IS TO CONVINCE YOU THIS IS TRUE. I'M NOT GOING TO MAKE any pretense of being unbiased in my presentation. Like an attorney defending a client, I intend to present the facts for my case in the strongest possible way. The only favor I ask is that you try to hear all the evidence before you make up your mind. Sometimes the whole *is* greater than the sum of its parts, and it's exceedingly rare that a single piece of evidence resolves all doubts on a topic. But ultimately the case will be yours to decide.

To help you do that, I've reproduced as many contemporary writings (shown in alternate type) as I could find. And occasionally, as above, I've capitalized what I want you to notice. It's one thing to read in the popular press that Court de Gébelin asserted Tarot encapsulates the wisdom of ancient Egypt, and another to learn, in his own words, that he discovered that fact in just fifteen minutes, while at a party! And the example of the four meanings of "Jerusalem" captures better than pages of discussion the difficulties of understanding medieval thought.

Original writings have an immediacy and candor about them.

Their authors had no way of anticipating us as their audience, and can't help revealing, warts and all, more truth than they imagined. Very few of these sources are in English. Most are written in Latin, or in medieval French, German, and Italian, riddled with obsolete words and odd spellings. I've translated some myself and used the translations of others when available, to make them accessible to English readers. For those of you who are better at languages than myself, I've reproduced my originals in the Translations section at the end of each chapter. The rest, as well as other studies I've consulted, can be found in the works cited in the Bibliography there.

Many materials can be also be found on the Internet. Medieval scholarship is exemplary in the way it uses on-line resources. There are several excellent e-mail lists and a half-dozen key web-sites which lead one to literally thousands of pages of medieval texts, and new pages are being added daily. For that reason, I've supplemented each Bibliography with a special Internet section giving URLs (http://www.etc...) which you may want consult. At the end of this chapter, you'll find some of the key sites from which you can begin your own searches.

Contemporary Illustrations

AGAIN, MY ILLUSTRATIONS ARE EITHER ORIGINALS OR ADAPTATIONS OF ORIGINALS. This means the youngest are contemporary with the American Constitution, while the oldest date from the time of the Magna Carta, to put matters in perspective. While some art works this old are truly magnificent, only a few that you'll see here can make that claim. Cards and manuscripts are frequently smudged, torn, or cut in two, and their execution may seem amateurish and sloppy. On the other hand, they're the real thing, so I've done a minimum of retouching to make them attractive to modern tastes. I have, however, altered contrasts to make their details visible.

My guiding principle with original sources has been to allow you to re-experience for yourself what passed for common knowledge in times long past – without the filter of "experts" of one persuasion or another. When you do, I'm confident that you'll agree with me the evidence leads to only one conclusion. Tarot tells the story of the Second Coming of Christ and the Millennium.

Bibliography

The (*New*) *Catholic Encyclopedia*, various editions, 15-17 Vols.

Louis Charbonneau-Lassay, "The Dolphin, "The Pelican, & The Lion." In *The Bestiary of Christ*, trans: D.M. Dooling, (Arkana, 1991).

Michael Dummett, "The Game of Tarot." In *The Game of Tarot from Ferrara to Salt Lake City*, (Gerald Duckworth and Co., 1980).

Antoine Court de Gébelin, "Du Jeu des Tarots, & Recherches Sur Les Tarots." In *Monde Primitif: analsé et comparé avec le monde moderne,* (Paris: 1781) Vol VIII.

Bruce M. Metzger, Michael D. Coogan, eds., *The Oxford Companion to the Bible*, (Oxford UP, 1993).

Gertrude Moakley, "The Waite-Smith Tarot." In *Bulletin of The New York Public Library*, Vol 58, No 10, Oct 1954, pp 471-5.

Jacobus de Voragine, "The Advent of the Lord." In *The Golden Legend: Readings on the Saints*, trans W. G. Ryan, (Princeton UP., 1993), Vol I.

Arthur Edward Waite, *The Pictorial Key to the Tarot*, reprint: (Barnes & Noble, 1995).

Internet

Note: There's no need to type this yourself. Current links to these and future sites, as they become available, can be found at: http://tarot-cards.com

Catholic Encyclopedia
http://www.knight.org/advent/cathen/

Christian Classics Ethereal Library
http://ccel.wheaton.edu/

Conference Fourteen
http://www.osb.org/osb/gen/topics/lectio/cassian/conf/book2/conf14.html#14.0

Ecole Initiative_Early Church Documents
http://www.evansville.edu/~ecoleweb/documents.html
Fathers of the Church
http://www.knight.org/advent/fathers/
Historische Ressourcen Im Netz (Mittelalter)
http://www.phil.uni-erlangen.de/~p1ges/ma_resso.html
Labyrinth Home Page
http://www.georgetown.edu/labyrinth/labyrinth-home.html
Medieval Sourcebook
http://www.fordham.edu/halsall/sbook.html
NetSERF: The Internet Connection for Medieval Resources
http://www.cua.edu/www/hist/netserf/home.htm
Online Medieval and Classic Library (DL SunSite)
http://sunsite.berkeley.edu/OMACL/
ORB: Online Reference Book for Medieval Studies
http://orb.rhodes.edu/
Types in Scripture
http://www.knight.org/advent/cathen/15107a.htm

Translations

1. Invité il y a quelques années à aller voir une Dame de nos Amies, Madame la C. d'H. qui arrivoir d'Allemagne ou de Suisse, nous la trouvâmes occupée à jouer à ce Jeu avec quelques autres Personnes. Nous jouons à un Jeu que vous ne connoissez sûrement pas... Cela se peut; quel est-il?... Le Jeu des Tarots... J'ai eu occasion de le voir étant fort jeune, mais je n'en ai aucune idée... C'est une rapsodie des figures les plus bisarres, les plus extravagantes: en voi-la une, par exemple; on eut soin de choisir la plus chargée de figures, & n'ayant aucun rapport à son nom, c'est le Monde: j'y jette les yeux, & aussi-tôt j'en reconnois l'Allégorie: chacun de quittér son Jeu & de venir voir cette Carte merveilleuse où j'appercevois ce qu'ils n'avoient jamais vû: chacun de m'en montrer une autre: en un quart-d'heure le Jeu fut parcouru, expliqué, déclaré Egyptien: & comme ce n'étiot point le jeu de notre imagination, mais l'effet des rapports choisis &

sensibles de ce jeu avec tout ce qu'on connoît d'idées Egyptiennes, nous nous promîmes bien d'en faire part quelque jour au Public; persuadés qu'il auroit pour agréable une découverte & un présent de cette nature, un Livre Egyptien échappé à la barbarie, aux ravages du Tems, aux incendies accidentelles & aux volontaires, à l'ignorance plus désastreuse encore.

2. Quant la femele foone
Le foon chiet a terre mort;
De vivre n'aura ia confort
Iusque li pere, au tierz iior
Le souffle et leche par amor;
En tel maniere le respire
Ne porreit aveir autre mire.

Autresi fu de Ihesu-Christ
L'umanité que por nos prist,
Que por l'amor de nos vesti,
Paine et travail pos nos senti;
Sa deité ne senti rien
Issi creez, i ferez bien.

Quand Deix fu mis el monument
Treis iorz i fu tant solement
Et au tierz ior le respira
Li pere, qui le suscita
Autresi comme li lion
Respire son petit foon.

3. Litera, gesta docet; quid credas, allegoria;
Moralis, quid agas; quo tendas anagogia.

24. Tarot and the Millennium

Chapter Two

Psychic Advisor

I DISCOVERED TAROT QUITE BY ACCIDENT. I HOST AN INTERNET WEBSITE, and was looking for a new feature to promote. Telephone psychic advisors are sort of an in-joke in Southern California right now. Heavily promoted on television, no one will admit to calling one, yet they're making money hand over fist for their owners. An Internet Psychic Advisor might be just the thing to attract web surfers to my site.

I hadn't given the subject much thought when I happened upon a mail order ad for a book on Tarot. This might be useful. Didn't psychics and fortune-tellers use Tarot cards? As I read the description in the catalogue, my brain conjured up visions of Gypsies and Lovers cards, vaguely recollected from old James Bond films. An aura of mystery enveloped the subject, and the cards themselves were exciting, a definite plus on the Internet where graphics count for a lot. Best of all, the book was on sale! That clinched the matter – and I added *The Pictorial Key to the Tarot* to my buy list.

When the order arrived, I set to work right away. I learned there are 78 cards in a Tarot deck, divided into four ordinary suits, and 22 special picture cards, like The Lovers card I remembered. Actually, ordinary is stretching it even for the ordinary suits, because if you do the math you'll see each of them contains fourteen cards, not thirteen like a standard deck. Two cards, a Knight and a Page, replace the Jack of standard decks. And instead of Clubs, Diamonds, Hearts and Spades, Tarot suits signs are Wands, Swords, Cups and Coins, or as my book called the latter, Pentacles.

But the 22 picture cards are the real show-stoppers. One of them, The Fool, sometimes looks a little like a Joker; but the rest have to be seen to be appreciated. They're so unique some people collect Tarot decks instead of stamps, coins or antique toys. But whatever their differences, all decks bear a similarity to one another, and their cards have standard names like The Wheel of Fortune, Hanged Man, Death, Star, etc., or their foreign language equivalents. And usually, they're numbered from one to 21; except for The Fool, which is often unnumbered, or card zero. The 22 picture cards are called the Major Arcana. The rest, naturally enough, are the Minor Arcana.

Many modern Tarot decks make the Minor Arcana cards picture cards too. This was the case in *The Pictorial Key* and is now a regular feature of fortune-telling decks. Before this, ordinary Tarot suits repeated their suit symbols one, two, three, etc. number of times, just like standard decks. And the decks were used for playing card games, and still are in parts of Italy and Switzerland today. These are the Tarot decks we'll be primarily concerned with.

Inventing the Psychic Advisor

THE FIRST THING MY INTERNET PSYCHIC ADVISOR WOULD NEED WAS SOME "BRAINS." I found everything required in the back of my Tarot book under a discussion of spreads, the term for how to lay out the cards, and what to say while doing so. There are many, many spreads, but fortunately after you learn one, the others are variations on what you already know. The spread most people learn first is the Celtic or ten-card spread, and it's worthy of further study.

The first step of the Celtic spread is to choose a card to repre-

A Knight and Page (*below*), in addition to the king and queen (*above*), make up the court cards of a Tarot deck.

sent the subject of the reading or querent. This can be as simple as choosing The Magician for a man or The High Priestess for a woman, or another card based on the subject's age, hair and eye color, or personality. The card reader picks this card and places it face up on the middle of the table where the reading takes place.

Next, the querent is asked to think of her question and (usually) shuffle the remaining cards. Since they always start out in numerical order this must be done thoroughly. If a card pops out while shuffling, it's considered a favorable sign, and that card is used in the reading.

Now we're ready for business. The reader takes the top card from the shuffled deck, places it face down on the card already there and says, "What covers her," or him, as the case may be. The next card is placed face down, crosswise to these two with the words, "What crosses her." The next four cards are then placed face down, around these three at: 12 o' clock, 6 o'clock, 3 o' clock, and 9 o'clock respectively, with the words: "What crowns her, What is beneath her, What is behind her," and, "What is before her." Finally, the last four cards are placed face down, in a column to the right of this constellation, with the words: "Herself, Her house, Her hopes and fears," and, "What will come."

The set-up completed, the following is all there is to fortune-telling: The Cover card is turned over, and this is a signal to talk about the influences the subject is under. Next the Crosses card is turned over and this is a signal to talk about obstacles; the Crowns card about goals; the Beneath card about foundations; the Behind card about the immediate past; the Before card about the near future; the Herself card about attitudes; the House card about environment; the Hopes card about desires; and finally the "What will come" card sums up the impact of all the previous factors.

The reader finishes by informing the querent this outcome will come to pass only if she continues on her present course. If she changes, it can change too.

You've probably noticed nothing has been said about Tarot – nor need there be. In 1770 the following advertisement appeared

Tarot suit signs are (*clockwise from top left*) Wands, Swords, Coins, and Cups shown here on the Aces.

in the Paris journal *The Front-Runner* (*l'Avant-Coureur*):

"Etteilla, or a Way to Amuse Oneself with a Card Deck.

> This amusement consists of discovering from combinations of cards in a deck, answers to various questions put forth. The game is called Etteilla which is an anagram of its author's name. Etteilla is also the name of the first and most important card in this game, which is made-up of thirty-three cards in all. On each of the cards are symbols with different meanings, and meanings differ by card and according to whether a card is dealt upright or reversed; producing a multitude of combinations to better accommodate the variety of responses one expects to get from such cards and to challenge those who enjoy themselves with these kinds of diversions...." [1]

The name of the game, 33 cards and publication date all tell us this is *not* Tarot. But here is the first description of a Tarot spread. After de Gébelin's work appeared, Alliette (the author's real name) increased the number of cards in his deck to 78 and called them *Tarots*, still retaining the *Etteilla* card. In 1783 and 1785 he republished his ad with a new title, "A Way to Amuse Oneself with the Tarot Card Deck." [2] Thus, Tarot's association with fortune-telling is purely accidental. If Alliette hadn't known about de Gébelin they might not have come together at all. As it turned out they became practically synonymous, through Alliette's popularizations, and later when Empress Josephine Bonaparte and French high society became infatuated with fortune-telling.

Actually, the whole business is just a two-person play, and a Tarot spread the script (complete with stage directions) which divides any question into meaningful acts and resolves them in a final curtain, something like this:

> SCENE I. *Card reader turns over the Cover card. It's The Wheel of Fortune.*

Card Reader: I'm sensing that insight and spiritual growth are most important for this person right now. The Wheel of Fortune reveals the presence of destiny, fortune, luck, and happiness around her. This is an excellent sign.
Querent: Thinking to herself... Yes, that's right.

SCENE II. *Card reader turns over the Crosses card. It's The Tower.*
Card Reader: The Tower indicates a change for the worse in this situation due to opposing forces of misery, distress, disgrace and ruin.
Querent: Go on.

SCENE III. *Card reader turns over the Crowns card. It's The Sun, reversed.*
Card Reader: The Sun, reversed, reveals her aims and ultimate object to be...

The above dialogue, taken from an actual reading by my Internet Psychic Advisor shows how it works. But there's a catch. Every time a new card is turned up, the reader knows the subject to talk about but not what lines to say. Somehow, the cards themselves have to provide this information.

If, for instance The Tower card turns up, the reader should stress: *misery, distress, indigence, adversity, calamity, disgrace, deception, and ruin* – or – *oppression, imprisonment, and tyranny*, according to whether the card is dealt right-side-up or upside-down (reversed). That's The Tower card's divinatory meaning. There are even Tarot decks with divinatory meanings written out on each card for beginners. Looking back at the dialogue, you can see how easy it was to combine the Crosses subject – obstacles – with The Tower card's divinatory meaning to build a convincing line for the reader to say.

The Tarot of Marseilles

THE LOGIC IN PLACE, IT WAS TIME TO ADD SOME GRAPHICS. AUTHENTIC IMAGES would be critical to the Psychic Advisor's impact and credibility. A check of the local telephone directory indicated no less than four New Age bookstores within 30 minutes driving distance of my home – one of the cultural advantages of living in Southern California. I called one and asked if they carried Tarot decks.

"Which one are you looking for?" the saleswoman asked.

I didn't have the slightest idea. "Something old," I said.

"Oh, then you probably want a Renaissance deck," she replied.

After a bit of going back and forth I learned they had about 25 different decks in stock, and I should come down and look them over to find what I wanted. I was tempted. But there were three other stores nearby, so I decided to call another.

When I asked how many decks the second store carried, their answer was, "Oh, about 125, I think."

That was the place for me! I asked for directions, and told them, "I'll be right down."

The store was in a new mini-shopping complex, sandwiched between a fast food outlet and dress shop. The windows were covered by thick, red drapes, and there were signs outside announcing "Help Wanted, Inquire Within", and offering the services of a fortune-teller.

As I entered the door, I heard the tinkling of bells and nearly choked on the heavy aroma of incense. Twenty years ago I'd bought meditation tapes in a place like this. Little had changed. Makeshift bookshelves covered the back walls and tables spilling over with crystals, incense holders, shiny brass medallions, tapes and videos crowded the entryway, making passage almost impossible. One thing was new, an entire wall of locked glass cases. The merchandise here must be expensive.

On a table in the middle, I found what I'd come for. Here were dozens of Tarot sets, a deck and a book, packaged together in black plastic vinyl for $25 to $35. Nearby were some imported wooden cases, resembling cigar boxes. I knew what these were for. You were suppose to wrap your Tarot cards in silk and keep them in a wooden case, out of sight and away from prying hands, lest they lose their powers for prognostication.

But I didn't need a set; I wanted a deck. And frankly it didn't look like there were 125 sets here. So, admitting defeat, I wandered back to the counter and asked, "I called about your Tarot decks, where do you put them?"

The sales clerk promptly marched me past the table where I'd been looking to two six-foot bookshelves on the back wall. "They're here," she said.

This was more like it. There were more decks than I cared to count, threatening to tumble off the shelves onto the floor below.

"Is there anything in particular you're looking for?" she offered.

"No, I'll just have to look," was all I could say.

I was being honest. The cards I needed would be reduced to tiny, postage-stamp sized images on a computer screen. They had to be attractive, yet clear and recognizable for what they were. Not many of these decks met my criteria. Most were far too elaborate and couldn't be reduced in size.

Two decks showed promise. They looked identical to me, but their names were different. They were obviously old. One said it was based on eighteenth-century woodcuts. The other, calling itself the Tarot of Marseilles, didn't mention any date, but is even older, dating from the seventeenth century. The two look alike because the first deck is derived from the second. In fact most modern decks are descendants of the Tarot of Marseilles, though it's not always obvious at first glance.

Pictures on the Tarot of Marseilles cards are simple and crude because they were originally printed from woodblocks and colored using stencils While it's difficult to call them attractive, they're definitely interesting. And they would be easy to reduce in size for display on a computer screen. I decided I wouldn't find anything better and took the deck to the sales counter.

When I got there, my fears about expensive merchandise were confirmed. A woman in line ahead of me placed a few items on the counter and shelled out over $100 without batting an eye. Then my turn came, and I handed the deck to the salesclerk.

"Just a moment," she said, and headed over to one of the locked

EIGHTEENTH-CENTURY TAROT OF MARSEILLES: MAGICIAN I, POPESS (HIGH PRIESTESS) II, EMPRESS III, AND EMPEROR IIII CARDS.

EIGHTEENTH-CENTURY TAROT OF MARSEILLES: POPE (HIEROPHANT) V, LOVERS VI, CHARIOT VII, AND JUSTICE VIII CARDS.

glass cases. She opened it up, and returning with a new deck in a plastic wrapper began to ring-up the sale.

"Oh no! What's this going to cost?" I thought.

"With tax that's $14," she said.

"Ouch! Four times as much as an ordinary deck," I said to myself. I smiled and paid for my purchase.

Me, a Fortune-teller?

TRANSFERRING THE CARD IMAGES TO THE COMPUTER SCREEN WENT MUCH AS I EXPECTED, except they were so tiny I couldn't read their names and numbers, so I removed them. And it was too much work to reproduce rounded edges, so I left the cards square. Both shortcuts, by a strange coincidence, made the cards appear even older than they are. Unlike modern ones, the oldest Tarot cards have no writing on their faces, and their edges are square.

For some reason, the Psychic Advisor would occasionally freeze and come to a complete halt. It took a long time to locate the source of the error because it occurred so seldomly. By the time I did, I'd had my fortune told many times, and pretty much knew the drill. I was just fixing the bug when my youngest son Craig, spying the clutter of books and papers piled around the computer, asked what I was working on. I explained briefly and showed him my Tarot deck, something I was sure he'd never seen before. I was only partially right. He thumbed through the cards and pulled out number thirteen, Death. "What's this one mean," he asked.

"Well, it's not as bad as it looks," I said, "it foretells the end or termination of something, but that could be making way for a new beginning somewhere else."

"Yeah, that's what it meant on the Simpsons on TV the other night," he replied. Apparently I had just passed some certification exam because his next question really floored me.

"Why don't you tell my fortune?" he said matter-of-factly.

Me, a fortune-teller! I barely knew the meanings of the cards. What if I came across one I didn't know? Not wanting to disap-

Eighteenth-century Tarot of Marseilles: Hermit VIIII, Wheel of Fortune X, Strength XI, and Hanged Man XII cards.

point him, I agreed, but not until I'd made profuse apologies in advance for the mistakes I was sure I'd make. That didn't seem to matter much to Craig. So we sat down at a table and began. I imagine a professional would have tried to impress him with some occult hocus-pocus at this point. But we knew each other too well for this, so I simply told him what I was doing step-by-step and what it was supposed to mean. That way, if he didn't like the reading, it was the cards' fault, not mine.

It soon became apparent that many of the cards he'd selected belonged to the Coins suit, which concern material and financial matters – a very apropos choice for a teen. Mid-way through the reading, I was interrupted by a high-pitched whine. "What's the matter," I asked.

"Mom's been on my case about that," he replied.

"Well, mom's usually right," I shot back. Hooray! Score, parents: 1, child: 0. For the first time since we'd begun I took my eyes off the cards and looked at him. He was literally on the edge of his seat. Mr. Cool Teen hadn't taken anything I'd said to him this seriously since he was five years old! A thought immediately crossed my mind. Why not fudge a bit on the next few cards and make the score parents: 2, child: 0? After all, it would be for his own good. But what if I got caught? Too risky. I was lucky to be doing this well.

We'd hardly finished, when he said, "Do it again."

I explained that, "It doesn't work that way. You're supposed to wait a while between reading for things to work themselves out."

That didn't matter. "Do it again, do it again," he insisted.

Regardless of this show of enthusiasm, I knew enough to quit leaving my audience wanting more, and refused an encore – satisfied that one person in this world considered me a genuine fortune-teller.

A complete novice like myself shouldn't have been this successful, after all, I was breaking the rules:

> "...the cards must be interpreted relatively to the subject, which means that all official and conventional meanings of the cards may and should be adapted to harmonize with the particular case in question... On this account it is more easy

EIGHTEENTH-CENTURY TAROT OF MARSEILLES: DEATH XIII, TEMPERANCE XIIII, DEVIL XIV, AND FOOL (*unnumbered*) CARDS.

to divine correctly for a stranger than for yourself or a friend."

— *The Pictorial Key to the Tarot*

These warnings presume that the reader is responsible for the card reading and Tarot cards only serve to enhance their intuitive and clairvoyant talents. Many professionals don't even bother learning divinatory meanings. They just look at a card and say what comes to mind.

This point of view leaves out the subject entirely. Having your fortune told can be a tremendous ego trip. For 20 minutes an expert in occult science will reveal hidden secrets about your most favorite person in the whole world – you. The strange surroundings, mysterious ritual, and exotic cards are all calculated to impress you with that expert's special powers. Under such conditions, it's difficult not to lose your head.

Circumstances like these are not unique to fortune-telling. Suppose you've been suffering from back pain for weeks and learn of a medical treatment that may help to alleviate it. Your doctor tells you a medication is still in the trial stage but she can get you into the evaluation program. You agree to participate and receive pills to take twice a day. Here, pain provides the motivation, while the clinical program, doctor and pill-taking regimen may impress you with the treatment's curative powers in much the way a Tarot reading might affect you.

Not many participants like to think about it, but in evaluations like these some of them will receive placebos – sugar-pills – and be encouraged to think they're receiving the latest wonder drug. More than half of these "controls" will report feeling better, and will believe the cure is effective. And a few may actually improve their condition by thought alone!

If doctors must subtract placebo effects before they present their conclusions on the effectiveness of a new drug, why shouldn't occultists be required to do the same thing before making claims about fortune-telling? Most likely the subject is the one who's (unwittingly) responsible for making the reading work. Sigmund Freud observed that some of his patients held the predictions of fortune-tellers in high regard, even when demonstrably false, when they satisfied the patient's unconscious wishes.

My own success was probably due to this placebo factor. Craig's interest had already been piqued before our session together and his curiosity, plus a few lucky "hits" on the cards, was all it took to convince him of my abilities. You can test this for yourself. Try my Psychic Advisor at http://tarot-cards.com on the Internet (be sure to include the hyphen). It makes no claims to clairvoyance, yet it has given many convincing readings – especially when subjects don't realize they're dealing with a computer program!

Bibliography

Henry-René D'Allemagne, "Etteilla vulgarisateur de la bonne adventure par les cartes à jouer." In *Les Cartes à Jouer du XIV au XX Siècle*, (Paris: Hachette et Cie, 1906), Vol I.

Carnegie, Dale, "Fundamental Techniques in Handling People." In *How to Win Friends and Influence People*, revised edition: (Simon & Schuster, 1981), Part One.

Sigmund Freud, "Dreams and the Occult." In *New Introductory Lectures on Psycho-Analysis,* (W. W. Norton & Co., 1939), Lecture 30.

Arthur Edward Waite, "The Greater Arcana and their Divinatory Meanings, & An Ancient Celtic Method of Divination." In *The Pictorial Key to the Tarot*, reprint: (Barns & Noble, 1995).

Internet

Note: There's no need to type this yourself. Current links to these and future sites, as they become available, can be found at: http://tarot-cards.com

Internet Psychic Advisor
http://tarot-cards.com/psychic.htm

U.S. Games Tarot & Cartomancy
http://member.aol.com/usgames/tarhome.htm

Translations

1. Etteilla ou la manière de se récréer avec un jeu de cartes. Cette récréation consiste à trouver par les combinaisons d'un jeu de cartes des réponses à diverses questions proposées. Ce jeu est appelé Etteilla qui est l'anagramme du nom de l'auteur. L'Etteilla est aussi le nom de la première et de la principale carte

de son jeu, qui est composé en tout de trente-trios cartes. Sur chacune de ces cartes sont marquées différentes significations et ces significations varient relativement à la carte qui suit et selon que la carte a été tirée droite ou renversée; ce qui doit produire une multitude de combinaisons, jeter beaucoup de variété dans les réponses que l'on se propose de faire au moyen de ces cartes, et occuper ceux qui se plaisent à ces sortes d'amusements....

2. Manière de se récréer avec le Jeu de Cartes nommeés Tarots.

Chapter Three

How Hard Can It Be?

THE PSYCHIC ADVISOR WAS RUNNING ON MY WEBSITE, BUT I WASN'T FINISHED. The Tarot of Marseilles deck I'd purchased contained two extra cards advertising a book and listing its contents. Many of its topics were unfamiliar and not discussed in the *Pictorial Key*. Perhaps something was missing from the Psychic Advisor too? I certainly didn't want to make any embarrassing mistakes.

I remembered seeing this book in the New Age bookstore on the shelf above the Tarot decks. So the next time Craig and I went out for chicken burritos at our favorite fast-food restaurant, we stopped by on our way home and picked up a copy. The new book, the *Tarot Classic*, was very different from the other. A friend once pointed out to me that books should be both inspirational and informational. By this classification, the *Pictorial Key* rates about 95 percent on the inspirational scale. The *Classic* was more balanced. Now, perhaps, I could figure this subject out.

That proved overly ambitious, but Court de Gébelin particularly impressed me. What a great writer! No wonder people believed everything he'd said. After I'd finished my reading, I laid the book aside and forgot about it, until one day while cleaning house, it turned up under a pile of papers. As I picked it up to put it away, I thought to myself, "I'll just read the de Gébelin part one more time."

As I did, the strangest idea came into my head. "How hard can it be?" I thought. "How hard can it be to figure out the meaning of the cards from their symbols?" The notion that many had tried and failed didn't enter my mind.

I found my Tarot deck and thumbed through the cards, searching for an interesting one. I settled on The World, the same card de Gébelin had used – though I gave the coincidence little notice.

THE WORLD CARD IN THE TAROT OF MARSEILLES DECK (*right*) SHOWS A PARTIALLY CLAD FIGURE STANDING ON ONE LEG, SURROUNDED BY AN OVAL WREATH.

The figure holds a short wand in each hand. At the four corners of the card, outside the oval, are an angel, bird, lion, and bull. All with wings.

Checking with a heraldry book under "Divine Beings, Saints, and Religious Symbolism," I discovered the bird was an eagle and the symbol of St. John the Apostle. The lion was associated with St. Mark, and the bull with St. Luke. I guessed, but couldn't confirm, the angel represented St. Matthew. So much for heraldry.

Next I got out a bestiary, a medieval zoology manual of mythical creatures: dragons, griffins, unicorns, and the deadly basilisk, reputed to kill with its breath. Reading about eagles, lions, and bulls only confirmed what I'd learned from heraldry and my guess about St. Matthew. But the more I read, the more I found references to ancient Egypt and Babylon. This line of inquiry was leading right back to where de Gébelin said it did!

Trying another approach, I skimmed each chapter of the book looking for clues. Ironically the very first chapter, which I'd skipped over before, provided the key. The picture there didn't look anything like The World card, but as I began to read I knew

I'd found what I was looking for.

THE TETRAMORPH, OR FOUR FORMS (*right*), WAS A CELESTIAL ANIMAL MADE-UP OF:

> "...four living creatures, full of eyes before and behind. And the first living creature was like a lion: and the second living creature like a calf: and the third living creature, having the face, as it were, of a man: and the fourth living creature was like an eagle flying. And the four living creatures had each of them six wings; and round about and within they are full of eyes."
>
> – *Revelation* 4:6-8

The World card shows the Tetramorph split into its four component parts surrounding God's throne, while my bestiary depicted it as one animal. If you know what you're looking at, you can see how one transforms into the other. If you don't, you'd hardly guess it.

Apparently, writers of the Old and New Testaments borrowed ancient Egyptian and Babylonian icons for their accounts of the Tetramorph, which early Christian writers again borrowed to represent the four Evangelists. Irenaeus, an early Church Father, championed this interpretation in 170 AD, and it was commonly accepted by the third century. Thus, the Egyptian God Horus became John's eagle; Sekhmet, Mark's lion; Ka (soul), Matthew's angel or man; and Apis, Luke's bull. Some claim that, like the Tetramorph, all four Egyptian animals are all incorporated together in the Sphinx. When we see these symbols today we think of their original, or final meanings – forgetting the connecting link. Here was de Gébelin's error and a valuable clue. The Tetramorph occurs in only two places in the Bible: *The Apocalypse of St. John the Apostle* (The *Book of Revelation* in Protestant Bibles) and *The Prophecy of Ezechiel*. This was were I should look next.

The *Book of Revelation*

THE *BOOK OF REVELATION* ATTRACTS ONLY OCCASIONAL NOTICE TODAY, as in Ingmar Bergman's film *The Seventh Seal*. But in the past it has been exceedingly popular. It is quintessential apocalyptic literature, recounting divine disclosures about the secrets of heaven and the end of history. The word *apocalypse* is derived from a Greek root meaning to uncover or reveal, hence the book's two different names. Here, I'll use *Revelation* when I talk about the book in the Bible, reserving the term *Apocalypse* for special, illustrated *Revelation* manuscripts – but usually they're synonymous.

The *Book of Revelation* is presented in the guise of a letter of warning and exhortation to seven churches in Asia Minor. After introductory admonitions to each church, John, the author, is summoned to heaven in God's presence. A scroll with seven seals sits beside God, which only Christ is worthy to open.

In Chapters Four through Seven, the seals are opened one by one, unleashing disaster after disaster. This sequence inspired Albrecht Dürer to create his famous print *The Four Horsemen of the Apocalypse*, depicting war, pestilence, famine, and death. In fact, many scenes from *Revelation* are celebrated in religious art: Christ with the scroll, and the Last Judgment, to name two.

In Chapters Eight through Fourteen, seven angels blow their trumpets and another series of calamities unfold. Afterwards, Archangel Michael defeats Satan in heaven, foreshadowing the appearance of Antichrist and the false prophet on earth.

Finally, in Chapters Fifteen through Twenty Two, seven angels pour vials filled with the "wrath of God" upon the earth, wreaking still more destruction. This purification sets the stage for a 1,000 year reign of Christ and his elect; at the culmination of which, Satan is defeated in a final battle between good and evil and the dead rise for judgment. The saved enter new Jerusalem, sent down by God from heaven, while the damned suffer a second death in a pool of fire for eternity.

Scholars disagree on whether the Seals, Trumpets and Vials series are distinct or represent different views of a single episode (termed recapitulation) because as the author John says:

> "I was IN THE SPIRIT on the Lord's day, and heard behind me a great voice, as of a trumpet, Saying: What thou seest,

Albrecht Dürer's *Four Horsemen of the Apocalypse*, depicting (*right-to-left*) war, pestilence, famine, and death.

write in a book, and send to the seven churches which are in Asia..."

— *Revelation* 1:10-11

"In the spirit," is Bible-speak for experiencing visions of religious ecstasy. Depending on how he got that way, a modern John might be arrested for doing the same thing. As a consequence, *Revelation* is full of loose ends, repetitions, and inconsistencies. St. Jerome aptly described the result: "As many mysteries, as words."[1]

Numbers pervade every chapter: ½ and 3½ – 2 through 7 – 10, 12, 24, 42, 144, 666, 1000, 1260, and 1600 – 7, 12 and 144 thousand – even 2×10,000×10,000 is there! *Revelation's* numerology is second to none. New Testament Greek made letters do double duty as numerals. Consequently every name could also be read as a number, a practice that continues in occult circles to this day. One of these numbers still holds us in its grip, the 1,000 years of the Millennium:

"Blessed and holy is he that hath part in the first resurrection. In these the second death hath no power; but THEY SHALL BE PRIESTS OF GOD AND OF CHRIST; AND SHALL REIGN WITH HIM A THOUSAND YEARS.

The REST OF THE DEAD LIVED NOT, till the thousand years were finished."

— *Revelation* 20:6 & 5

As the text makes clear, the Millennium was reserved for God's elect. Resurrection and the Last Judgment for the rest of mankind occurred after it was over.

The Millennium could begin at any time. The Middle Ages expected it in 1200, 1260, 1290, 1348, 1360, 1387, 1396, and 1417. Contrary to popular opinion today, not everyone was excited about its prospects in the year 1000 or 1033 (1,000 years after Christ's death). Church doctrine opposed a literal interpretation of *Revelation* and the Millennium then. St. Augustine taught:

"...there [are] also two resurrections, one, the first and spiritual resurrection, which has place in this life and preserves us from coming into the second death; the other, the second,

> which does not occur now but in the end of the world, and which is of the body."
>
> — *City of God* 20:6

St. Augustine also thought a 1,000 year reign for the elect smacked too much of a party:

> "THOSE WHO... HAVE SUSPECTED THAT THE FIRST RESURRECTION IS FUTURE AND BODILY, have been moved, among other things, specially by the number of a thousand years, as if it were a fit thing that the saints should thus enjoy a kind of Sabbath-rest during that period... and that for this purpose the saints rise, viz., to celebrate this Sabbath.
>
> This opinion would not be objectionable, if it were believed that the joys of the saints in that Sabbath shall be spiritual, and consequent on the presence of God; for I myself, too, once held this opinion.
>
> But, as THEY ASSERT THAT THOSE WHO THEN RISE AGAIN SHALL ENJOY THE LEISURE OF IMMODERATE CARNAL BANQUETS, furnished with an amount of meat and drink such as not only to shock the feeling of the temperate, but even to surpass the measure of credulity itself, SUCH ASSERTIONS CAN BE BELIEVED ONLY BY THE CARNAL."
>
> — *City of God* 20:7

For St. Augustine and most Christians before 1100, the millennial kingdom was the current reign of the Church, and the first resurrection was resurrection from sin through baptism. They held that, just as God had created the world in six days and rested on the seventh; the world would have six ages of one 1,000 biblical (not chronological) years before Christ's Second Coming. The First Age began with Adam, the Second with the Flood, and the Third with Abraham. The Fourth Age began with David or sometimes Moses, the Fifth with the Babylonian Captivity, and the Sixth with Christ

The world was still in the Sixth Age, and whether Christ's Second Coming would bring about a seventh, Sabbath Age, or not, was an open question. St. Augustine thought not, others like St. Jerome weren't so sure.

Searching for More Clues

I BEGAN TO READ THROUGH *REVELATION* LOOKING FOR CLUES TO THE IDENTITIES OF THE TAROT CARDS – and wasn't disappointed. The Tower card portrays a stone tower blasted apart by a fiery lightning bolt. Two men fall from the crumbling structure, and many small circles – some say they're sparks – stream down on both sides. Two passages in *Revelation*, from the Trumpet and Vial series respectively, captured this feeling:

> "...there were THUNDERS and voices and LIGHTNINGS, and A GREAT EARTHQUAKE. And the seven angels, who had the seven trumpets, prepared themselves to sound the trumpet. And the first angel sounded the trumpet, and there followed HAIL AND FIRE, mingled with blood, and it was cast on the earth..."
>
> – *Revelation* 8:5-7

> "And there were LIGHTNINGS, and voices, and THUNDERS, and there was A GREAT EARTHQUAKE, such an one as never had been since men were upon the earth, such an earthquake, so great... And GREAT HAIL, like a talent, came down from heaven upon men: and men blasphemed God for the plague of the hail: because it was exceeding great."
>
> – *Revelation* 16:18-21

Thunder, lightning, and hail represent the mood of The Tower card very well. The latter actually clarifies the scene; those so-called sparks look more like hail than sparks. But an earthquake? To my knowledge no one had ever suggested one before. On the other hand, perhaps it's shown too. What *would* an earthquake look like on a Tarot card?

The Star Card

THE STAR CARD PORTRAYS A LARGE STAR SURROUNDED BY SEVEN SMALLER STARS in the sky. Below, a nude woman pours water from two urns into a river or pond, while in the background a black bird sits atop a tree.

In *Revelation*, the smaller stars represent angels:

Eighteenth-Century Tarot of Marseilles: Tower XVI, Star XVII, Moon XVIII, and Sun XVIIII cards.

"The SEVEN STARS ARE THE ANGELS of the seven churches."
— *Revelation* 1:20.

And a large, single star occurs in the Trumpet series:

"...the third angel sounded the trumpet, and A GREAT STAR fell from heaven, burning as it were a torch, and it fell on the third part of the RIVERS, and upon the FOUNTAINS OF WATERS: And the name of the star is called Wormwood. And the third part of the WATERS became wormwood; and many men died of the waters, because they were made bitter."
— *Revelation* 8:10-11

Comparison with The Tower card suggests there should be a Vial series reference too. But there's no mention of a star in the Vial series. However, there are two water references:

"And the third [angel] poured out his vial upon the RIVERS and the FOUNTAINS OF WATERS; and there was made blood."
— *Revelation* 16:4

"And the sixth angel poured out his vial upon that great RIVER EUPHRATES; and dried up the WATER thereof, that a way might be prepared for the kings from the rising of the sun."
— *Revelation* 16:12

Perhaps *river*, *water(s)*, and *fountains of waters* provided the connection between the two series that I expected? Certainly there are plenty of water clues on the card itself. But what about the bird? There's mention of that too:

"And I saw an angel standing in the sun, and he cried with a loud voice, saying to ALL THE BIRDS that did fly through the midst of heaven: Come, gather yourselves together to the GREAT SUPPER OF GOD: That you may EAT THE FLESH of kings, and the flesh of tribunes, and the flesh of mighty men, and the flesh of horses, and of them that sit on them, and the flesh of all freemen and bondmen, and of little and of great."
— *Revelation* 19:17-18

Revelation's bird is a symbol of death. In the Middle Ages, bodies of executed criminals were publicly exposed after death where they were scavenged by ravens and crows – hence the association. Peter Brueghel the Elder uses this symbolism in his paintings *The Road to Calvary* and *The Triumph of Death*. In *Revelation*, warriors slain in battle meet a similar fate.

It appeared that Tarot's Star card depicted the horrific scene of an angel poisoning life-sustaining waters as a punishment from God while other angels watched on. The fact I could find matches for all the card's symbols lead me to believe I was on the right track.

The Moon Card

THE MOON CARD SHOWS A MAN-IN-THE-MOON SURROUNDED BY INVERTED TEARDROPS in the sky. Two facing dogs, baying at the moon with their tongues sticking out, dominate its center. Behind them, cut off by the card's edges, are two towers. A lobster, more familiar in medieval times as a crab, swims in a pond in the lower third of the card. As before, there is a Trumpet series reference:

> "And the fourth angel sounded the trumpet, and the third part of the sun was smitten, and the third part of the MOON, and the third part of the stars, so that THE THIRD PART OF THEM WAS DARKENED, and the day did not shine for a third part of it, and the night in like manner."
>
> – *Revelation* 8:12

And, likewise, a Vial series reference using *darkened* as an intermediate keyword:

> "And the fifth angel poured out his vial upon the seat of the beast; and his kingdom BECAME DARK, and they gnawed their tongues for pain..."
>
> – *Revelation* 16:10-11

This might explain why dogs (beasts) and their tongues are so prominently featured. For like the Satan (the archbeast), they are associated with lies:

> "Without are DOGS, and sorcerers, and unchaste, and murderers, and servers of idols, AND EVERY ONE THAT LOVETH AND MAKETH A LIE."
>
> – *Revelation* 22:15

The Vial series reference may also shed light on the teardrop objects. They could be drops of the "wrath of God" poured from the angel's vial. And the towers might represent the beast's kingdom.

However most of the card is pure astrology. The *Book of the Seven Planets* was a popular work on astrology which first appeared in about 1410. Made up of illustrations with accompanying poems on facing pages, its poem for the moon begins:

> "Luna, the moon and last [seventh] planet,
> I'm called; and I influence things that come to be.
> Cold and damp are my attributes,
> By nature inconstant all the time.
> The Crab governs my house,
> So, my likeness stands in there...." [2]

THE LAST TWO LINES REFER TO THE ACCOMPANYING ILLUSTRATION (*opposite page*) WHERE LUNA AND THE SAME CRAB AS ON THE MOON CARD ARE PROMINENTLY FEATURED.

The moon embraced water and change, and Cancer the Crab was her sign. Remove the dogs and towers, and Tarot's Moon card could serve as the accompanying illustration for the portion of Luna's poem reproduced here.

The Sun Card

THE SUN CARD SHOWS A SOLAR FACE IN THE SKY SURROUNDED BY INVERTED TEARDROPS like The Moon's. Below, two partially clad figures stand in front of a stone wall. The sun shares the same Trumpet series reference with the moon given earlier, but now there's also an explicit Vial series reference:

> "And the fourth angel POURED OUT HIS VIAL UPON THE SUN, and it was given unto him to afflict men with heat and fire: And

LUNA'S, ILLUSTRATION FROM A *Book of the Seven Planets.*

> men were scorched with great heat, and they blasphemed the name of God, who hath power over these plagues, neither did they penance to give him glory."
>
> – *Revelation* 16:8-9

This unambiguously connects pouring from the vial with the sun, confirming the teardrops as the "wrath of God," both here, and on The Moon card. With no modification at all, the Vial series reference above could serve a caption for Tarot's Sun card.

The Opening of the Sixth Seal

ADDITIONALLY, THE TOWER, STAR, MOON AND SUN CARDS ALSO SHARE a common Seal series reference:

> "And I saw, WHEN HE HAD OPENED THE SIXTH SEAL, and behold there was a great EARTHQUAKE, and the SUN became black as sackcloth of hair: and the whole MOON became as blood: And the STARS from heaven fell upon the earth, as the fig tree casteth its green figs when it is shaken by a great wind..."
>
> – *Revelation* 6:12-13

This ties all four cards together and relates them to the opening of the sixth seal, which, as will become apparent later, is the reason why these cards are in the Tarot deck. And note, it's an earthquake – not thunder, lightning, and hail – through which The Tower's connection is established.

The World Card Revisited

THE JUDGEMENT CARD LOOKED LIKE IT BELONGED IN *REVELATION* TOO. But despite its name, Judgement portrays resurrection which is only implied there:

> "The rest of the dead lived not, till the thousand years were finished."
>
> – *Revelation* 20:5

So, any analysis would have to wait for further data.

EIGHTEENTH-CENTURY TAROT OF MARSEILLES: JUDGMENT XX, AND WORLD XXI CARDS (*below*).

THAT LEFT ONE QUESTION UNANSWERED, "Where did The World card belong?" One possibility was at the beginning of *Revelation* where the Tetramorph is first described. But the symbolism doesn't support this. The central figure on its card was obviously neither God, Christ, nor the Apostle John.

THOSE IMAGES (*right*) HAVE BEEN WELL KNOWN SINCE THE FIFTH CENTURY.

Perhaps only the throne was intended, as in:

> "...and in the midst of the throne, and ROUND ABOUT THE THRONE, WERE FOUR LIVING CREATURES, full of eyes before and behind..."
>
> — *Revelation* 4:6

This description matches the outside of the card. If that was the case, a passage at the end of *Revelation*, in the holy city of new Jerusalem, was the only place where the throne itself was important:

> "And he [an angel] showed me a river of water of life, clear as crystal, proceeding from THE THRONE OF GOD and of the Lamb. In the midst of the street thereof, and on both sides of the river, was the tree of life, bearing twelve fruits, yielding its fruits every month, and the leaves of the tree were for the healing of the nations. And there shall be no curse any more; but the THRONE OF GOD and of the Lamb shall be in it, and his servants shall serve him."
>
> — *Revelation* 22:1-3

New Jerusalem was mentioned before in Chapter One, where it stood for the anagogic or mystical meaning of Jerusalem. The World card is simply anagogy in pictures. The figure at its center reminded me of Christian and Hopeful entering the holy city two centuries later in *Pilgrim's Progress*:

> "Now you must note that THE CITY stood upon a mighty hill, but the pilgrims went up that hill with ease, because they had these two men to lead them up by the arms. Also, THEY HAD LEFT THEIR MORTAL GARMENTS behind them in the river, for though they went in with them, they came out without them."
>
> — *Pilgrim's Progress*, end of Part I

The soul was frequently depicted as a nude figure in religious art. So, The World card's central figure might be the soul of one of the elect in the holy city. Its wands and one-legged stance echo The Magician's wand and The Hanged Man's crossed legs, suggesting a connection between these three cards. Indeed, later I'll show that these three neatly summarize Tarot's central message.

Altogether, I had detailed picture-word correspondences for five Tarot cards, each pointing to the *Book of Revelation.* But other cards like The Pope and The Wheel of Fortune couldn't possibly be from the Bible. What could they have in common with *Revelation*?

Bibliography

St. Augustine, "Concerning the Last Judgment and the declarations regarding it in the Old and New Testaments." In *The City of God*, Marcus Dods, tr (Edinburgh: T. & T. Clarke), Book XX.

E. A. Wallis Budge, "Figures of Gods." In *The Mummy: Chapters on Egyptian Funereal Archaeology*, reprint: (Collier Books, 1972).

John Bunyan, *The Pilgrim's Progress from This World to That Which Is to Come*, reprint: (Dodd Mead, 1979), First Part.

Louis Charbonneau-Lassay, "The Tetramorph, & The Sphinx." In *The Bestiary of Christ*, D. M. Dooling, Tr., (Arkana, 1992).

Richard K. Emmerson, "Antichrist and Medieval Apocalypticism." In *Antichrist in the Middle Ages: A Study of Medieval Apocalypticism, Art, and Literature*, (U. Washington Pr., 1981).

Richard K. Emmerson, Bernard McGinn, eds., "Part II: The Apocalypse in Medieval Art." In *The Apocalypse in the Middle Ages*, (Cornell UP, 1992).

St. John, "The Apocalypse of St. John the Apostle." In *Douay-Rheims Bible: Translated from the Latin Vulgate* (Baltimore: 1899).

Jim Harter, "Pre-Christian Angels, & Angels in Early Christian Iconography." In *The Ultimate Angel Book*, (Gramercy Bks., 1995).

Stuart R. Kaplan, *Tarot Classic*, (U.S. Games Systems, Inc., 1972).

Heinrich Keller, *Mittelalteriches Hausbuch: Bilderhandschift des 15. Jahrhunderts mit vollstandigen Tert und facsimilierten ubbilddungen*, reprint: (George Olms Verlag, 1986).

Willi Kurth, ed., *The Complete Woodcuts of Albrecht Dürer*, (Dover Pubs., Inc, 1963).

Lionello Puppi, Peter Brueghel's *Triumph of Death & Road to Calvary*. In *Torment in Art: Pain, Violence and Martyrdom*, (Rizzoli, 1991), p 113-115.

Carl-Alexander von Volborth, "Divine Beings, Saints, Religious Symbolism." In *Heraldry: Customs, Rules and Styles*, (New Orchard Eds., 1991).

Internet

Note: There's no need to type this yourself. Current links to these and future sites, as they become available, can be found at: http://tarot-cards.com

Apocalypse of St. John
http://www.knight.org/advent/cathen/01594b.htm
City of God
http://www.knight.org/advent/fathers/1201.htm
Albrecht Dürer
http://www.knight.org/advent/cathen/05209c.htm
HOLY BIBLE
http://www.cybercomm.net/~dcon/drbible.html
Holy Bible_Douay Rheims Version
http://davinci.marc.gatech.edu/catholic/scriptures/douay.htm
IPBE LIBRARY BUNYAN
http://www.iclnet.org/pub/resources/text/ipb-e/epl-bu.html
St. Irenaeus
http://www.knight.org/advent/cathen/08130b.htm
St. Jerome
http://www.knight.org/advent/cathen/08341a.htm
Millennium and Millenarianism
http://www.knight.org/advent/cathen/10307a.htm
The *Planets and Their Children*
http://www.englib.cornell.edu/mhh4/planets/planets.html
Seraphim
http://www.knight.org/advent/cathen/13725b.htm

Translations

1. quot verba, tot mysteria.

2. Luna der monat der letzst planet naß,
Heiß ich und wurd dingt die sein laß.
Kalt und feucht mein wurdung ist,
Naturlich unstet zu aller frist.

Der krebs mein hawβ besessen hat,
So mein figur dor inne stat.

Chapter Four

Let's Kill All the Lawyers.

SOMETHING MORE WAS NEEDED IF I WAS GOING TO DISCOVER THE IDENTITIES of the remaining cards. Fortunately, I owned a book that might help, a study of English wayfaring life in the fourteenth century, the time when playing cards first entered Europe. Of course England was the wrong place to be looking, but I was searching more for clues than answers at this point and hoped that English and Italian life were not too different then. Besides, I was going to read the book anyway.

I'd started it a few years back, but was put off by Part I, English Roads, 140 pages of them. But now, Part II, Lay Wayfarers:

- *Herbalists, Charlatans, Minstrels, Jugglers and Tumblers*
- *Messengers, Itinerant Merchants and Peddlers*
- *Outlaws, Wandering Workmen, and Peasants out of Bond*

– looked promising for leads on The Fool and Magician. And Part III, Religious Wayfarers:

- *Wandering Preachers and Friars*
- *Pardoners*
- *Pilgrims and Pilgrimages*

– might shed light on The Hermit. So I began again.

This time I made it past Roads, but nothing clicked until I reached John Ball and his fellow itinerant preachers in Part III. According to contemporary accounts:

> "They preach... not only in churches and churchyards, but also in markets, fairs, and other open places where a great congregation of people is... which persons do also preach diverse matters of slander, to engender discord and dissension betwixt divers estates of the said realm as well spiritual as temporal, in exciting of the people, to the great peril of all the realm."
>
> – *English Wayfaring Life*

What was all the commotion about? How could religious men constitute a fifth column? Traditionally the relation between Church and state emphasizes their peaceful co-existence:

> "And Jesus answering, said to them: Render therefore to Caesar the things that are Caesar's and to God the things that are God's."
>
> – *Mark* 12:17

Ball preached another interpretation, captured by a popular ballad of the time:

> "Whan Adam dalf [dug] and Eve span,
> Who was then a gentilman?"

– a reading which, as events were to prove, transformed Marx's "opiate of the masses" into a revolutionary manifesto. Here was a group nearly outside the pale of history, with extensive contacts throughout society, and an agenda at odds with the establishment. Could they create and popularize something like Tarot? And were they interested in *Revelation*? I had only to read to find out.

Excommunicate Hedge Priest

On June 6, 1381 John Ball languished in the Archbishop's prison in Maidstone 20 miles southeast of London, unaware of the events of the previous week and a citizen's army marching to free him. Arrested as an excommunicate, he'd been incarcerated since late April.

Originally a priest at St. Mary's Abbey in York, he became a hedge priest with no church and no charge. For 20 years he preached evangelical poverty and attacked the established clergy and their property whenever and wherever the opportunity arose. He proposed to:

> "...get rid of all the lords, and archbishops and bishops, and abbots, and priors and most of the monks and cannons, saying there should be no bishop in England save one archbishop only, and that he himself would be that prelate... and that their possessions should be distributed among the laity."
>
> — *Anonimal Chronicle*

As early as 1366 he was cited before the Archbishop of Canterbury, accused of preaching manifold errors and scandals, and imprisoned. This was only a temporary setback. After his release the Archbishop complained:

> "...he had slunk back into our diocese, like the fox that evades the hunter, and feared not to preach and argue... there beguiling the ears of the laity by his invectives, and putting about scandals concerning our own person, and those of other prelates and clergy, and (what is worse) using dreadful language concerning the Holy Father himself [the pope] such as shocked the ears of good Christians."
>
> — *The Great Revolt*

The Peasant's Revolt of 1381

WHO WAS COMING TO HIS RESCUE? AN ARMY OF TAX-PROTESTERS. England's Hundred Year's War with France had the country strapped for cash and £160,000 was needed to continue the fighting. In 1377 and 1379 officials had collected a tax of four pence a head from common laborers. Now that amount almost tripled in the poorest counties – the equivalent of a month's wages. With the collusion of local officials, many resorted to tax evasion. Comparing names between the old and new tax rolls, government overseers reported the number of taxpayers was down by 20 to 50 percent. Single women: widows, aunts, sisters and daughters were especially under-reported. To remedy the shortfall, the government empowered new commissioners to return to the counties and collect what had been missed. For more than a month, townships grumbled and settled up. But in late May the townspeople of Fobbing in Essex told auditors they had a receipt showing they'd paid the tax, and ran them out of town.

On June 2, when a special prosecutor appeared to punish the guilty parties, the government learned how much it had underestimated the seriousness of the situation. Armed citizens halted the proceedings, bullied the prosecutor into handing over a list of jurors giving testimony, and razed the houses and beheaded as many on the list as they could find. They also beheaded three court clerks, stuck their heads on poles, and marched them around to neighboring villages. Over the next few days sympathetic riots sprang up in surrounding townships as mobs seized and burned records, deeds, and court-rolls. Court officials and anyone connected with the hated tax were in danger of their lives.

What had started as a tax revolt had unleashed all the pent-up frustrations of English lower class life. Historians cite a scarcity of laborers to work the land – brought on by the Black Death – and harsh laws restricting their ability to bargain for fair wages as its cause. And undoubtedly this was a factor. Succeeding waves of plagues at ten to fifteen year intervals kept the population in check, so that the problem worsened year after year.

But, this doesn't explain why Londoners eagerly joined the

revolt, nor why Cambridge University came under attack, nor the murders of Flemish woolen craftsmen at Lynn. These acts speak of a more widespread dissatisfaction throughout society. Two years before the king had been forced to issue the statute:

> "Item, of devisors of false news and reporters of horrible and false lyes, concerning prelates, dukes, earls, barons, and other nobles and great men of the realm, and also concerning the chancellor, treasurer, clerk of the privy seal, steward of the king's house, justices of the one bench or of the other, and of other great officers of the realm about things which... were never spoken, done, nor thought...
>
> From henceforth none be so hardy to devise, speak, or to tell any false news, lyes, or other false things of prelates, lords, and of other aforesaid, whereof discord or any slander might rise within the same realm."
>
> – *English Wayfaring Life*

As the lower classes saw it, rich nobles, prelates, and foreigners were a pack of greedy scoundrels, who with lawyers and judges as their henchmen, were leading the country into ruin. They were political criminals deserving punishment – death by beheading. That was the glue that bonded them together.

According to the confession of Jack Straw, the leaders of the army coming to Ball's rescue planned to take the king hostage, and under his authority arrest and execute the rich and powerful throughout the realm. Churchmen would be included too – all but the mendicant orders:

> "Mendicants alone, living in the country, would suffice for the holy celebrations and congregations of the entire land."[1]
>
> "...and when there was no one greater or stronger or more learned than ourselves surviving, we would have made such laws as pleased us..."
>
> – *The Great Revolt*

There's no doubt that some mendicants played a role in the revolt. Their doctrine of poverty had influenced John Ball and was derided by critics as Christian communism:

> "They preach men of Plato and prove it by Seneca,
> That all things under heaven ought to be in common:
> And yet he lies, as I live, that to the unlearned so preacheth."
> – *Piers Plowman, 23*

Evangelical poverty had split the mendicant orders. While practical churchmen aspired to build magnificent churches and acquire wealth for their orders, otherworldly ones looked forward to a time when the Church would return to simple poverty. They were the troublemakers, who:

> "...used oftentimes on the Sundays after mass, when the people were going out of the minster, to go into the cloister and preach, and made the people to assemble..."
> – Froissart's *Chronicles*

This was dangerous business. Sympathizers acknowledged one another with watchwords like: "John the Miller grinds small, small, small," to which the reply was, "The King's son of heaven shall pay for all."

John Ball Hath Rungen Your Bell

ON JUNE 7, 1381 BANDS FROM ALL OVER KENT CONVERGED ON MAIDSTONE and released Ball from the Archbishop's prison. He spent the next few days writing rhyming letters drumming up support for the revolt in progress:

> "John Ball, priest of St. Mary's,
>
> Greets well all manner of men, and bids them in the name of the Trinity, Father, Son, and Holy Ghost, to stand together manfully in truth. Maintain the truth and the truth will maintain you.

Now reigneth Pride in price,
And Covetise is holden wise,
And Lechery withouten shame,
And Gluttony withouten blame,
Envye reigneth with treason,
And Sloath is take in grete season.

God give aid, for now is the time. Amen."

"John Schepe [Ball],

Some time St. Mary's Priest of York, and now of Colchester, greeteth well John Nameless, and John the Miller, and John the Carter, and biddeth them that they beware of guile in borough, and stand together in God's name, and biddeth Piers Plowman go to his work, and chastise well Hobbe the Robber [Robert Hales], and take with you John Trueman [Wat Tyler] and all his fellows, and no mo[re], and look that ye shape you to one head and no mo[re]."

"John Ball greeteth you well all,

And doth you to understand that he hath rungen your bell.

Now right and might, will and skill. Now God haste you in every thing. Time it is that Our Lady help you with Jesus her son, and the Son with the Father, to make in the name of the Holy Trinity a good end to what has begun.

Amen, Amen, for Charity Amen."

— *The Great Revolt*

As a result of the outrage over the tax, and Ball's grass roots campaign, as many as 100,000 men mustered to march on London by June 11th. In comparison, London's population was just 40,000 then. This fact erased any doubts in my mind about how effective itinerant preachers could be at promoting ideas and causes.

The army set out in two groups, one from Essex east of London, and Ball's group from Kent to the south. Ball was not its leader. At Maidstone, a Wat Tyler took charge. Little is known about him other than what transpired in the following week, but he was a born leader, and possibly a retired soldier from the skills he showed in discipline and organization.

The rebel advance impressed even their enemies. Tyler had them organized into companies by towns, and they marched more than 70 miles in under two days. Along their route they made forays into the surrounding countryside collecting old bows, swords, billhooks, staves and axes with which to arm themselves, and cattle, sheep, and hens for food – some men actually paying for what they took.

Everyone they met was challenged by: "Wyth whome haldes you?" and made to swear, "Wyth Kynge Richarde and wyth the trew communes," that is, themselves. On their way they encountered the Queen Mother, her carriage stuck in the mud. Marchers put their shoulders to the wheels of the 20 foot behemoth, freed it, and allowed her to proceed to London and safety unhindered. Whatever their leaders intentions, the rank and file was not anti-royalist.

Later at Blackheath, six miles south of London, Ball delivered a famous sermon which captures the spirit of their enterprise. Froissart's *Chronicles* gives the following account of it:

> "Ah, ye good people, the matters goeth not well to pass in England, nor shall not do till everything be common, and that there be no *villains* nor gentlemen, but that we may be all united together, and that the lords be no greater masters than we be.
>
> What have we deserved, or why should we be kept thus in servage? We be all come from one father and one mother, Adam and Eve: whereby can they say or shew that they be greater lords than we be, saving by that they cause us to win and labour for that they dispend? They are clothed in velvet and camlet furred with grise, and we be vestured with poor cloth: they have their wines, spices and good bread, and we have the drawing out of the chaff and drink water: they

dwell in fair houses, and we have the pain and travail, rain and wind in the fields; and by that that cometh of our labours they keep and maintain their estates: we be called their bondmen, and without we do readily them service, we be beaten; and we have no sovereign to whom we may complain, nor that will hear us nor do us right.

Let us go to the king, he is young, and shew him what servage we be in, and shew him how we will have it otherwise, or else we will provide us of some remedy; and if we go together, all manner of people that be now in any bondage will follow us to the intent to be made free; and when the king seeth us, we shall have some remedy, either by fairness or otherwise."

— Froissart's *Chronicles*

He concluded with, "Whan Adam dalf and Eve span..." and his audience answered him, chanting, "small, small, small..."

What Happened Next

JUST THIS MUCH WAS ENOUGH TO ANSWER MY QUESTIONS ABOUT ITINERANT PREACHERS – powerful catalysts for social change – and any connection with *Revelation* – none. Plus, there's a bonus. John Ball's story turns up again in literary and folk history in ways which may shed light on Tarot's forgotten past. But to appreciate the analogy it's necessary to know what actually happened, so it can be compared with these other versions.

When the rebels arrived at London, they found the city gates and London Bridge shut against them, and fourteen-year-old King Richard II attempted to parley from a barge in the middle of the Thames. When this failed the rebels responded by petitioning for a list of "political criminals" to be handed over: John of Gaunt, the king's uncle and regent; Sir Simon Sudbury, chancellor of England; Sir Robert Hales, treasurer of England; Sir John Fordham, clerk of the Privy Seal; Sir Robert Belknap, chief justice of the King's Bench; Sir Ralph Ferrers; Sir Robert

Plessington, chief baron of the Exchequer; John Legge, king's Sergeant-at-arms; and Thomas Bampton, the poll-tax commissioner for Fobbing.

Richard, of course, refused. But his options quickly dwindled when rebel sympathizers betrayed the city gates and once inside, rebels began to break open prisons and systematically destroy properties connected with the names on their list:

> "And at this time, as it was said, the mob of London set fire to and burnt the fine manor of [JOHN OF GAUNT'S] Savoy."
>
> "...the commons of Essex came to Lambeth near London, a manor of the Archbishop of Canterbury [SIMON SUDBURY], and entered into the buildings and destroyed many of the goods of the said Archbishop, and burnt all the books of register, and rules of remembrances belonging to the Chancellor, which they found there."
>
> "They went into the Temple church [associated with ROBERT HALES] and took all the books and rolls and remembrances, that lay in their cupboards in the Temple, which belonged to the lawyers, and they carried them into the highway and burnt them there."
>
> — *Anonimal Chronicle*

This was primarily a demonstration of political will. Property and records were its target. Discipline was so strict that looters were executed on Wat Tyler's orders.

Against this threat, the king and his ministers decided upon a ruse. They would promise the rebels anything to get them out of London; later it would be easy enough to renege on some pretense or another. Accordingly, the king proclaimed a meeting at Mile End, east of London, for the next day. There, a crowd of 60,000 demanded:

> "...for the future no man should be in serfdom, nor make any manner of homage or suit to any lord, but should give rent

of four pence an acre for his land. They asked also that no one should serve any man except by his own free will, and by terms of an ordinary contract."

— Froissart's *Chronicles*

To which King Richard promised:

"Sirs, I am well agreed thereto. Withdraw you home into your own houses and into such villages as ye came from, and leave behind you of every village two or three, and I shall cause writings to be made and seal them with my seal, the which they shall have with them, containing everything that ye demand; and to the intent that ye shall be the better assured, I shall cause my banners to be delivered into every bailiwick, shire and countries."

— *Ibid*

Thirty clerks wrote out letter patents sealed with the king's seal to this effect. After receiving theirs, many men departed for home as requested.

Meanwhile, Tyler, Ball and others had slipped away, joining four hundred men surrounding the Tower of London where the king's ministers were holding out, and:

"...entered into the Tower and brake up chamber after chamber, and at last found the Archbishop of Canterbury, called Simon [Sudbury]... and strake off his head, and also they beheaded the lord of Saint John's [treasurer, Robert Hales] and a Friar Minor [lawyer, Sir William Appleton]... and a sergeant-at-arms called John Legge; and these four heads were set on four long spears and they made them to be borne before them through the streets of London and at last set them a-high on London bridge, as though they had been traitors to the king and to the realm."

— *Ibid*

This act only makes sense if the executions were part of an organized political program. It was also the signal for a massacre of foreigners. Over 150 rich Fleming and Lombard merchants residing within the city died that day.

Though the situation seemed hopeless, Richard was to rid himself of Tyler and his army at Smithfield the following day. Summoned to another parley, Tyler added to his demands, many of which we consider basic rights nowadays:

> "...there should be no outlawry in any process of law, and that no lord should have lordship save civilly, and that there should be equality among all people save only the king... that there should be only one bishop in England and only one prelate, and all the lands and tenements now held by them should be confiscated, and divided among the commons, only reserving for them a reasonable sustenance. And... that there should be no more *villeins* in England, and no serfdom or *villeinage*, but that all men should be free and of one condition."
>
> — *Anonimal Chronicle*

In the course of this exchange, a valet in the king's retinue provoked a quarrel, boasting, "...he knew him [Tyler] for the greatest thief and robber in all Kent." When William Walworth, the Mayor of London, attempted to place Tyler under arrest the latter stabbed at him. Tyler's blow was deflected by the mayor's concealed armor, while Walworth:

> "...drew his cutlass, and struck back at the said Wat, and gave him a deep cut on the neck, and then a great cut on the head. And during this scuffle one of the king's household drew his sword, and ran Watt two or three times through the body, mortally wounding him. And he spurred his horse, crying to the commons to avenge him, and the horse carried him some four score paces, and then he fell to the ground half dead..."
>
> — *Ibid*

Seeing what had happened, the rebels made their bows ready. Young King Richard saved the day by his quick thinking and bravery. Spurring on his horse, he rode into the crowd crying, "Sirs, what aileth you? Ye shall have no captain but me. I am your king. Be all in rest and peace," and lead them away to Clerkenwell Fields to the north.

This gave Walworth precious time to raise a force of loyal citizens over the next 30 minutes. Returning to Smithfield with his recruits, Walworth found Tyler dying in St. Bartholomew's hospital for the poor and had him carried out of the building and beheaded. The head was stuck on a pole and carried to where the king was surrounded by rebels. Confronted by an armed force of 7,000 men and the grim reminder of Tyler's fate, the rebels decided their best remedy lay in surrender. Some fled out of the city gates, while others were given an armed escort across London Bridge out of town. Only a few of the boldest dared to remain.

London was safe but the revolt was still in progress, as men from Mile End carried revolution back to their home counties. In Hertfordshire they even fought under the banners they'd received there. But now officials were organized, and pursuing a divided opposition. A week after Smithfield, Richard told a delegation seeking confirmation of their Mile End charters, "*Villeins* ye are still, and *villeins* ye shall remain." By July he was secure enough to annul all the concessions he'd granted.

John Ball was captured in Coventry and tried in St. Albans on July 13, 1381. He freely admitted writing incendiary letters and his part in the rebellion, but denied any of it was blameworthy and refused to ask for a pardon. He was hanged and drawn and quartered two days later.

Two Hundred Years Later

WHEN WE NEXT ENCOUNTER JOHN BALL, HIS DEEDS ARE PART OF A COMPOSITE CHARACTER larger than life. Jack Cade was a real, historical figure portrayed in Shakespeare's play the *Second Part of King Henry the Sixth.* Like Ball and Wat Tyler, he was a usurper who captured London in 1450 after his men ambushed a royal army and sent the king scurrying for safety. Two days later, Londoners threw him out again after an all-night battle on London Bridge. But compared with Ball and Tyler, Cade was bourgeois. His troops included a number of gentlemen and squires, and even two members of Parliament!

Perhaps the Bard couldn't find enough material in Holinshed on him, or didn't find it interesting enough. In any case much of what passes for Jack Cade in *King Henry the Sixth*, including the best lines of the play, comes from the peasants rebellion of 1381:

> **Cade:** There shall be in England seven halfpenny loaves sold for a penny: the three-hooped pot shall have ten hoops; and I will make it a felony to drink small beer: all the realm shall be in common ... there shall be no money; all shall eat and drink on my score; and I will apparel them all in one livery, that they may agree like brothers.
>
> **Dick:** The first thing we do, let's kill all the lawyers.
> **Cade:** Nay, that I mean to do. Is not this a lamentable thing, that of the skin of an innocent lamb should be made parchment? that parchment, being scribbled o'er, should undo a man? Some say the bee stings: but I say, 'tis the bee's wax; for I did but seal once to a thing, and I was never mine own man since.
>
> **King:** How now! what news? why comest thou in such haste?
> **Messenger:** The rebels are in Southwark; fly my lord! ... His army is a ragged multitude of hinds and peasants, rude and merciless ... All scholars, lawyers, courtiers, gentlemen, they call false caterpillars and intend their death.
>
> **Cade:** So, sirs: now go some and pull down the Savoy; others to the inns of court [Temple]; down with them all ... Away, burn all the records of the realm: my mouth shall be the parliament of England ... And henceforward all things shall be in common.
>
> **Cade:** I thought ye would never have given out these arms till you had recovered your ancient freedom: but you are all recreants and dastards, and delight to live in slavery to the

nobility. Let them break your backs with burthens, take your houses over your heads, ravish your wives and daughters before your faces...

– *Second Part of King Henry the Sixth, Act IV*

Much of the dialogue is hyperbole, but in 1381 *they really did kill all the lawyers!* And the lord chancellor and treasurer too. The character that emerges in Shakespeare's play is part John Ball, part Jack Cade – but no one seems to notice.

Vague Echoes

IN CONTRAST TO THE ABOVE, WE WOULD PROBABLY NEVER REALIZE THE FOLLOWING refers to John Ball, except that his name is explicitly mentioned. Once it is, however, we can appreciate its deeper significance. A rhyme still current in the south of England goes:

"John Ball Shot Them All

John Patch made the match,
John Ball shot them all!
John Clint made the flint,
John Ball shot them all!
John Puzzle made the muzzle,
John Ball shot them all!
John Crowder made the powder,
John Ball shot them all!
John Block made the stock,
John Ball shot them all!
John Wyming made the priming,
John Ball shot them all!
John Brammer made the hammer,
John Ball shot them all!
John Scott made the shot,
John Ball shot them all!"

Since both match and flint (different ways of igniting gunpowder) are mentioned, the rhyme was composed long after the actual events, probably between 1620 and 1650. To someone unfamiliar with what happened in 1381 it must seem like so much doggerel. But it has a kind of rough logic to it. John Ball and his fellows confronted the establishment of their time. He, and they, *really did shoot them all.*

This, and my other readings, convinced me that I should be looking for an Italian *Giovanni Palla* or *Ballo* if I was going to make further progress in understanding Tarot's origins.

The Payoff

JOHN BALL AND ITINERANT PREACHERS WERE ON MY MIND, BUT I HADN'T DECIDED where to look next, when Craig announced after dinner one evening, "There's a school band practice in 45 minutes, do you want to drive me over? If not, it's OK. I don't really need to go."

"Sure, I'll take you," I answered.

Since it was only a one hour practice and a fifteen minute drive it made sense to stay till he'd finished. I decided to browse in a nearby bookstore while I waited. Inside the store, on my way to the computer section, I passed a large history collection – seven rows high and three shelves wide. I had plenty of time. I might as well check for books on itinerant preachers.

The collection was completely unorganized, but that didn't matter since I didn't know what I was looking for anyway. So, starting with the top shelf, I began to work right to left towards the bottom. Somewhere about the third shelf, I began to wonder, "Even if there's something here, what are the odds I'll find it?" But I kept on going, and going... and going. Finally on the middle of the bottom shelf, as I was crawling along the floor, I glimpsed the word *Bible* sandwiched between *World War II* and *General Custer*.

Here it was! I pulled a small paperback from the shelf to get a better look. The full title, written on two lines, was: *The English Bible and the Seventeenth-Century Revolution.* Rats! Charles I and Oliver Cromwell. Wrong country and 200 years too late! Still, I had it out and, "If you can't be with the one you love, love the one you're with," – Stephen Stills. So I began skimming for interesting topics.

John Ball and Wat Tyler were listed in the index at the back. The book was recent and practically every page listed five or six citations – obviously a piece of scholarship. Section VI of the first chapter, "A Biblical Culture," talked about preaching and the spoken word being more important than print. Perhaps some of this was true for the fourteenth and fifteenth centuries as well? Little did I know, in spirit much of it was, witness the earlier quote from *Pilgrim's Progress.* In any case, the book looked interesting enough to read on its own merits.

I placed it under my arm and glanced at my watch. Ten minutes till I had to pick up Craig! My search had taken much longer than I'd planned. There was no time for the computer section now. To kill a few minutes, I went over to the bargain table. What was this? A book on Ancient Egypt, and another on the Vikings, in fact, a whole set of historical titles. I opened one. It was a reprint of a nineteenth-century work. I guessed that they all were. These can be quite good, but you have to be careful their "facts" aren't out of date. Altogether there were about a dozen titles, and I was pressed for time, but one on the end stood out: *Legendary and Mythological Art.*

I flipped through the pages. Dozens and dozens of religious drawings: angels, saints, Christians and lions, whizzed by. I came to a stop on page seventeen. There was the drawing of the Tetramorph from my bestiary. I looked at my watch; five minutes to go. I looked at the sale price, four dollars. Sold! I paid for my two acquisitions and was on my way in time to pick up Craig.

The next day, in the "The Reign of the Saints" chapter of the *English Bible* I discovered that seventeenth-century England had a fascination with the *Book of Revelation.* Zealots predicted the Second Coming of Christ would occur in 1650 or shortly thereafter. And after the English Civil War got underway, they began to link its events with passages from *Revelation* and the *Book of Daniel.* Radicals, even Quakers, were urging Cromwell to lead his armies to overthrow the Antichrist, who they identified as the pope in Rome. But my most valuable discovery was that chapter's first citation:

"Cohn, The Pursuit of the Millennium, *passim*."

Norman Cohn's book proved to be the Rosetta Stone for which I'd been searching. It describes the myths and legends which unlock the rest of Tarot's symbolism, and would broaden my focus from *Revelation* to Millennium. You might wonder, then, why I refer to it so seldomly. Unfortunately, Cohn writes about northern Europe, and only occasionally mentions in passing lands south of the Alps. Thus, I've had to piece together the details of the story for Italy – the birthplace of Tarot – from other sources using his work as a guide. That said, its time time to get down to the actual work of deciphering Tarot's message.

Bibliography

Henry Bett, *Nursery Rhymes and Tales: Their Origin and History*, (London: Methuen 1924).

William M. Bowsky, ed., *The Black Death: A Turning Point in History?* (Robert E. Krieger Pub., 1978).

Clara Erskine Clement, *A Handbook of Legendary and Mythological Art*, reprint: (Bracken Books, 1994).

Norman Cohn, *The Pursuit of the Millennium: Revolutionary Millenarians and Mystical Anarchists of the Middle Ages*, (Oxford UP, 1970).

Jean Froissart, *The Chronicles of Froissart*, trans John Bourchier, (New York: Harvard Classics, 1910).

Christopher Hill, *The English Bible and the Seventeenth-Century Revolution,* (Penguin Books, 1993).

J.J. Jusserand, *English Wayfaring Life in the Middle Ages: XIVth Century*, trans Lucy Toulmin Smith, reprint: (Corner House Pub., 1974)

Charles Oman, "The Anonimal Chronicle of St. Mary's York." In *The Great Revolt of 1381*, (London: Oxford UP, 1906).

Internet

Note: There's no need to type this yourself. Current links to these and future sites, as they become available, can be found at: http://tarot-cards.com

2 KING HENRY VI
http://www.gh.cs.usyd.edu.au/~matty/Shakespeare/texts/histories/2kinghenryvi_0.html

Anonimalle Chronicle: English Peasants'Revolt, 1381
http://www.fordham.edu/halsall/source/anon1381.html

Froissart's *Chronicles*
http://etext.lib.virginia.edu/cgibin/browse-mixed?id=FroChro&tag=public&images=images/modeng&data=/lv1/Archive/eng-parsed

Ordinance of Laborers, 1349
http://www.fordham.edu/halsall/seth/ordinance-labourers.html
Statute of Laborers, 1351
http://www.fordham.edu/halsall/seth/statute-labourers.html

Translations

1. Soli mendicantes vixissent super terram qui suffecissent pro sacris celebrandis aut conferendis universae terrae.

Chapter Five

Ludus Cartarum, the Game of Cards

UNTIL NOW I'VE FOCUSED ON HOW I LEARNED TAROT'S MEANING. But having a notion, and proving it's true, are two different matters. It doesn't count how you make a discovery. It's even OK to guess (intelligently). But you can't stop there. Nothing I've said so far can withstand serious criticism. It's all been based on the Tarot of Marseilles deck, which while old, is a relative newcomer as far as Tarot goes. And many older Tarot decks use different symbolism. So what I propose to do, is to start over from the beginning and do it right – guided by the insights of the earlier chapters.

European Beginnings

STUDENTS OF TAROT ARE FORTUNATE. TWO AUTHORS HAVE PUBLISHED almost every reference to its history in a few readily available volumes. Stuart R. Kaplan began this task in 1978 with *The Encyclopedia of Tarot*, which has now grown to several volumes. And in 1980, Michael Dummett published *The Game of Tarot From Ferrara to Salt Lake City*. These books are indispensable for the serious student, and the authors complement one another.

Mr. Kaplan is the president of U.S. Games Systems, and has managed to make a business of his hobby and vice versa. He approaches his subject from a collector's standpoint and illustrates almost every imaginable facet of Tarot – not just cards – but milestones in its history as well. This is both his strength and weakness. His collection is huge, and since he publishes in stages, his organization can be difficult to follow until you understand the subject. Characteristic of his approach, each volume has only a single page of conclusions.

Michael Dummett is listed in *The Oxford Companion to Philosophy* as a philosopher of language, logic, and mathematics, and this point of view characterizes his approach. He focuses on the Tarot card game, but manages to cover nearly the same range as Kaplan, with the difference that on practically every one of his pages you'll find a conclusion.

These two authors have done such an excellent job of weighing the evidence about the origin of playing cards, how they reached Europe, and the first Tarot decks, etc., I'm going to take most of their findings as established fact. If you want to know more about why we believe what we do about Tarot, read their accounts. With that said, the earliest records of playing cards in Europe which withstand scrutiny date from 1377. For the most part they're mere mentions in decrees and account books:

1379, Covelluzzo's *Chronicle for Viterbo*: "In the year 1379 there was brought to Viterbo the game of cards, which in the Saracen language is called *nayb*."[1]

1380, Barcelona inventory of goods: "...a game of cards, of which there are forty-four pieces."[2]

1382, Decree of Barcelona: "You may not amuse yourself by playing with dice, or tiles [boardgames], or cards..."[3]

1392, Charles Poupart's accounts: "Given to Jacquemin Gringonneur, painter, for three decks of cards, gilt, colored, and variously ornamented for the king's amusement, fifty-six Parisian *sols*." [4]

There's one important exception. In 1377 Johannes von Rheinfelden, a German monk, discussed the new pastime of playing cards as a metaphor for moral instruction. In doing so, he tells his readers, and us, much about the cards of his day. Frequently, his commentary is edited to the point where it's almost quoted out of context. Therefore, I'm going to give it at length here:

> "Hence it is that a certain game, called the game of cards, has come to us in this year, viz the year of our Lord 1337. In which game the state of the world as it is, is excellently described and figured. But at what time it was invented, where, and by whom, I am entirely ignorant. But this I say, that it is of advantage to noblemen and other persons of leisure; they may do no worse, especially if they practice it courteously and without money...
>
> Wherefore I, brother John, the least in the Order of Preachers [Dominicans], a German by birth, sitting as it happened, abstractedly at table, revolving in my mind one way and another the present state of the world, there suddenly occurred to me the game of cards; and I began to think how it might be closely likened to this state of the world. And it seemed to me very possible that it had a likeness to the world.
>
> Therefore, trusting in the Lord, I determined to compile a treatise on the subject, and began it on the following day, hoping by God's aid to complete it And should persons find some passage in it not easy to understand, but obscure and difficult, let them get out of their boat at Burgheim and enter it again at Rinveld [i.e. skip it], and proceed reading the treatise as before, until they come to the end of it...
>
> The subject of this treatise may be compared with the game of chess, for in both there are kings, queens, and chief nobles, and common people, so that both games may be treated in a moral sense.

And in this treatise I propose to do three things: first to describe the game of cards itself, as to the matter and mode of playing it; second to moralize the game, or teach noblemen the rule of life; and third, to instruct the people themselves, or inform them of the way of laboring virtuously. Wherefore it seemed to me the present treatise ought to be entitled 'Of Morals and Everyday Ethical Instruction' (De Moribus et Disciplina Humanae Conversationis).

The first part will have six chapters. In the first, will be stated the subject of the game and styles of play. In the second, it will be shown that in this game there is a moral action of virtues and vices. In the third it will be suggested that it is of service for mental relief and rest to the tired. In the fourth it will be shown that it is useful for idle persons, and may be a comfort to them. In the fifth will be treated the state of the world, as it is in respect to morals. In the sixth will be demonstrated the divisors of the number sixty, and the properties of numbers."

Brother John has the following to say about the cards themselves:

"In the game which men call the game of cards, they paint the cards in different manners, and they play with them in one way and another. The common form, as it first came to us is thus: Four kings are depicted on four cards, each of whom sits on a royal throne. And each one holds a certain sign in his hand, of which signs some are reputed good, but others signify evil. Under the kings are two *marschalli*, the first of whom holds the sign upwards in his hand, in the same manner as the king; but the other holds the same sign downward in his hand.

After this are another ten cards, outwardly of the same size and shape; on the first of which, the aforesaid king's sign is placed once [Ace]; on the second, twice [Deuce]; and so on for the others, up to and including the tenth card. So each king becomes the thirteenth, and there are altogether fifty-two cards.

There are others who play in the same manner with queens, and with as many cards as has been already said for kings. There are also others who arrange the cards, so that there are two kings with their *marschalli* and other cards, and two queens with theirs in the same manner. Again, some take five, others six kings, each with his *marschalli* and other cards, according to as it pleases them, and thus the game is varied in form by many.

Also there are some who make the game with four kings, eight *marschalli* and the other common cards, and add besides four queens with four attendants; so that... the number of the cards will then be sixty. This manner of distributing the cards and this number pleases me most, for three reasons: first, because of its greater authority; second, because of its royal fitness; and third, because of its more becoming courteousness."

— *The History of Playing Cards*

We probably wouldn't feel out of place using this deck today. Scholars are disturbed by the many styles of play described and note the earliest manuscript dates from 1429, not 1377 (three others from 1472 also exist). Some suggest a later copyist brought it up to date as he reproduced it. But this seems unlikely. Even from what's given here it's apparent the sixth part of the treatise has been included because of games with sixty cards, and updating wouldn't have been a simple touch-up job. But we needn't be too concerned, the history of Tarot probably begins around 1429 anyway.

Islamic Origins

THE RAPID SPREAD OF CARDS THROUGHOUT EUROPE SUGGESTED TO Hellmut Rosenfeld that cards must have been introduced from somewhere else. Language clues suggested the Islamic world. Playing cards were first called *naibi* in Italy, *nahipi* in southern France, and *naips* in Spain (they're still called *naipes* there today) – all variations on the Islamic word *na'ib*, the

Mameluke word for viceroy. The Mameluke word for playing cards was probably *kanjifah*. That Europeans would confuse the name of the entire deck with one for a single card is understandable if cards were of foreign origin. There's even evidence that both European and Islamic cards were once used interchangeably. An inventory of goods for Valentina Visconti in 1408 lists: "...one deck of Saracen cards; some decks from Lombardy."[5]

The only problem with this theory is that no one had ever seen an early Islamic playing card. Eventually, forty-eight cards from a fifty-two card deck of Mameluke Egypt was discovered by L. A. Meyer in the *Topkapi Sarayi* Museum in Istanbul. But it wasn't as old as early European decks. Finally, fragments of even earlier Islamic cards were identified, and the theory corroborated.

The Istanbul cards are curious in one respect; like many Islamic coins, they have no portraits. The rank and suit of the king (*malik*), viceroy to the king (*na`ib malik*), and second viceroy (*thani naib*) are indicated by inscriptions at their bottoms. This brings up the question, "Why do European cards have portraits if they were borrowed from Mameluke cards with none at all?" The answer seems to be that the court cards of the Istanbul deck were made by overpainting inscriptions on what were originally number cards and additional cards were borrowed from other decks to replace the changed suit cards. So perhaps this deck isn't entirely typical of the ones introduced into Europe.

In contrast, the suit signs of the Istanbul and early European cards are quite similar. The Mameluke suits are Swords, Polo Sticks, Cups, and Coins; similar to the suits on the Tarot of Marseilles. Europeans, however, didn't have the slightest idea of what Polo Sticks were, and changed them to Wands. This is the oldest, so-called Latin, suit system. The standard American deck: Clubs, Diamonds, Hearts and Spades employs French suits, while the Swiss use: Shields, Flowers, Bells, and Acorns, and the Germans: Hearts, Leaves, Bells, and Acorns.

These other suits first appeared in the last quarter of the fifteenth century, although their individual symbols had appeared a quarter-century earlier. Before this, suit signs could be quite variable, especially in Germany.

Records of Tarot

SO FAR I'VE BEEN TALKING ABOUT ORDINARY PLAYING CARDS. THE FIRST MENTION OF TAROT comes from Ferrara, Italy. Registries there dated 1442 mention: "one pair [i.e. pack] of *trionfi* cards,"[6] and the purchase of: "four pair of *trionfi* cards."[7] Similar references occur in the years 1452, 1454, and 1461.

Trionfi or *triumphi* is the original name for Tarot. This was changed to *tarocchi* after 1510 or thereabouts, when *triumphi* began to be used for any card game played with trumps. The word trump is just a corruption of *triumphi.* Tarot or *Tarau* is a French variant of *tarocchi.* A reference from Milan makes it clear *triumphi* refer to Tarot cards, and not ordinary playing cards:

> "To Antonio Trecho, treasurer
>
> As soon as this is received, I want you to send, by a mail rider, two decks of *triumphi* cards, the finest you can find; AND IF YOU DO NOT FIND TRIUMPHI, PLEASE SEND TWO OTHER DECKS OF PLAYING CARDS, of the finest there are. Do this so we have them here for all day Sunday, which will be the 13th of this month.
>
> From Lodi, the 11th of December 1450.
>
> Vicecount Francesco Sforza,
>
> signed by his own hand. *Ci`ao.*" [8]

Just as the best description of ordinary playing cards comes from a moral treatise, the best description of *triumphi* comes from a collection of sermons: *Very Useful Sermons On Games* (*Sermo Perutilis de Ludo*) composed some time between 1450 and 1480. Under the heading of Misleading Games, is found:

> "The third kind of game is, of course, *triumphs.* There's nothing in this world, pertaining to games, as repugnant to God as this game of *triumphs.* It's clear, indeed, that every disgrace to the Christian faith is manifest in its play. For so-called *triumphi,* should be accounted as creations of the devil; because in no other game do spirits of perdition con-

> quer like in this one. So that mere gods, angels, planets, and cardinal virtues capture and thereby slander and defame the true lights of the world, the pope and emperor; which is absurd, and the greatest disgrace to Christendom to play this game. There are 21 *triumphs* which are arranged in 21 levels of depth from one another.
>
> The first is called The Trifle (and is least of all), 2. The Empress, 3. The Emperor, 4. The Popess (O misfortune that contradicts Christian faith! O pontiff, how can this be?), 5. The Pope (who ought to be worshiped by all, and they make this joke of their leader.), 6. Temperance, 7. The Lovers, 8. The Chariot or little World, 9. Strength, 10. The Wheel of Fortune (that is: I reign, I reigned, I am without reign), 11. The Hunchback, 12. The Hanged Man, 13. Death, 14. The Devil, 15. The Arrow, 16. The Star, 17. The Moon, 18. The Sun, 19. The Angel, 20. Justice, and 21. The World, created by God the Father."

A little later the sermon also mentions:

> "The Madman, worth nothing except to follow suit." [9]

The order of the cards in the sermon differs from the standard Tarot of Marseilles ordering. And some card names, marked by bullets in the table (*opposite page*), are different. In this book I'll use the sermon's card order, but retain standard Tarot names, except for The Popess and Pope cards where the older names are more revealing than the modern euphemisms.

Early Tarot Decks

SO FAR I'VE SPOKEN OF WRITTEN RECORDS. WHAT ABOUT TAROT DECKS? If you think about how many cards you've saved from years past, you might think it's a miracle any have survived at all. Early cards have come down from three sources. Many of the survivors are *objets d'art* created by noted artists of the time and handed down from collector to collector. These are hand painted

Sermon Card Names

Standard Name	Sermon Name
• The Magician	The Trifle (*El bagatella*)
The Empress	The Empress (*Imperatrix*)
The Emperor	The Emperor (*Imperator*)
• The High Priestess	The Popess (*La papessa*
• The Hierophant	The Pope (*El papa*)
Temperance	Temperance (*La temperentia*)
The Lovers	The Lovers (*L'amore*)
• The Chariot	The Chariot (*Lo caro triumphale*) or little World (*mundus parvus*)
Strength	Strength (*La forteza*)
The Wheel of Fortune	The Wheel (*La rotta*)
• The Hermit	The Hunchback (*El gobbo*)
The Hanged Man	The Hanged Man (*Lo impichato*)
Death	Death (*La morte*)
The Devil	The Devil (*El diavolo*)
• The Tower	The Arrow (*La sagitta*)
The Star	The Star (*La stella*)
The Moon	The Moon (*La Luna*)
The Sun	The Sun (*El sole*)
• Judgment	The Angel (*Lo angelo*)
Justice	Justice (*La justicia*)
The World	The World (*El mondo*)
• The Fool	The Madman (*El matto*)

and incorporate heraldic and other insignias of the families who originally commissioned them. Some mass produced cards, printed from woodblocks and colored using stencils, have survived too. Not usually in deck form, but even better, as uncut sheets. Because the stiff paper used for cards was expensive, remainders were sometimes reused for book linings. Some turned up years later when the books were rebound. Presumably, more await discovery. Finally, a few individual cards have been recovered from the bottom of wells and other locations protected from oxidation.

A substantial number of *triumphi* exist from the first century or so of their manufacture. Cards get worn and lost, so there are no complete decks. Those with the most surviving Major Arcana cards are listed in the table (*opposite page*). If all 78 Tarot cards were included, the table would look a little different.

The decks of the first five columns are hand-painted. Those in the first three columns are linked with the Visconti and Sforza families of Milan, Italy while those in the fourth and fifth columns come from Ferrara, Italy and France respectively. They were all originally unnumbered, but Roman numerals were later added to the French deck.

The remaining five decks are printed. Those in columns six and seven are also unnumbered. The deck in column eight is numbered from I to IIX (12), while only The World card of the deck in column nine is unnumbered. The deck in the last column is the oldest deck to have Tarot of Marseilles numbering.

In the table, cells with no entries indicate missing cards. Those with an X indicate original cards; R, replacement cards; and C, copies of other cards. The printed decks, except for the one of the last column, are really uncut sheets, though I'll refer to them as decks for simplicity. An F means that only a fragment of a card is visible on a sheet. For convenience, I've also listed the beginning page of the *Encyclopedia of Tarot* where each deck is illustrated.

Only true decks have popular names. Sheets typically go by the museum and collection they belong to. Thus the Washington deck in the table is really: 1951.16.7 (PR) B-19823 in the Washington National Gallery of Art's Rosenwald collection. Sometimes copies of sheets belonging to the same "deck" are held by several institutions. At the risk of introducing more confusion, I've chosen to refer to these decks by the cities in which their sheets currently reside. This solves most of the cumbersome name and multiple copies problems and makes remembering them a bit more manageable.

Early Tarot Decks with the Most Surviving Major Arcana Cards

Card	Visconti-Modrone	Visconti-Sforza	Lombardy	d'Este	Charles VI	Paris	New Haven	Washington	Budapest	Catelin Geofroy
1 The Magician		X	C	X			X	X	X	X
2 The Empress	X	X	C				X	X	X	X
3 The Emperor	X	X			X		X	X	F	X
4 The Popess		X	C				X	X	X	X
5 The Pope		X	C	X	X		F	X	X	X
6 Temperance		R	C	X	X		F	X	F	X
7 The Lovers	X	X	C		X		F	X	F	
8 The Chariot	X	X	C		X	X	F	X	F	X
9 Strength	X	R	C		X		F	X	F	
10 The Wheel of Fortune		X	C			X	F	X	X	
11 The Hermit		X	C		X	X		X	X	X
12 The Hanged Man		X	C		X	X	F	X	X	X
13 Death	X	X	C		X	X		X	X	X
14 The Devil						X	F	X	X	
15 The Tower					X	X	F	X	X	X
16 The Star		R		X		X	X	X	F	
17 The Moon		R		X	X	X	X	X	X	
18 The Sun		R	C	X	X	X	F	X	X	
19 Judgment	X	X	C		X	X		X	X	X
20 Justice		X			X		F	X	X	
21 The World	X	R		X	X	X		X	X	
0 The Fool		X	C	X	X		F		X	
Encyclopdia of Tarot vol I	88	65		117	112	128		130		132
Encyclopdia of Tarot vol II	26		13				286		272	303

X: Original Card
C: Copy of Original
R: Replacement Card
F: Partial Fragment

The Visconti-Sforza Family of Decks

BECAUSE OF THEIR ATTRACTIVENESS AND ACCESSIBILITY, SCHOLARS have paid most attention to the hand-painted decks. In fact, many theories about Tarot were formulated with only these in mind. For this reason, they deserve additional comment.

Conventional wisdom makes the Visconti-Modrone deck the oldest of those listed. It's also a little different from the others; it contains extra Major Arcana cards representing the theological virtues: Faith, Hope, and Charity. And it adds two Queen's attendants, a Mounted Lady and Maid, to each of the four suits, bringing the number of cards per suit to sixteen. On the other hand, it provides some of the best clues to the meaning of Tarot, so I've included it here. This deck currently resides at Yale University's Beinecke Library.

The Visconti-Sforza deck in the second column has attracted more attention than the others because of its beauty and completeness. Only its Devil and Tower cards are missing. This statement is misleading, however, since six cards are later replacements and may not be faithful to the symbolism of the originals. And personally, I find it to be the most enigmatic deck of all. The cards of the Visconti-Sforza deck are divided between three owners: The Pierpont Morgan Library in New York, and the Accademia Carrara and the Colleoni family in Bergamo, Italy.

The Lombardy deck in the third column is a more or less faithful copy of the Visconti-Sforza deck and provides no new information, except to clarify faded and ambiguous images. The fact that even replacement cards are copied makes it the most recent of these three decks.

Heraldry establishes the relative dating of the Visconti-Sforza family of decks, of which there are fifteen decks, and 271 cards extant. Comparing these cards with Visconti coins and a *Book of Hours* painted for Gian Galeazzo (1351-1402) and Filippo Maria (1392-1447) Visconti reveals numerous personal and heraldic devices [sunbursts, a dove, the motto: *A bon droyt*, a ducal crown with fronds and the Visconti viper (*opposite page*)] on all of them, leaving no doubt about a Visconti connection. On the

Visconti-Modrone and the Brambilla (48 surviving cards including The Emperor and The Wheel of Fortune) decks actual dies derived from Filippo Maria's gold *fiorino* coin, bearing his initials *FI* and *MA,* were used to stamp coin images on the cards of the Coins suit. Hence these two decks are traditionally said to belong to him.

A fountain and three interlinked rings, identified as Francesco Sforza's (1401-1466) devices, on the Visconti-Sforza cards are cited as justification for attributing ownership of this deck to him. But the logic is not as clean as before; the same fountain also appears prominently on some Visconti-Modrone cards, and three interlinked rings were a popular symbol for the Trinity.

THE VISCONTI VIPER ON A SILVER *pegione* COIN OF MILAN, CIRCA 1400 (*about the size to a quarter*).

Three years after Filippo Maria Visconti died without a male heir, Francesco Sforza, who had married Filippo's daughter Bianca Maria, re-conquered Milan to become its fourth duke. Afterwards he used the devices of both his and his wife's families as a mark of legitimacy. Filippo Maria was the last ruler of Milan who's legitimacy was unquestioned. Subsequent rulers, including the Spanish as late as the seventeenth century, continued to employ Visconti devices. This may be the real reason why the cards are loaded with Visconti symbols. Nevertheless, the Visconti-Modrone deck is customarily identified as belonging to Filippo Maria Visconti, and the Visconti-Sforza deck to Francesco Sforza.

The D'Este Deck

THE ESTE COAT-OF-ARMS ON THE QUEEN OF SWORDS ESTABLISHES THE PROVENANCE OF THIS DECK. Actually, this card may be The Empress. Why else would she bear different arms from both the King and Knight of Swords? And hold a different style of sword? In any case, the arms allow us to fix an earliest date that the deck could have been painted.

The original Este family arms were a white eagle with a gold crown on a blue field (*Azure an eagle argent armed, beaked and crowned or*) as seen on the escutcheon in the center of the queen's shield (*opposite page*). In 1431, Charles VII granted to Niccolo d'Este the right to quarter this with three gold *fleurs-de-lys* on a blue field with a red and silver border (*Azure three fleurs-de-lys or* a *bordure indented gules and silver*) – bottom left and top right of the shield. On May 18, 1452 Emperor Frederic III granted Borso d'Este the county of Rovigo and the title of imperial vicar, at which point the arms added a black imperial eagle – top left – and another two-headed eagle – bottom right (*Quarterly 1. Or an eagle sable, 2 and 3. Azure three fleurs-de-lys or and a bordure indented gules and silver, 4. Per pale azure and or a two-headed eagle per pale silver and sable en surtout Este*). In later versions, as on the d'Este card, the Rovigo eagle was replaced by a second imperial eagle (also two-headed). In 1474 Pope Sixtus IV grant-

THE ARMS OF THE D'ESTE QUEEN OF SWORDS CARD (*about actual size*) PROVES THIS DECK DATES FROM AFTER 1508.

ed Ercole I d'Este the papal keys – bottom center – on a vertical red stripe down the center of the shield. Finally, in 1508 Alfonso I, duke of Ferrara, became the papal standard-bearer (*gonfalonier)*, and the papal tiara – top center – was added to the keys. Although Alfonso lost his title the next year, he and his descendants retained the insignia. Thus, the arms portrayed on the Queen of Swords card could not have been painted before 1508 when the final papal tiara was added.

While only the last fact is required to establish an earliest date for the d'Este deck, the detailed history of changes allows us to definitively state it wasn't painted earlier, as some have suggested. If it had, the shield would look quite different. The d'Este deck is held by Yale University's Beinecke Library.

The Charles VI Deck

THE CHARLES VI DECK IS A MISNOMER. CHARLES VI RULED FRANCE from 1380 to 1422, probably a century before the deck bearing his name was made. If one were to rename it after a French monarch today, Francis I would be a better choice – as can be inferred from the history of coins and medals.

In 1438, the Byzantine emperor John VIII Palaelogus came to Italy with a religious delegation to discuss uniting the Greek and Roman Churches and the defense of Constantinople against the Ottoman Turks. Nothing lasting came of the talks, but at the time artist Vittore Pisano, or Pisanello, cast a bronze portrait medal – copies still exist – of John wearing a marvelous hat. The medal became the talk of Italy, and was so popular that Pisanello was kept busy making portrait medals for the rest of his life.

In the 1450s both Francesco Sforza and King Ferdinand I of Naples issued coins (*testone*) bearing portraits. The fashion caught on, and in the following decades larger portrait coins were issued by Galeazzo Maria Sforza, fifth duke of Milan; Niccolo Tron, doge of Venice; and Ercole I and Borso d'Este, dukes of Ferrara. Eventually portrait coins became so common they're now used to mark the boundary between medieval and Renaissance coinage.

When did portrait coins reach France? The first French *testone* features Louis XII on a 1514 coin of Milan. It was created by Caradossa, the same artist and engraver the Sforzas used. Louis was a descendant of Valentina Visconti and claimed the Milanese duchy through her. Valentina was the sister of Filippo Maria Visconti, the last Visconti duke. The terms of her marriage contract stipulated that in the absence of a male heir, Milan would pass to her descendants. There were male heirs; Filippo of course, and his brother Giovanni. But they both died without male heirs, opening the way for French claims to Milan. Meanwhile, Francesco Sforza reconquered the duchy for himself and his wife, *née* Bianca Maria Visconti, setting in motion a medieval soap opera with geopolitical consequences. France pressed her claims and occupied Milan from 1499 till 1522. This gave French kings ample opportunity to become acquainted with Italian culture, *testone* and Tarot included.

Portrait coins first appear in France itself, during the reign of Francis I, Louis' cousin and successor. Francis also campaigned in northern Italy, winning a decisive victory at Marignano in 1515 and suffering a crushing defeat at Pavia in 1525, resulting in his capture and the end of French power in Italy. He was Valentina Visconti's grandson and added Duke of Milan to his titles.

Furthermore, Francis was a connoisseur of Italian culture and eagerly imported it to France. He began the Louvre's collection with twelve paintings from Italy, including works by Titian, Raphael, and Leonardo da Vinci, of which the most famous is the Mona Lisa or *La Joconde*. And Leonardo spent his last years in France in his employ. In 1528 Francis' sister-in-law, Renée, married Ercole II d'Este, the son of the Duke of Ferrara. Ercole's brother Cardinal Ippolito d'Este was a favorite of the French court and received numerous gifts from the king. The French-Ferrara infatuation was mutual. An English history of Italy written in the 1540's says of Ercole, then Duke:

> "By his father's days he married Madame Renée, daughter unto Louis XII, French king, a very gracious lady ... and of devotion is altogether French, so that if there should happen

> any business in Italy between the [Habsburg] emperor and French king his part is like to be therein."
>
> – *The State of Ferrara*

It's likely that Tarot was carried to France at the same time as portrait coins, by the same people, and that the Charles VI deck, like the d'Este one, dates from 1520-40.

The Charles VI deck currently resides at the Bibliothèque Nationale in Paris. I've used line-drawings rather than photographs to illustrate it in this book. These are much clearer than photographs, and I would have done the same for the other hand-painted decks if I could.

The Printed Decks

OTHER THAN WHAT'S COVERED IN THE TABLE, THE MOST IMPORTANT FACT about the printed decks is where they're located, so scholars familiar with them by their catalogue names can identify what I'm talking about. If this isn't you, feel free to skip this section as it won't be used again.

Two different sheets of cards from the Paris deck survive. One is held by the Louvre, and the other by the Bibliothèque d'Ecole Nationale Supérieure des Beaux-Arts. The New Haven cards, like so many others here, are part of Yale University's Cary Collection in the Beinecke Library. And as noted above, the Washington deck is held by the Washington National Gallery of Art. Most of the sheets comprising the Budapest deck reside at the Szépmüveszeti Múzeum in Budapest, although a few duplicates were sold to the Metropolitan Museum of Art in New York. Finally, the Catelin Geofroy deck (a true deck) is the only one with a date – 1557. And Catelin Geofroy, the manufacturer's name, appears on the aces of its suits. It's currently held by the Museum für Kunsthandwerk in Frankfurt am Main, Germany.

Tarot of Marseilles Decks

SINCE TAROT OF MARSEILLES DECKS ARE FREQUENTLY MENTIONED, it's appropriate to give some of their history too. Marseilles got off to a late start as a card manufacturing center. Tax records for the year 1605 fail to include it as such, and it appears for the first time in the records for 1631. In contrast, card making had prospered in the nearby cities of Toulouse, Avignon and especially Lyon, since the mid-fifteenth century. By the mid-eighteenth century, however, Marseilles had caught up and was an important production center with an export trade. It's estimated there were eleven card manufacturers with thirty workers then, producing 2,700 gross (390,000) decks per year. Accounts relate:

> "In 1730 we cardmakers only made cards of the French, Madrid, large Club, Lima, and Tarot kinds... The French cards were also called the 'Marseilles design'; and we made around 130 cases of 5 gross each per year, and sold them at 24 *livres* per gross. These cards were consumed in Marseilles, with the exception of a dozen cases, which were exported.
>
> The large Club and Madrid cards were made exclusively for the Spanish; and we made almost as many of these as of French cards, and sold them at 60 *livres* per gross.
>
> We also made, each year, six cases of Tarot of Marseilles, of which a quarter were exported. Each Tarot deck was valued at 10 *sous*." [10]

Working the numbers for just the city of Marseilles, there were approximately twenty-five ordinary card decks sold for every Tarot deck, and the latter were three times as expensive as regular decks.

Who Played Tarot?

THIS NATURALLY LEADS TO THE QUESTION, "WHO FIRST PLAYED TAROT?" The small number of decks sold suggests an aristocracy. And the surviving hand-painted decks were surely made for nobles and their courts. The chance hypothesis says the game of Tarot originated there and spread to the general population a generation later.

Its proponents cite two arguments. First, since the earliest ordinary cards were hand-painted, hand-painted Tarot cards must be from the earliest Tarot decks. That a number of them are connected with the Visconti's, who also turn up in the early accounts of Tarot, seems to confirm this. A second argument focuses on production. Some nobles employed full-time card painters to supply their courts. It would matter little whether painters were painting Tarot or ordinary cards. On the other hand, woodblocks for mass produced decks would require a certain level of sales before they could return profits to their creators. It's argued that the risk of introducing a novelty item like a Tarot deck would be too great for ordinary card manufacturers to bear until the cards had already become popular in the noble's courts.

Both arguments are subtlely influenced by the perception that surviving hand-painted decks are examples of very early Tarot decks. But, you've already seen this is false for the d'Este deck and probably the Charles VI one too. And there are reasons to believe it's false for the others as well.

Evidence From the Death Card

CRITICAL EVIDENCE COMES FROM THE DEATH CARD, WHICH EXCEPT on the Visconti-Sforza and Catelin Geofroy decks, depicts a skeleton rider with a scythe. This convention has been the subject of considerable scrutiny because of its influence upon Albrecht Dürer's print *The Four Horsemen of the Apocalypse* shown earlier. Art historians believe that the image of death as a skeleton rider (without the scythe) first appeared in illustrated Apocalypses from the Low Countries shortly after 1400. The scythe is even older. In the 1330's Giotto replaced the hand sickle, familiar from the hammer and sickle on the flag of the former Soviet Union, with a large scythe in his frescoes for the Peruzzi chapel of Santa Croce in Florence, Italy.

As far as known, the rider and scythe came together for the first time in a series of German woodcut illustrations in 1478-9, 1483 and 1485, for the Cologne (Quentell), Nüremberg (Kolberger) and (*above*) Strausberg (Grüninger) Bibles.

That the convention was unknown before this date can be inferred from the *Très Riches Heures* Book of Hours created for the Duke of Berry. The original was left unfinished and completed by the artist Jean Colombe some time between 1485 and 1489.

Particularly interesting are two of Colombe's illustrations: *The Funeral of Raymond Diocrès* (Folio 86v) and *The Horseman of Death* (Folio 90v). Both depict numerous skeleton figures representing death, including death riding a unicorn and death with a scythe. Thus, Colombe knew the component parts, but failed to combine them together. Few artists to this day have resisted the temptation to do so. Either Colombe demonstrates a remarkable independence or he just wasn't aware of the convention.

The German Bible woodcuts did capture the attention of other European artists. Historians speculate that Albrecht Dürer saw and was influenced by the Kolberger print in his illustrations of the Apocalypse published in 1498 and re-issued in 1515, where he substituted a pitchfork for the scythe.

EARLIER, HE HAD PORTRAYED DEATH AS A SKELETON RIDER HOLDING A BONE IN HIS 1493 ILLUSTRATION (*right*) FOR: "ON HOPING FOR AN INHERITANCE," CHAPTER 94 OF SEBASTIAN BRANT'S *Ship of Fools* (*Narrenschiff*).

Similar experiments were tried by other artists in the last decade of the fifteenth century. *The Triumph of Death* fresco in the National Gallery at Palermo painted at this time shows the fourth horseman with a bow and arrow. Another, portrayed in the *Romance of the Rose* (*Roman de la Rose*) painted for Louise of Savoy, at the Bodleian Library in Oxford (Ms. Douce 195 f.22), carries a spear.

By the first quarter of the sixteenth century, the scythe had won out as the accepted convention. Not before the mid-fifteenth century, as we would otherwise have to believe, if the skeleton rider with a scythe on the Visconti-Modrone Death card was painted for Filippo Maria Visconti who died in 1447. Thus, the Visconti-Modrone deck's dating by heraldry and iconography are at odds.

Confirmation From The Lovers Card

BUT THIS OVERLOOKS FRANCIS I, THE LAST VISCONTI. FOR VERY much the same reasons as Francesco Sforza 70 years earlier, he needed to establish his legitimacy by wrapping himself in the Visconti mantle. The cards are his. The Visconti-Modrone Lovers card (*following page*) supports this contention. The Visconti viper and Savoy arms – white cross on a red field (*gules, a cross argent*) – around the card's canopy, and other heraldic devices, suggest it commemorates the marriage of a Visconti groom and a Savoy bride. Attempts to identify the groom as Filippo Maria Visconti make the woman his second wife, Maria of Savoy, in a marriage of political convenience, never consummated.

On the other hand, Francis I's mother, Louise of Savoy, was one of the most powerful figures in his court, served as regent while he was on his Italian campaigns, and actively participated in foreign affairs until her death in 1531. She could be the bride, and his father, Charles, count of Angoulême, the Visconti groom – offering "proof" of Francis legitimate claim to Milan. The French used Visconti heraldry extensively. The viper and gold *fiorino* coin of the Visconti-Modrone deck also appear on Louis XII's and Francis I's coins for Milan, as does the Visconti ducal crown and imperial eagle.

Identifying the bride as Louise of Savoy also permits the conclusion, often put forward and rejected, that the Visconti-Modrone deck is an early, 105 card Minchiate deck with its Faith, Hope, and Charity cards. Minchiate, an offshoot of Tarot, was invented around 1530, so this conclusion is impossible for cards belonging to Filippo Maria Visconti – but now it fits. By implication, the other surviving hand-painted and printed decks with skeleton rider Death cards, are circa 1520-40 too.

It's even possible that all the hand-painted decks are associated with Francis I and the d'Estes of Ferrara. In addition to Tarot

THE VISCONTI-MODRONE LOVERS CARD (*about actual size*).

decks, elaborate hand-painted ordinary decks, executed in a similar style, survive from this time. All might have been commissioned as political favors by or for people like Cardinal Ippolito d'Este, a favorite of the French court. This could explain why so many similar Visconti-Sforza decks exist.

Who Could Afford Tarot Cards?

PROPONENTS FOR THE CHANCE HYPOTHESIS TACITLY ASSUME COMMON PEOPLE couldn't afford Tarot cards. This contradicts evidence that ordinary decks were extremely popular and easy to come by, even in Tarot's earliest days. Cardmakers (*kartenmacher*) are mentioned in registries for Ulm, Germany in 1402; Augsburg, Germany in 1418; and Tournai, Belgium in 1427.

An account of a sermon delivered from the steps of Saint Peter's Church in Bologna, Italy on May 5, 1423 relates that Saint Bernardino of Sienna preached so fervently to his audience that they made a bonfire of their dice, board games, and cards on the spot before the magistrates – prompting a tearful cardmaker present at the scene to complain:

> "My Father, I make cards, and I have no other trade; in preventing the exercise of my art, you remove the means of earning my livelihood and supporting my family."
>
> "If you know only painting," responded the saint sweetly, "then paint this image." [11]

And he held up a radiant sun with the letters IHS which stand for the name of Christ. The saint's advice proved useful to the poor cardmaker, who grew rich selling the image which has since became the symbol of Saint Bernardino.

A SIMILAR SERMON BY JOHN CAPISTRAN AT NUREMBERG, GERMANY IN 1452 (*below*) WAS EVEN MORE SUCCESSFUL – 3,640 BACKGAMMON GAMES, 40,000 DICE, AND A LIKE NUMBER OF CARDS WERE COMMITTED TO THE FLAMES.

Woodblock printing, used in card manufacture, originated in the Low Countries, perhaps as early as the 1420's. By the mid-fifteenth century, cardmakers virtually everywhere were using it. This is all the technology a cardmaker needs. Manufacturers stayed with woodblocks and colored stencils till the mid-nineteenth century – in some places even longer. All this adds up to the fact that by the early days of Tarot:

- Cardmaking was a profession,
- The required technology for mass production was known and in use,

- Many ordinary people owned cards, which they could afford to pitch into bonfires, and
- Even if nobles were their best customers, cardmakers needed sales to ordinary customers to stay in business.

Francesco Sforza's letter of 1450, and the Ferrara registries confirm the fact that some nobles and courts bought their cards from cardmakers.

This points to the conclusion that popular markets led rather than lagged sales to the nobility. Under such conditions, one of the cardinal rules of business says to increase sales you should either sell your old product to new customers, or sell a new product to your old ones. The many novel and unique decks surviving from before card suits became standardized suggest cardmakers adopted the later strategy. Tarot would be a natural in such circumstances. And they weren't really that expensive. Even if they cost three or four times as much as an ordinary deck, like the Marseilles decks mentioned earlier, people then were accustomed to pooling their resources to afford what, as individuals, they couldn't buy for themselves. The higher cost of a Tarot deck could have easily been shared among the players.

Why Aren't All Decks Numbered?

SEQUENCE IS EVERYTHING IN THE GAME OF TAROT. *TRIUMPHI* (EXCEPT FOR THE FOOL) capture every card in the ordinary suits and any trump of lower rank. When several trumps are played on a single hand, the highest wins the trick. So, for instance, if the King of Coins were led, followed by The Lovers and The World, the latter would win.

Numbering makes knowing card order so easy its absence on more than half the early decks is a puzzle to us. We shouldn't forget, however, that in the past not everyone handled numbers as effortlessly as we do today. Nevertheless, the question remains, "How did early players know which trump card to play from their hands? And who won the trick?" I believe the cards tell a story familiar to everyone in northern Italy, be they dukes, artisans, or pilgrims relaxing after a day's journey. And a memory technique, known since antiquity and popular in the middle ages, used this story to recall the ranking of the cards.

As explained to me by my college speech professor many years ago, the idea is to pick a sequence of things you do every day, and associate items you want to remember with the steps in that sequence. Humorous or unusual associations seem to work best. Then, when you want to recall an item, you mentally go through your sequence and retrieve it with your humorous clue. It works. After twenty minutes practice, everyone in the professor's class could recite the names of thirty other classmates.

For example, suppose I want to learn the names of the primary colors of the spectrum – red, orange, yellow, green, blue, indigo, and violet. For my sequence, I recall the things I do before I go to work each morning: get out of bed, turn on the radio, exercise, brush my teeth, shave, shower, get dressed, etc. I might associate the primary colors with this sequence as follows:

1. Get out of bed and get *red*-dy,
2. That's a nice musical *orange*-ment on the radio,
3. I exercise till I *yell-ow!* (no pain, no gain),
4. I brush my teeth so they won't be *green*,
5. When I shave, in the mirror my eyes look *blue*,
6. To be clean, I must *indigo* shower, and
7. I think I'll put on my *violet* socks today.

If I want to remember the fifth color of the spectrum I think: *Five* – shave – mirror – eyes – *blue*, and I have it!

Can the same technique work for a card game? Yes! When it's used in reverse. And if you use the characters and events of a story everyone knows by heart as your sequence, you can play immediately, with no practice, and everyone will agree on card order. Images on the cards take the place of humorous and unusual clues. If you have doubts about this, before you've finished this book I'll teach you the story Tarot used and you can judge for yourself. Or, if you're too impatient to wait that long, take a look at the nine out-of-order cards on the opposite page and prove it to yourself...

Although you've never seen them before, using what I've just said, almost everyone knows how to arrange these cards in their proper order. Hint: *think of the pledge of allegiance.* You can check your answers at the end of this chapter.

The ancient Greeks invented this art, called artificial memory. According to legend, the poet Simonides of Ceos spoke at a banquet for a Scopas of Thessaly. In his speech, Simonides was as generous in his praise of the gods as to Scopas. So, when it came time to collect his fee, his peeved employer paid only half the agreed amount, telling him,"Collect the other half from the gods."

After the party got in full swing, Simonides was called outside for a moment to see two young men who had asked to speak with him. While he was out, the roof of the banquet hall collapsed, killing all the guests inside. Their bodies were mangled beyond recognition, but Simonides – spared by the gods – identified all of them for their families from where they had been sitting, using the technique I've just described.

The Greeks were fond of making up clever stories like this to explain the origins and principles of various arts. They're probably not true, but impossible to forget. As in the story, buildings were frequently the inspiration for sequences of places (*loci*) in which to store images (*imagines*). A part of rhetoric, artificial memory passed down to later ages in the writings of Cicero, Quintillian, and an anonymous author who dedicated his treatise to his patron (*Ad C. Herennium*):

> "Artificial memory uses places and images. By places we mean things that are naturally or artificially compact, complete and distinctive, that we can easily grasp and extend using our natural faculties, for example, a temple, promenade, nook, arcade or the like. Images are certain shapes or symbols or likenesses of the objects we want to remember; because if we want to retain in memory a horse, lion, or eagle, it is necessary to place its image in a certain place."[12]

St. Thomas Aquinas re-introduced the art of memory to the Middle Ages in his *Commentary On* [*Aristotle's*] *Memory and Reminiscence* (*De Memoria et Reminiscentia Commentarium*). His observations quickly found their way into a comprehensive summary (*summa*) of examples for the use of Dominican preachers. From there it spread to other orders. As a reminder of the sub-topics of his sermon, the fourteenth-century Franciscan John Ridevall pictured Idolatry as:

> "A disfigured woman, blind, ears mutilated,
> announced by a trumpet [as a criminal],
> face deformed and racked with disease."[13]

Some moral treatises written in vernaculars for the masses were even provided with appendices on the art of memory, with the admonition: "Now that we have provided the book to be read, it remains to hold it in memory." The technique was in use throughout the Middle Ages and Renaissance to enable clerics, lawyers and politicians to speak for several hours on a topic without requiring notes.

The fifteenth and sixteenth centuries were the golden age of artificial memory systems. And the most famous treatise among many was the *Phoenix, or Artificial Memory* (*Phoenix, sive artificiosa memoria*) by Peter of Ravenna, first published in Venice in 1491. The Phoenix was a legendary bird which lived five hundred years, burned itself to ashes on a pyre, and then rose alive from the ashes to live another period – hence the title. The last important memory system was developed by Giordano Bruno, who was burned at the stake as a heretic in Rome on February 17, 1600.

Card Sequence Example

AFTER A LITTLE THOUGHT, MOST PEOPLE ARRIVE AT SOMETHING LIKE THE FOLLOWING card order, with a high statistical correlation:

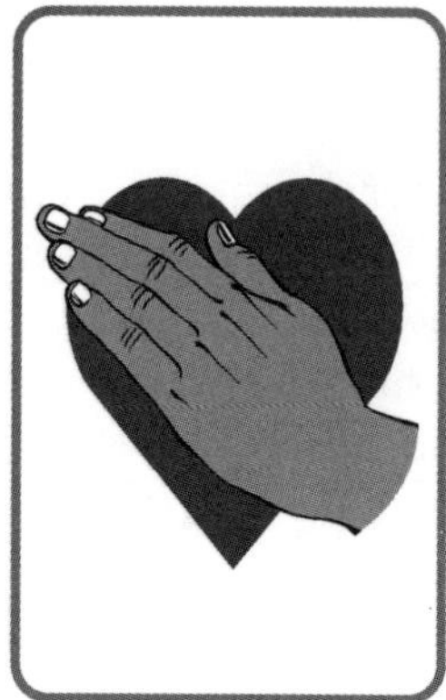

I pledge allegiance...

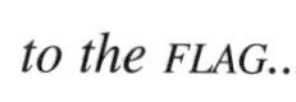

to the FLAG...

of the UNITED STATES OF AMERICA,

and to the REPUBLIC for which it stands.

[A. M. Willard's painting *The Spirit of '76* – note the figures are standing]

ONE NATION,

[*Reverse* of the Great Seal
of the United States,
– found on the One Dollar bill]

under GOD,

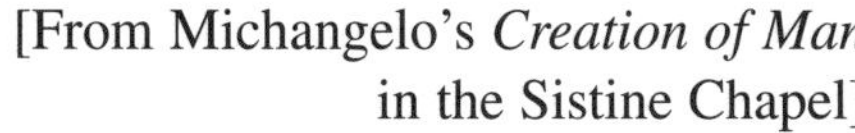

[From Michangelo's *Creation of Man*
in the Sistine Chapel]

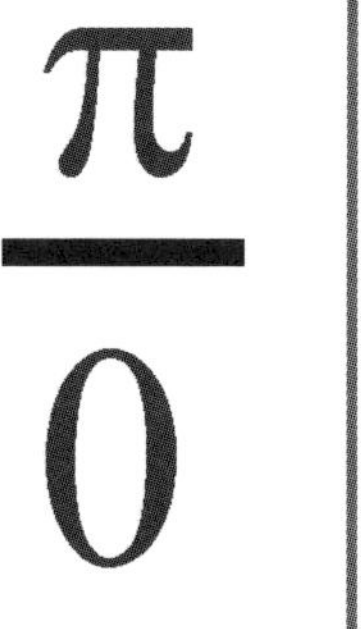

INDIVISIBLE,

[Division by zero is impossible]

with LIBERTY...

[Liberty Bell in Independence Hall,
Philadelphia]

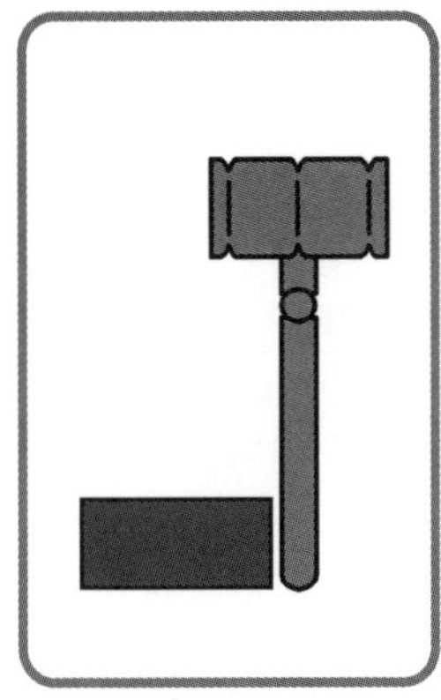

and JUSTICE *for all.*

[Judge's gavel]

The example is an excellent model of the phenomena at work in the larger set of 21 Tarot cards. One can't help noticing, for instance, that most of these cards have the "look" of illustrations from a high school Civics textbook. This is a consequence of the *pledge of allegiance* organizing theme. The implications for Tarot, in view of the Popess, Pope, Devil, and (from their connection with *Revelation*) the Tower, Star, Moon, Sun, Judgment and World cards, shouldn't be lost sight of. Divergences from this trend, like the $\pi/0$ card, which wanders into Algebra, result when the story requires a specific clue outside the customary domain of its theme. Tarot's Wheel of Fortune card will prove to be an analogue of this.

As my older son Keith points out, some people conclude the sequence is a rebus and make the very first card:

I...

[Eye for I]

– omitting the *One Nation* reference. As you'll see in Chapter Fourteen, something similar occurs with Tarot's Justice card. Both cards can be found in either of two distinctly different positions because there are two equally compelling interpretations of their meanings, even when their identities are perfectly clear.

Bibliography

E. A. Bond, "The History of Playing Cards." In *Athenaeum*, No. 2621, 19 January, 1878, pp 87-8.

Henry-Rene D'Allemagne, *Les Cartes A Jouer du XIV au XX Siècle*, (Paris: Hachette et Cie, 1906), Vols I & II.

_____, *Antique Playing Cards: A Pictorial Treasury*, C. B. Grafton, ed., (Dover Pubs., 1996).

Giacomo Bascapè & Marcello del Piazzo, "Insegne e Simboli, Araldica Pubblica e Privata Medievale e Moderna," *Ministero per i beni culturali e ambientali*, (Roma: 1983).

Michael Dummett, *The Game of Tarot from Ferrara to Salt Lake City*, (Gerald Duckworth & Co., 1980).

Michael Dummett & Kamal Abu-Deeb, "Some Remarks on Mameluke Playing Cards." In *Journal of the Warburg and Courtauld Institutes*, Vol xxxvi, 1973, pp 106-28.

Robert Friedberg, "Italy: Ferrara, Milan, & Naples." In *Gold Coins of the World: From Ancient Times to the Present, 6th Edition*, (Coin & Currency Institute Inc., 1992).

Phillip Grierson, "Jettons, Tokens, Medals." In *Numismatics*, (Oxford UP, 1975).

Ted Honderich, ed., "Dummett, Michael." In *The Oxford Companion to Philosophy*, (Oxford UP, 1995).

Stuart R. Kaplan, *The Encyclopedia of Tarot*, (U.S. Games Systems, Inc., 1994), Vols I & II.

Willi Kurth, ed., *The Complete Woodcuts of Albrecht Dürer*, (Dover Pubs, Inc, 1963).

Stanley Lane-Poole, "Medals." In *Coins and Medals: Their Place in History and Art*, reprint: (Argonaut Inc., 1968).

Nicholas Mayhew, "The End of the Middle Ages." In *Coinage in France: From the Dark Ages to Napoleon*, (Seaby, 1988).

Millard Meiss, Jean Longnon, and Raymond Cazelles, *The Très Riches Heures of Jean, Duke of Berry*, (George Braziller, 1989).

Millard Meiss, and E. W. Kirsch, *The Visconti Hours*, (George Braziller, 1972).

Gertrude Moakley, "The Tarot Trumps and Petrarch's *Trionfi*." In *Bulletin of The New York Public Library*, Vol 60, No 2, Feb. 1956, pp 55-69.

_____, *The Tarot Cards Painted by Bonifacio Bembo for the Visconti-Sforza Family: An Iconographic and Historical Study*, (New York Public Library, 1966).

Erwin Panofsky, *The Life and Art of Albrecht Dürer*, (Princeton UP, 1955).

David S. Parlett, "A Good Deal of History, & Tarot Games." In *The Oxford Guide to Card Games*, (Oxford UP, 1990).

John Porteous, "The Renaissance and the Baroque." In *Coins*, reprint: (Ocyopus Books, 1973).

Robert Steele, "A Notice of the Ludus Triumphorum and Some Early Italian Card games." In *Archaeologia*, Vol 57, 1900, pp 185-200.

_____, "Early Playing Cards, Their Design and Decoration." In Jornal of the Society of Arts, No 2,522., Vol XLIX., March 22, 1901, pp 317-323.

William Thomas, "Of the State of Ferrara." In *The History of Italy: (1549)*, George B. Parks, ed. reprint: (Cornell University Pr, 1963).

Frances A. Yates, "The Three Latin Sources for the Classical Art of Memory, & Medieval Memory and the Formation of Imagery." In *The Art of Memory*, (Pimlico, 1992).

Internet

Note: There's no need to type this yourself. Current links to these and future sites, as they become available, can be found at: http://tarot-cards.com

Books on Memory and Mnemonics
http://library.wustl.edu/~spec/rarebooks/semeiology/memory.html

Cimabue and Giotto
http://ubmail.ubalt.edu/~pfitz/ART/REN/vasari1.htm

Albrecht Durer
http://www.knight.org/advent/cathen/05209c.htm
FAQ for Playing-Cards Mailing List
http://www.cs.man.ac.uk/playing-cards/faq.html
Heraldry in Pre-Unification Italy
http://128.220.1.164/heraldry/topics/national/italy2.htm
IHS
http://www.knight.org/advent/cathen/07649a.htm
International Playing Card Society - Brief History of Playing-Cards
http://www.pagat.com/ipcs/history.html
LES TRES RICHES HEURES DU DUC DE BERRY
http://humanities.uchicago.edu/images/heures/heures.html
Leonardo da Vinci
http://ubmail.ubalt.edu/~pfitz/ART/REN/vasari14.htm
Leonardo da Vinci
http://www.knight.org/advent/cathen/15440a.htm

Translations

1. Anno 1379 fu recato in Viterbo il gioco delle carte, che in Saracino parlare si chiama Nayb.

2. unum ludum de nayps qui sunt quadrazinte quatuor pecie

3. Uno gos jugar a nengun joch de daus, ni de taules, ni de naips

4. Compte de Poupart: à Jacquemin Gringonneur, peintre, pour trois jeux de cartes à or et diverses couleurs, de plusieurs devises, pour porter devers ledit seigneur pour son esbattement, lvj. Sols parisis.

5. ung jeu de quartes sarrasines; unes quartes de Lombardie.

6. pare uno de carte da trionfi.

7. quattro paia di carticelli da trionfi.

8. Antonio Trecho texaurario
Voliamo, subito recevuta questa, per uno cavallaro ad posta, ne debbi mandare doe para de carte de triumphi, della più belle poray trovare; et non trovando dicti triomphi, voglie mandare doe altre para de carte da giocare, pur delle più belle poray havere. Quale fa che habbiamo qui domenica per tutto el dì, che serà adì xiij del presente.
Data Laude, die xj decembris 1450.
Francesco Sfortia Vicecomes manu propria subscripsit. Cichus.

9. De tertio ludorum genere, scilicet triumphorum. Non est res in hoc mundo quod pertineat ad ludum tantum Deo odibilis sicut ludus triumphorum. Apparet enim in eis omnis turpitudo Christiane fidei ut patebit per ipsos discurrendo. Nam dicuntur triumphi, sic, ut creditur, a dyabolo inventore intitulati, quia in nullo alio ludo ita triumphat cum animarum perditione, sic in isto. In quo non solum Deus, angeli, planete, et virtutes cardinales vituperose ponuntur et nominantur, verum et luminaria mundi, scilicet Papa et Imperator, compelluntur, quod absurdum est, cum maximo dedecore Christianorum, in ludum intrare. Sunt enium 21 triumphi qui 21 gradus alterius scale in profundum inferi mittentis.

Primus dicitur El bagatella (et est omnium inferior). 2, Imperatrix. 3, Imperator. 4, La papessa (O miseri quod negat Christiana fides. O pontifex cur, &c.). 5, El papa (qui debet omni sanctitate polere, et isti ribaldi faciunt ipsorum capitaneum). 6, La temperentia. 7, L'Amore. 8, Lo caro triumphale vel mundus parvus. 9, La forteza. 10, La rotta (id est rengo, regnavi, sum sine regno). 11, El gobbo. 12, Lo impichato. 13, La morte, 14, El diavolo. 15, La sagitta. 16, La stella. 17, La luna. 18, El sole. 19, Lo angelo. 20, La justicia. 21, El mondo cioe Dio Padre.
El matto sive nulla nisi velint.

10. En 1730, nos cartiers ne fabriquaient plus que des cartes à la Française, à la Madrid, à grands Bastons, de Lima et des Tarots... Les cartes françaises étaient appelées aussi 'Portrait de Marseille'; il s'en faisait environ 130 caisses de 5 grosses, année commune, et elles se vendaient 24 livres la grosse. Ces cartes se

consommaient à Marseille, à l'exception d'une douzaine de caisses seulement, qui passaient à l'étranger. Les cartes à grands bâtons et à la Madrid se fabriquaient pour l'usage exclusif des Espagnols; on en faisait à peu près autant que des cartes françaises et elles se vendaient 60 livres la grosse. On fait aussi, année commune, six caisses de tarots à Marseille, dont un quart passait à l'étranger. Chaque jeu de tarot valait 10 sous.

11. Un fabricant de cartes, ruiné par la conversion subite des Bolonais, vint tout en larmes trouver saint Bernardin et lui dit: 'Mon Père, je fabriquais des cartes, et je n'avais pas d'autre métier; en m'empêchant d'exercer mon art, tu m'ôtes les moyens de gagner ma vie et de soutenir ma famille. - Si tu ne sais que peindre, réspondit le saint, avec douceur, peins cette image.' En même temps, il lui fit voir un soleil rayonnant ayant au milieu les lettres IHS, si souvent employées pour désigner le nom du Christ. Le conseil du saint fut utile au pauvre peintre; il s`enrichit en vendant cette image, qui est devenue depuis le symbole de saint Bernardin."

12. Constat igitur artificiosa memoria ex locis et imaginibus. Locos appellamus eos qui breviter, perfecte, insignite aut natura aut manu sunt absoluti, et eos facile naturali memoria conprehendere et amplecti queamus: ut aedes, intercolumnium, angulum, fornicem, et alia quae his similia sunt. Imagines sunt formae quaedam et notae et simulacra eius rei quam meminisse volumus; quod genus equi, leonis, aquilae memoriam si volemus habere, imagines eorum locis certis conlocare oportebit.

13. Mulier notata, ocultis orbata,
aure mutilata, cornu ventilata,
vultu deformata et morbo vexata.

Chapter Six

Pictures Worth 10,000 Words

MANY STUDENTS OF TAROT ASSUME ALL PRESENT DECKS DERIVE from a single original deck which no longer exists. I was skeptical of this idea myself; I thought an underlying story is all that's needed to explain the images on Tarot cards. Imagine my surprise, then, when I found it!

Not an actual deck of cards, but illustrations from the *Book of Revelation*. Such depictions are as old as the fifth century. By the tenth century they had grown into elaborate cycles of 70 to 90 standardized scenes with parallel biblical commentaries, bound into books called Apocalypses. Thus my "deck" is a theoretical construct. As I'll show, Tarot's story is a sequel to *Revelation's*. So it's reasonable to expect that Tarot's and *Revelation's* images and symbolism should be related. The essence of a sequel or series is that characters and personalities from an earlier work are re-used, so plot development can proceed immediately without the need to establish background and motivation. Because Tarot borrows just characters – not plot – only pieces and parts of *Revelation* scenes appear on its cards. Tarot cards are tokens for *Revelation's* ideas, people and places, "images" of the artificial memory systems described in the last chapter.

Later, I'll go into the circumstances of my discovery and the meaning of this source for the history of Tarot. For now, I'll merely call this original deck Ancestor, and stress it possesses great authority, both for the appearance of early Tarot cards and their meanings. As you look at Ancestor's cards, don't be put off by their religious symbolism, it's actually of great help in decipherment. Ancestor predates many of the conventions of Renaissance art on the early Tarot decks, so once a correspondence between Ancestor and these decks is established obscurities in both often vanish. This correspondence is usually clear from the subjects portrayed. Tarot's Tower card, for instance, shows a falling tower, hail, men, and a lightning bolt. Ancestor too shows a falling tower, hail, men, etc. The style and arrangement of elements between them differ markedly, but there's no doubt they correspond just from the list of objects portrayed.

The format I'll usually follow is to manufacture "Tarot cards" by cutting and pasting relevant portions of scenes from Ancestor. To document what I've done, I typically follow each "card" with the original scene from which it came. But only the former are intended to be compared with Tarot cards. The originals are usually too cluttered with extraneous "plot" information to see what's important. I've also removed labels, comments, and hand-drawn borders from the originals, except where they help to clarify what's going on. With that said, it's time to revisit the six Tarot cards considered in Chapter Three.

The Tower Card

CHAPTER THREE WAS BASED ENTIRELY ON THE TAROT OF MARSEILLES DECK. Thus, conceivably, everything learned there might have to be discarded. However, the cards of the New Haven deck look strikingly similar to those of the Tarot of Marseilles. So perhaps the insights gained earlier apply equally to the New Haven and other decks.

ALTHOUGH ONLY PARTLY VISIBLE, THE NEW HAVEN TOWER CARD

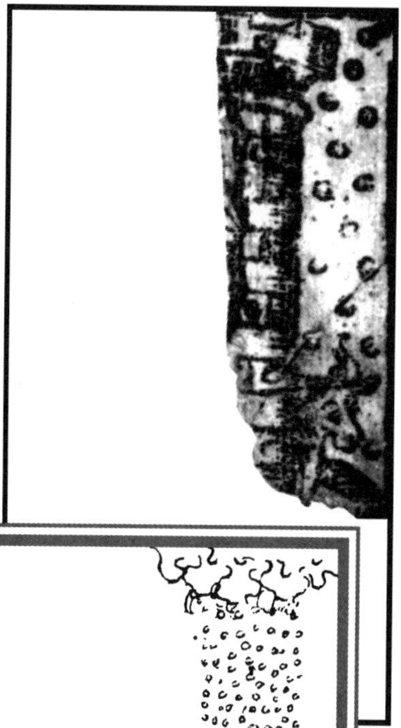

(*top right*) SHOWS A ROUND TOWER, FALLING MAN? AND HAIL LIKE THE MARSEILLES CARD (*above*).

A lightning bolt could be out of view on the left-hand-side, but there's very little room at the top of the card for one.

ANCESTOR'S CARD (*right*) SHARES THESE FEATURES AND IS IN COMPLETE AGREEMENT WITH THE MARSEILLES.

It matches the Marseilles card item for item: the main tower, its canted top, hail, and falling men.

THE MARSEILLES CARD'S LIGHTNING BOLT IS VISIBLE ON ANCESTOR'S FULL ILLUSTRATION (*opposite page*)

It's the vial filled with the "wrath of God" held by *Revelation's* seventh angel of the Vial series. With a little imagination it's even possible to see the tip of this vial on the Marseilles card.

THE SAME TIP IS SEEN ON THE BUDAPEST CARD (*right*), ALTHOUGH NOW THE MEN AND HAIL ARE MISSING.

COMPARE THIS WITH THE CHARLES VI CARD (*left*) AND YOU'RE IN FOR A SURPRISE.

The massive destruction there with no apparent cause seems puzzling. But if I say the scene depicts an earthquake, its meaning becomes clear. This card uses the earthquake reference I couldn't account for earlier.

THE WASHINGTON (*right*) AND PARIS DECKS PROBABLY ALSO DEPICT EARTHQUAKES, THOUGH THE PRESENCE OF SUNS COMPLICATES THEIR INTERPRETATION.

Thus, the surviving early Tower cards all portray one or another of the agents of destruction: earthquake, lightning, thunder, fire, and hail, described in *Revelation* and portrayed in Ancestor – confirming that they all depict the same event.

The Star Card

THE NEW HAVEN STAR (*opposite, top left*) CARD CLOSELY RESEMBLES THE MARSEILLES CARD (*opposite, top right*).

There are only slight differences between them: the number of small stars, and a bird on the latter.

ANCESTOR'S CARD (*right*) PORTRAYS A SIMILAR SCENE, ILLUSTRATING THE THIRD ANGEL FROM *Revelation's* TRUMPET SERIES.

Here, the figures are drinking, not pouring from their vessels. The waters are poisoned on all three representations however, all that changes is the point-of-view.

THE ANGEL SO PROMINENTLY FIGURED ON THE EARLY TAROT CARDS IS ONLY VISIBLE ON ANCESTOR'S FULL SCENE (*above*).

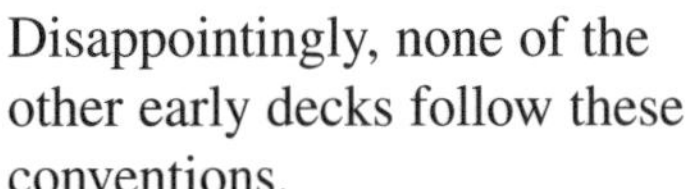

Disappointingly, none of the other early decks follow these conventions.

The Paris and D'Este (*above*) cards portray religious and astrological themes reminiscent of the three Magi. The Visconti-Sforza and Budapest (*top right*) cards show figures holding stars above their heads, while the Washington card (*right*) reduces to a single star in the clouds, suggesting the visionary atmosphere of *Revelation*.

Only a star is common to all the decks. The same is true of the moon on The Moon card. Why? I believe it's because the heavenly bodies by themselves are enough to recall the harbingers of the sixth seal – earthquake, sun, moon, and stars – the *raison d'être* for these cards in the Tarot deck. As long as they were present, card makers were free to add whatever additional symbolism they liked to their cards. The new meanings simply enhanced the sixth seal meaning. This was almost bound to happen anyway, since moon and star have so many rich associations. This situation is unique to these subjects and no other Tarot cards vary as much from Ancestor and one another as they do.

The Moon Card

AT FIRST GLANCE THE NEW HAVEN MOON (*left*) CARD DIFFERS FROM THE MARSEILLES CARD (*right*) ONLY IN MINOR DETAILS: THE DOGS, AND DROPS OF THE "WRATH OF GOD."

But these omissions change it's meaning completely! Without them, any connection with the *Book of Revelation* vanishes, and what is left is pure astrology: the moon, crab and water from the *Book of the Seven Planets*.

Furthermore, there's no Ancestor illustration for this card. In the picture suggested by *Revelation,* where the fifth angel pours its vial on the seat of the beast, Ancestor portrays the beasts as men – not animals – with their tongues sticking out. And the seat there is a throne. The overall effect is a visual pun, similar to what is occasionally seen on medieval coins and heraldry.

The Moon cards from the early decks are similar to their Star counterparts:

THE D'ESTE (*top left*), CHARLES VI (*above*), AND PARIS CARDS PORTRAY ASTROLOGICAL THEMES; THE VISCONTI-SFORZA AND BUDAPEST (*left*) CARDS, SHOW FIGURES HOLDING MOONS ABOVE THEIR HEADS,

...WHILE THE WASHINGTON CARD (*right*) IS CONTENT WITH A SIMPLE MOON.

I attribute the extreme variability of this card to the fact that *Revelation* only mentions the moon in a general way. There was no specific Trumpet or Vial reference to guide illustrators in its "proper" depiction.

The Sun Card

THE NEW HAVEN SUN (*right*) CARD IS ONLY PARTLY VISIBLE, BUT CLEARLY SHOWS THE SAME DROPS OF THE "WRATH OF GOD" SURROUNDING THE SUN AS THE MARSEILLES (*left*) CARD.

It's not clear, however, whether one or two figures, as on the Marseilles card, are portrayed. The number of people depicted is the chief difference between The Sun cards of the early decks:

THE BUDAPEST AND WASHINGTON (*opposite, top left*) CARDS SHOW ONLY A SUN. THE VISCONTI-SFORZA, CHARLES VI (*opposite, right*) AND PARIS CARDS ADD ONE FIGURE TO THE SCENE, WHILE THE D'ESTE (*opposite, bottom left*) AND MARSEILLES INCREASE THIS NUMBER TO TWO.

ANCESTOR'S CARD (*above*) SHOWS THREE!

And portrays the fourth angel from *Revelation's* Vial series identified in Chapter Three. At the top of the illustration is the word *sun* (*sol*), so there's no mistaking what it represents.

Thus, unlike the Star and Moon cards, Sun cards again follow Ancestor's precedent. This is even more apparent when you cover the angel on the left, and perhaps the figure on the right.

The Judgment Card

ANCESTOR IS UNUSUAL IN SHOWING THE DEAD RISING FROM THEIR GRAVES. As previously mentioned, *Revelation* only talks only about judgment, the rewards of heaven and punishments of hell. Because it's not explicitly mentioned, resurrection is seldom depicted in Apocalypse pictures. Another thing you won't find is trumpets – even in Ancestor. These come from the *Gospels*, not *Revelation*:

"And he shall send his angels with a trumpet and a great voice: and they shall gather together his elect from the four winds, from the farthest parts of the heavens to the utmost bounds of them."

— *Matthew* 24:31

It's likely that the prelates and kings on Ancestor's card (*left*) became angels with trumpets on Renaissance Tarot cards. Additionally, the Visconti-Modrone Justice card (*right*) carries the message: *Rise to Judgment* (*Surgite ad judicium*) at its top, making it clear it depicts the resurrection that precedes the Last Judgment.

THE FULL RESURRECTION SCENE IN ANCESTOR IS JUST A WIDER VERSION OF THE CARD SHOWN BEFORE.

As for the other early cards, only the hand-paint-ed Charles VI card (*above*) rivals the sophistication of the Visconti-Sforza decks,

... the printed Budapest (*top right*), Washington (*right*), Paris and Catelin Geofroy cards simplify the scene to a single angel.

The World Card

MY EARLIER INTERPRETATION FOR THE TAROT OF MARSEILLES SUGGESTED a connection between The World card and the new Jerusalem:

> "And I saw a NEW HEAVEN and a NEW EARTH. For the first heaven and the first earth was gone, and the sea is now no more. And I John saw THE HOLY CITY, THE NEW JERUSALEM, coming down out of heaven from God..."
>
> – *Revelation* 21:1-2

Ancestor interprets these lines literally.

ABOVE THE CIRCLES TO THE LEFT IN ITS FULL ILLUSTRATION (*opposite page*) ARE THE WORDS: NEW HEAVEN (*caelum novum*) AND NEW EARTH (*terra nova)* IN MEDIEVAL LATIN.

THE TRANSFORMATION USED TO CREATE ANCESTOR'S CARD (*left*) SHOWS NEW JERUSALEM AT THE CENTER OF THIS NEW EARTH

– the same convention as on the Visconti-Sforza card (not shown). Christ and an angel are in heaven above the clouds, holding dialogue banderoles, the medieval equivalent of cartoon balloons.

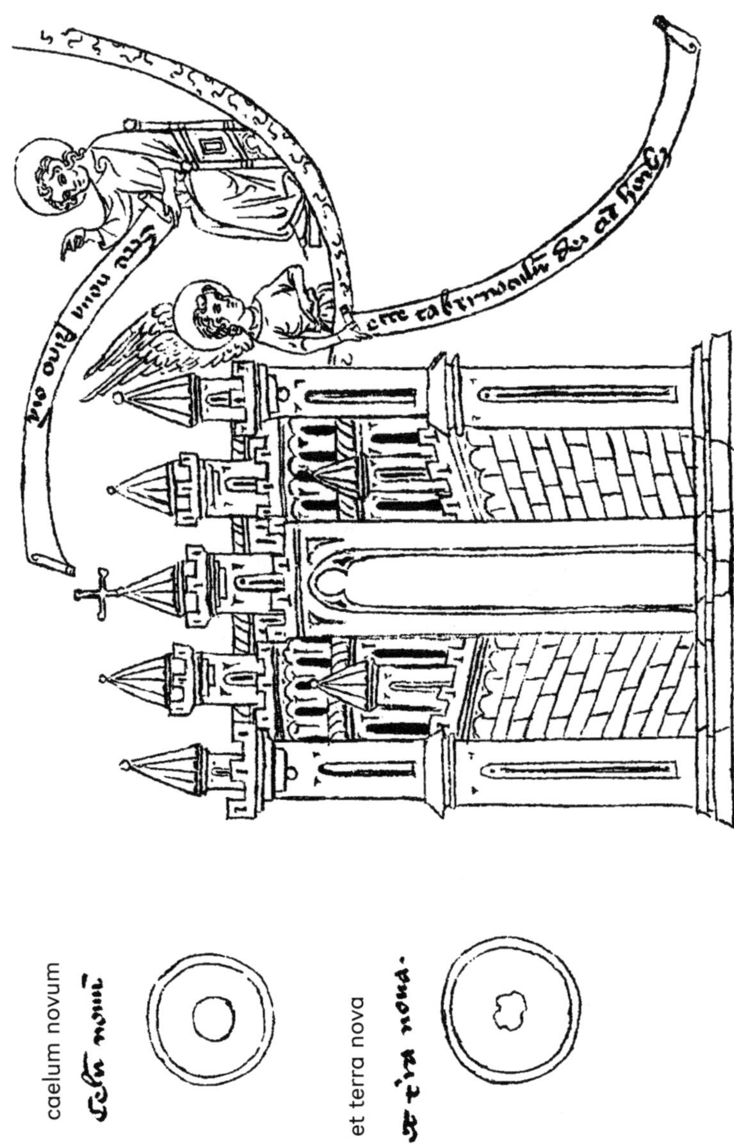
caelum novum
et terra nova

Thus, the wreath or circle on the Marseilles and other World cards, is not mere decoration. It is an essential feature, marking the boundary of the new earth, which is further elaborated inside. On the Marseilles card, this scene depicts one of God's elect, while on Ancestor's, the Visconti-Sforza and Guildhall (London) cards, new Jerusalem is portrayed there.

The latter is described in the fourteenth-century poem *The Pearl*:

> "As John the Apostle saw it with sight,
> I saw that city of great renown,
> Jerusalem so new and royally dight,
> As it was lit by the heavens around.
> The borough was of fiery gold bright,
> Like gleaming glass burnished brown...
>
> The city stood above – a square,
> As long, as broad, as high – so fair;
> The streets of gold like glass all bare,
> Walls of jasper that gleamed like glair...
>
> As John himself writes, yet more I saw:
> Each part of that place had three gates;
> So twelve altogether I could espy,
> Their portals bedecked with rich plate,
> And each gate of a stone,
> A perfect pearl that never fades..." [1]

The last mentioned "pearly gates" seem to be the only part of the heavenly city remembered today.

The Visconti-Modrone World card (see Chapter Eleven) also portrays the new Jerusalem as a city, a "little Venice" with sea-port and canals. At its center is a knight on a charger, holding a large banner. Above the scene, an angel in the clouds holds a staff and crown, the insignia of imperial authority. This may signify more than just new Jerusalem, and I'll return to it later.

THE D'ESTE WORLD (*below*) HAS IT ALL: ANGEL, INSIGNIA, NEW JERUSALEM (*the bride*) AND A DOVE (*symbol for the Holy Spirit*).

It quite literally repeats the anagogic message I inferred for the Tarot of Marseilles in Chapter Three:

> "And THE SPIRIT and THE BRIDE say: Come. And he that heareth, let him say: Come. And he that thirsteth, let him come: and HE THAT WILL, LET HIM TAKE THE WATER OF LIFE, FREELY."
>
> – Revelation 22:17

– testimony to what card imagery meant to Renaissance Italians who knew how to interpret it. And many did.

THE CHARLES VI (*above*), WASHINGTON (*top left*), AND BUDAPEST (*left*) DECKS REPLACE THE NEW JERUSALEM WITH SEMI-PASTORAL SCENES OF THE NEW EARTH.

The Paris deck goes even further, substituting symbols of the elements: earth, air, fire, and water for the new earth. And most decks portray angels with scepters and orbs – announcing the heavenly kingdom is at hand.

Pictorial Proof

PICTURE EVIDENCE IS AT THE SAME TIME THE MOST CONVINCING AND MOST DIFFICULT there is. There's no way of establishing if a picture correlation is a one in a hundred, in a thousand, or a million proposition. I can only point out that for five out of six cards considered so far, I can cut up and re-arrange Ancestor's illustrations to make Tarot cards that players would have no difficulty using. And in the remainder of this book, I'll increase that number to seventeen. At some point this surpasses sheer coincidence and must inspire conviction. If you don't agree, I suggest you attempt what I've done with any set of illustrations of your choosing, and discover for yourself how difficult it is.

At this point, we've caught up to where we were with the Tarot of Marseilles at the end of Chapter Three. In reality, we've far ahead of that. Before, we were looking for clues to what Tarot might be about; now we have a definite idea of what it means and a powerful method for proving it. And we've tested both, gaining considerable insight in the process. So let's review what's been found so far:

- The Tower and World cards have been spectacular successes. All the early decks follow Ancestor's precedents, and we've gained additional understanding of their symbolism which we couldn't have learned in any other way.

- The Sun and Judgement cards likewise follow Ancestor's example. And while we don't get additional insight into their symbolism, we should consider ourselves lucky. Based on *Revelation*, we shouldn't expect to find anything about Judgment at all.

- The Star card confirms our earlier conjecture for the Tarot of Marseilles, but doesn't carry over to other Tarot decks.

- Finally, The Moon card defies analysis, neither confirming nor denying Ancestor.

The latter shouldn't be surprising, and other cards to follow will do the same. As long as only a few are like this, it's still possible to reach viable conclusions. Based on iconography and other clues The Moon card appears to be related to the others as in the diagram:

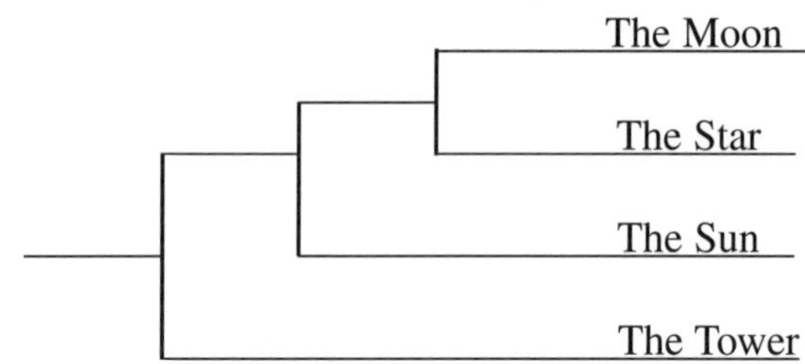

– where close branches indicate a close degree of relation. The fact that we can draw conclusions for the other cards in the diagram carries over to The Moon as well, at some level. And the same is true of the deck in its entirety.

Finally, the possibility must be considered that some of the above successes are fortuitous. Nothing can be done about that. But the chance that all of them are, seems remote. Even more remote is the possibility that all seventeen of the associations for the entire Tarot deck are mere chance. We haven't – and won't – found outright contradictions to the Second Coming hypothesis. That would immediately put an end to our speculations. That said, it's time to put methodology aside and forge ahead with finding meanings for the remaining cards.

Internet

Note: There's no need to type this yourself. Current links to these and future sites, as they become available, can be found at: http://tarot-cards.com

The *Pearl*
http://etext.lib.virginia.edu/etcbin/browse-mixed-new?id=AnoPear&tag=public&images=images/modeng&data=/lv1/Archive/mideng-parsed
Resurrection
http://www.knight.org/advent/cathen/12792a.htm

Translation

83: As John the apostle hit sygh wyth syght,
I syghe that cyty of gret renoun,
Jerusalem so nwe and ryally dyght,
As hit was lyght fro the heven adoun.
The borgh was al of brende golde bryght,
As glemande glas burnist broun...

86: As John devysed yet I saw thare:
Thise twelve degres wern brode and stayre;
The cyté stod abof ful sware,
As longe as brode as hyghe ful fayre;
The stretes of golde as glasse, al bare,
The wal of jasper that glent as glayre...

87: As John hym wrytes yet more I syghe:
Uch pane of that place had thre yates;
So twelve in poursent I con asspye,
The portales pyked of rych plates,
And uch gate of a margyrye,
A parfyt perle that never fates.

Chapter Seven

New Confirmation

JUST LOOKING AT THEM, SUGGESTED THAT OTHER CARDS LIKE THE DEVIL might be from *Revelation* too. But the text was too ambiguous to confirm this. Even cardinal virtues were religious subjects in the Middle Ages. St. Thomas Aquinas devotes numerous articles to them in the second part of his *Summa Theologica,* and the Visconti Book of Hours mentioned earlier shows a (rare) scene of God on his throne surrounded by the cardinal and theological virtues. Now that I had pictures, it might repay the effort to investigate this subject anew. Indeed it did. Not only did I find new associations, but I uncovered an important principle for interpreting Ancestor's cards – one which has to be seen to be believed.

The Devil Card

EITHER THE DRAGON, BEAST, FALSE PROPHET, GOG, OR SATAN MIGHT be portrayed on The Devil card. To help decide, I looked for illustrations in Ancestor with legacy to the portrayal on the early Tarot decks. One illustration seemed especially appropriate. It depicted:

"And the rest of the men, who were not slain by these plagues, did not do penance from the works of their hands, that THEY SHOULD NOT ADORE DEVILS."

— *Revelation* 9:20

ITS PEDESTAL (*left*) SUGGESTED A SIMILAR ONE ON THE TAROT OF MARSEILLES (*right*).

And worshiping figures hinted at a spiritual bond with the devil, expressed on the Marseilles by a rope binding the demons. "And they worship demons" (*Et demonia adorant*) is written on the illustration, suggesting that worship is just as important as *devil.*

A SECOND INSIGHTFUL ILLUSTRATION (*opposite page*) DEPICTED:

"...and they adored the beast, saying: Who is like to the beast? and who shall be able to fight with him? And there was given to him a mouth speaking great things, and blasphemies: and power was given to him to do TWO AND FORTY MONTHS."

— *Revelation* 13:4-5

Forty-two months is the length of Satan's reign on earth during the last times, so there's no mistaking who's referred to, but there seem to be two of him. If you look carefully at the angels on Ancestor's Tower, Star, and Sun illustrations, you'll see they have two heads – representing two interpretations: one, a character from *Revelation*, and the other, a real-life person in history who corresponds to them.

On this illustration, the real-life beast at the far left with horns is Mohammed, and the figure with claws standing next to him is the "image" or "form" of the beast – Satan himself. This is all spelled out by the comments which I've left untouched on the picture. Mohammed's two horns represented his claim to possess both wisdom and holiness.

The sun-like ball at the top of the illustration is "fire from heaven," representing holy scripture from which he took much of his teaching, although it was "wrongly" applied. The two figures at the right are Saracens (Moslems), and a faithful Christian sitting on a rock is about to be martyred for refusing to worship (adore) the beast.

IN VIEW OF THESE FACTS AND THE PARIS AND THE FRAGMENTARY NEW HAVEN (*right*) CARD,

...which doesn't depict babies being speared in their bassinets, but rather the Devil collecting souls (which were represented as small naked figures in medieval art), it's likely that the Devil's minions are as important in these illustrations as he, and the cards are really about followers of the Devil.

ANCESTOR'S FULL ILLUSTRATION (*below*) SHOWS EVEN MORE FOLLOWERS,

...WHILE THE WASHINGTON (*left*) AND BUDAPEST (*right*) DEVIL CARDS POSSIBLY MISS THE POINT BY DEPICTING SATAN ALONE.

The Death Card

MOST EARLY TAROT DECKS PORTRAY DEATH AS THE FOURTH HORSEMAN OF THE APOCALYPSE.

ON THE VISCONTI-MODRONE, CHARLES VI (*left*), WASHINGTON, PARIS AND BUDAPEST (*right*) CARDS, HE'S SHOWN AS A SKELETON RIDER WITH A SCYTHE (USUALLY) TRAMPLING PEOPLE UNDERFOOT.

Only the Visconti-Sforza and Catelin Geofroy cards are an exception, showing Death alone, standing with a bow, and spade and scythe, respectively.

ANCESTOR (*opposite page*) ALSO DEPICTS THE FOURTH HORSEMAN AS A RIDER – THE ROMAN EMPEROR DOMITIAN, INFAMOUS FOR HIS PERSECUTIONS OF CHRISTIANS – TRAMPLING A MAN WITH HIS HORSE.

No skeleton or scythe appears there because Ancestor predates both conventions, which only became widespread after 1500. The illustration also contains a bonus; Strength, supposedly one of the cardinal virtues, is shown together with the horseman.

SURPRISINGLY, ANCESTOR'S CARD (*below*) ILLUSTRATING:

> "And the first [angel] went, and poured out his vial upon the earth, and there fell a sore and grievous wound upon men, who had the character of the beast..."
>
> — *Revelation* 16:2

– ALSO MATCHES THE TAROT OF MARSEILLES DEATH CARD (*right*) PORTRAYING A SKELETON REAPING WITH A SCYTHE.

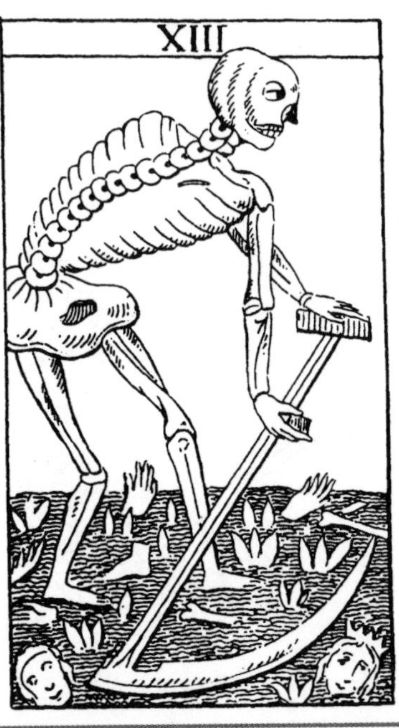

This is readily seen upon mentally substituting a skeleton for the angel and scythe for the vial.

The illustration unequivocally establishes the convention of heads strewn about the ground as a representation of death, which is used several times in Ancestor. Thus again, Ancestor anticipates all representations for Death on the early decks.

The Temperance Card

THE PRESENCE OF THE STRENGTH CARD IN ANCESTOR SUGGESTED other cardinal virtue cards might be there also. In particular, the pitchers on the Temperance card indicated it might refer to *Revelation,* where:

> "One of the four living creatures gave to the seven angels seven golden vials, full of the wrath of God..."
>
> — *Revelation* 15:7

ANCESTOR'S CARD (*right*) COMPLETELY BORE THIS OUT.

Thus, Temperance is really about reward and punishment, and the purification of the earth in preparation for the Millennium:

> "...thy wrath is come, and the time of the dead, that they should be judged, and that THOU SHOULDEST RENDER REWARD TO THY SERVANTS THE PROPHETS AND THE SAINTS, and to them that fear thy name, little and great, AND SHOULDEST DESTROY THEM WHO HAVE CORRUPTED THE EARTH."
>
> — *Revelation* 11:18

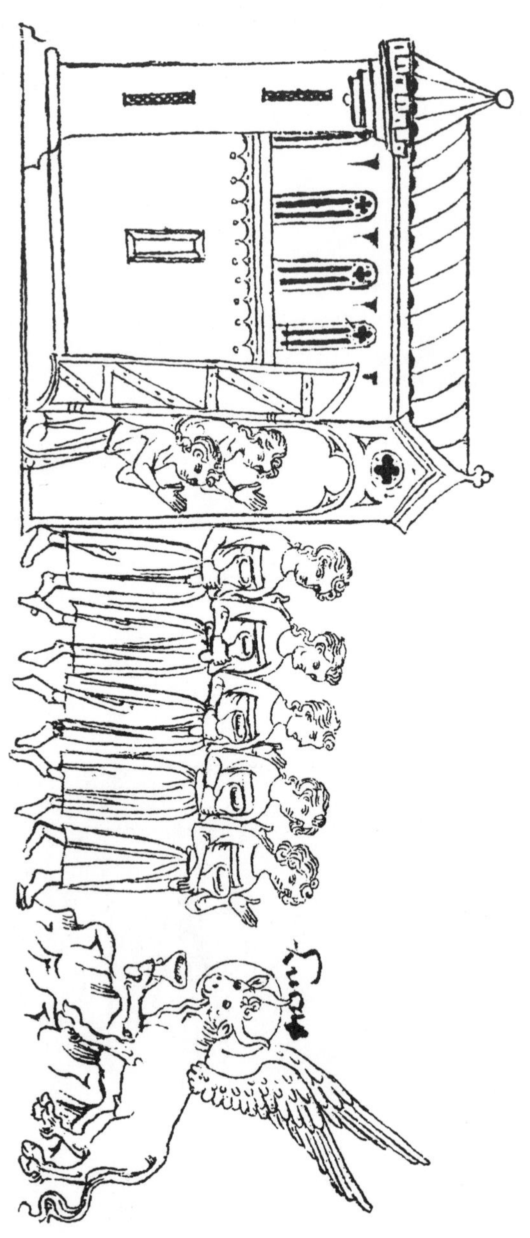

On Ancestor's full illustration (*above*) St. Luke distributes the vials to the angels.

The New Haven (*top left*), Budapest (*top right*), Charles VI (*bottom left*), D'Este (*bottom right*) and Catelin Geofroy decks all portray Temperance as a sitting woman pouring a liquid between two pitchers.

On the Visconti-Sforza and Marseilles decks she's standing as in Ancestor. Otherwise any differences between Temperance cards are merely stylistic.

The Justice Card

TO identify the last cardinal virtue card, I used the *Legendary Art* book I'd purchased while waiting for Craig's band practice to finish. The primary purpose of Christian art was to teach. Sculpture, mosaics, paintings, tapestries and stained glass windows were St. Augustine's "books of the simple" (*libri idiotarum*) and liberally decorated Church walls, floors and ceilings. Artists' first duty was to render spiritual truth. To do this, they developed a special language of icons and symbols – like the dove on the d'Este World card – which elevated and enhanced Christian art for those who understood them. Today, the same symbols often appear gauche and out of place to us, who do not.

Symbols were of two kinds: the first was associated with a person, as an aid in identifying them, while the second applied to any image and expressed a feeling or sentiment – like an olive branch as an emblem of peace. I hoped some Tarot cards contained symbols of the first kind that could help identify their characters.

One such association wasn't hard to find. Listed under Symbols of Angels was the note: *"the attributes of Michael are the sword and scales."* My experience with Temperance had made me skeptical of the cardinal virtue cards, and here was more

proof. Under St. Michael I found more details: He is the patron saint of the Church, and will expel Satan from heaven, hence the sword. And, he is lord of the souls of the dead; at judgment, he decides their merits, presenting the good to God and casting the wicked to torment. In this second aspect he is portrayed with scales, in one pan a (praying) virtuous soul and in the other, a damned sinner or demon. Frequently the demon is attempting to tip the scales in his favor. I'd seen arms for St. Michael in my heraldry book, but there he was portrayed with staff and scales so I'd missed the connection.

Today, and in the Apostle John's day, the third horseman of the Apocalypse with his scales represents famine.

BUT IN ANCESTOR (*below*) HE'S PORTRAYED HOLDING A GIANT SCALES AND WEIGHING SOULS.

So, just as the first horseman was often identified with Christ in medieval exegesis, Ancestor confirms that the third horseman was synonymous with St. Michael then.

The Justice card is mistakenly portrayed as a cardinal virtue. It really represents St. Michael and (the Last) Judgment, while the Judgment card represents resurrection. This confusing state of affairs explains why the Justice card occurs between the Judgment and World cards in some Tarot decks. That is their sequence of occurrence in the last times.

AS FOR EARLY TAROT DECKS, THE PRINTED WASHINGTON JUSTICE CARD (*top right*) LOOKS LIKE A DELIBERATE COPY OF THE HAND-PAINTED CHARLES VI (*top left*) ONE. (The same is true of all their cardinal virtue cards.)

EVEN THE BUDAPEST CARD (*right*) IS NOT ALL THAT DIFFERENT.

Only the Visconti-Sforza card (*not shown*), breaks the monotony with a horse and rider at the top.

The Popess (High Priestess) Card

THE POPESS HAS TRADITIONALLY BEEN VIEWED WITH SUSPICION BECAUSE OF THE TRIPLE PAPAL CROWN SHE WEARS, AS ON THE WASHINGTON CARD (*right*).

Witness the scorn for The Popess in the sermon on games given in Chapter Five.

Her identification with the Pope Joan legend is another instance of this. Thoroughly discredited now, it was more or less believed in the Middle Ages, and eagerly seized upon by Protestants to discredit Catholics during the Reformation. According to a thirteenth century version related by Martin Polonus:

> "After Leo IV, John Anglus, a native of Metz, reigned two years, five months, and four days... He is related to have been a female, and, when a girl, to have accompanied her sweetheart in male costume to Athens; there she advanced in various sciences, and none could be found to equal her. So, after having studied for three years in Rome, she had great masters for her pupils and hearers. And when there arose a high opinion in the city of her virtue and knowledge, she was unanimously elected Pope.
>
> But during her papacy she became in the family way by a familiar. Not knowing the time of birth, as she was on her way from Saint Peter's to the Lateran she had a painful delivery, between the Coliseum and Saint Clement's Church, in the street.

> Having died after, it is said that she was buried on the spot, and therefore the Lord Pope always turns aside from that way, and it is supposed by some out of detestation for what happened there. Nor on that account is she placed in the catalogue of the Holy Pontiffs, not only on account of her sex, but also because of the horribleness of the circumstance."
>
> — *Curious Myths of the Middle Ages*

Protestants painted an even blacker picture. The familiar became a cardinal, and her child the Antichrist:

> "Some say the child and mother died on the spot, some that she survived but was incarcerated, some that the child was spirited away to be the Antichrist of the last days. A marble monument representing the papess with her baby was erected on the spot, which was declared to be accursed for all ages."
>
> — *Ibid*

ONE PROTESTANT TRACT, JOHANN WOLFII'S *Remarkable Tales* (*Lect. Memorab. Lavingae*) PUBLISHED IN 1600 (*opposite page*) SHOWS ALL THREE ON A GALLOWS AT THE ENTRANCE TO HELL.

ALMOST 100 YEARS EARLIER, MARTIN LUTHER HAD DECLARED that the whore sitting on the beast in *Revelation* was not only the symbol of Roman paganism in St. John's time, she was the symbol of it's diabolical successor, the Roman papacy, in his own.

Lucas Cranach gave concrete form to this idea when illustrating Luther's 1522 translation of the New Testament, the so-called *Septembertestament*, in which the whore wears the papal crown (*following page*). This was removed in later editions, but in Luther's 1534 translation of the Bible, the crown appeared again on the heads of the whore and the dragon.

Pope Joan with her son and the cardinal hanging on a gallows before the jaws of hell.

LUCAS CRANACH'S ILLUSTRATION OF MARTIN LUTHER'S SYMBOL OF THE PAPACY – THE WHORE SITTING ON THE BEAST FROM *Revelation*

The Woman Clothed With the Sun

LUTHER'S INTERPRETATION MAKES THE POPESS A SYMBOL FOR AN INSTITUTION, while the Pope Joan legend identifies her as a (fictitious) person. Which approach is correct? Ancestor and *Revelation* side with Luther. Two women are prominent there: the "whore of Babylon," and a "woman clothed with the sun." They were identified with the Empire and the Church, respectively, in medieval exegesis – though the latter seems more like the Virgin Mary to us:

> "And a great sign appeared in heaven: A WOMAN CLOTHED WITH THE SUN, and the moon under her feet, and on her head a crown of twelve stars: And being with child, she cried travailing in birth, and was in pain to be delivered...
>
> And there was seen another sign in heaven: and behold a great red dragon, having seven heads, and ten horns: and on his head seven diadems: And his tail drew the third part of the stars of heaven, and cast them to the earth: and the dragon stood before the woman who was ready to be delivered; that, when she should be delivered, he might devour her son.
>
> And SHE BROUGHT FORTH A MAN CHILD, WHO WAS TO RULE ALL NATIONS with an iron rod: and HER SON WAS TAKEN UP TO GOD, AND TO HIS THRONE."
>
> — *Revelation* 12:1-5

Perhaps the thousands of medieval cathedrals dedicated to the Virgin or featuring a Lady Chapel set aside as her shrine offer a clue to the medieval reading. Female statues at the Notre Dame and Bamberg Cathedrals, crowned and wearing sovereign's robes, are known as "*L'Eglise*" and "*Ecclesia*." For whatever reason, in medieval art a woman with a book, unless she's a saint with her own writings, is a symbol of the Church. Significantly, a book (the Bible) is the most constant feature on Popess cards in early Tarot decks.

The dragon mentioned above was identified in medieval times with the persecutions of the Church, and we'll meet it again later.

ANCESTOR (*opposite page*) ILLUSTRATES THE WOMAN CLOTHED WITH THE SUN AND THE DRAGON QUITE LITERALLY.

Right down to *"the third part of the stars of heaven,"* which it portrays as eight X-ed out, and eighteen normal circles within a cartoon balloon, representing fallen and normal stars. (One more X-ed out star is required to get the math right!)

Symbol Substitution

AT FIRST SIGHT, THE CARD CONSTRUCTED FROM ANCESTOR'S ILLUSTRATION (*left*) HARDLY LOOKS LIKE TAROT'S POPESS – LIKE THE ONE ON THE BUDAPEST (*right*) CARD, FOR EXAMPLE.

Far from being a defeat, this is an opportunity to learn a valuable new lesson – symbol substitution. This important precept takes some getting use to, but repays the effort.

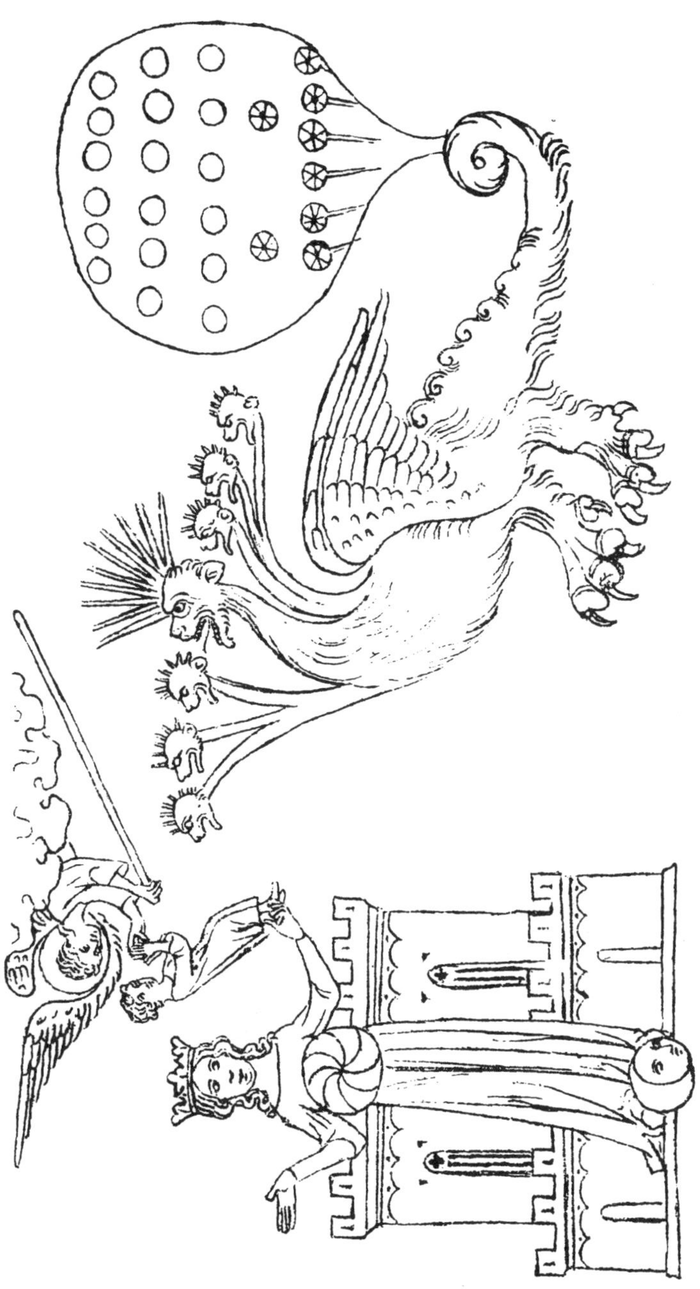

I used this concept before, when I spoke about the Death card and asked you to mentally substitute a skeleton figure for an angel, and scythe for a vial. There, Tarot's symbols didn't exist in Ancestor's time so it was appropriate to change them. Here, I'm fairly certain of the Popess representing the Church, so it makes sense to ask what's required to transform Ancestor into a conventional Tarot card. Apparently, its symbols are too explicit and were replaced by more subtile ones.

Let me emphasize, this principle isn't an invitation to invent anything one might please. It states a one-to-one relationship between symbols in Ancestor with symbols on Tarot cards. The direction of change is from religious to secular, and there's always a logical connection between the two.

Consider Ancestor's and Tarot's Popess card for instance. The principal subject of each is a woman. On Ancestor she holds Christ, and on the other a Bible – his book (the New Testament at least). On both she wears a crown, which on Popess cards becomes a triple one. On Ancestor she's decked out with the sun and moon, which are replaced by crosiers, papal keys, etc., on Tarot cards.

A MONK ON THE NEW HAVEN CARD (*right*) MAY EVEN CORRESPOND TO THE ANGEL ON ANCESTOR'S ILLUSTRATION.

Thus, the symbols correspond one-for-one and are related. Viewed in this way, what was strange at first sight now increases confidence in the initial interpretation: The Popess in Tarot represents the medieval Church.

Bibliography

Clara Erskine Clement, "Symbols of Angels, & St. Michael." In *Legendary and Mythological Art*, reprint: (Bracken Books, 1994).

Richard Kenneth Emmerson, "Antichrist in the Renaissance." In *Antichrist in the Middle Ages: A Study of Medieval Apocalypticism, Art, and Literature*, (U. Washington Pr., 1981).

Sabine Baring Gould, "Antichrist and Pope Joan." In *Curious Myths of the Middle Ages*, (London: Longman's, Green & Co., 1894), abridgement: Edward Hardy ed., (Barns and Noble, 1994).

C. M. Kauffmann, *An Alter-Piece of the Apocalypse from Master Bertram's Workshop in Hamburg*, (London, 1968).

Kathryn Henkel, *The Apocalypse: University of Maryland Art Gallery Exhibition Catalog*, (College Park, 1973).

Van Der Mere, "Albrecht Dürer." In *Apocalypse: Visions from the Book of Revelation in Western Art*, (Alpine Fine Arts, 1978), Chapter XVII.

Internet

Note: There's no need to type this yourself. Current links to these and future sites, as they become available, can be found at: http://Tarot-Cards.com

Devil
http://www.knight.org/advent/cathen/04764a.htm

Ecclesiastical Art
http://www.knight.org/advent/cathen/05248a.htm

Fortitude
http://www.knight.org/advent/cathen/06147a.htm

Justice
http://www.knight.org/advent/cathen/08571c.htm

Last Judgment
http://www.knight.org/advent/cathen/08552a.htm
St. Michael the Archangel
http://www.knight.org/advent/cathen/10275b.htm
Popess Joan
http://www.knight.org/advent/cathen/08407a.htm
Prudence
http://www.knight.org/advent/cathen/12517b.htm
Religious Painting
http://www.knight.org/advent/cathen/11395a.htm
Temperance
http://www.knight.org/advent/cathen/14481a.htm

Chapter Eight

Prophets and Apostles

The Strength Card

I HAD ALREADY SEEN THE STRENGTH CARD WITH ITS LION ON ANCESTOR'S ILLUSTRATION FOR THE FOURTH HORSEMAN (*right*).

I decided to try it next. The lions I remembered most from Sunday school were from Daniel in the lion's den:

> "And Daniel answering the king, said: O king, live for ever: My God hath sent his angel, and hath SHUT UP THE MOUTHS OF THE LIONS, and they have not hurt me."
>
> — *Daniel* 6:21-22

BINGO! THIS IS PRECISELY WHAT THE FIGURE ON THE NEW HAVEN (*right*) AND MOST OTHER CARDS IS DOING – SHUTTING A LION'S MOUTH. BUT NOT ON THE CHARLES VI (*left*) AND WASHINGTON DECKS; PILLARS, NOT LIONS, APPEAR THERE.

How can the latter cards be accounted for? Looking up Daniel under Symbols of the Virgin in *Legendary Art* lead me to Nebuchadnezzar's dream:

"Thou, O king, sawest, and behold there was as it were a great statue: this statue, which was great and high, tall of stature, stood before thee, and the look thereof was terrible. The head of this statue was of fine gold, but the breast and the arms of silver, and the belly and the thighs of brass. And

> the legs of iron, the feet part of iron and part of clay. Thus thou sawest, till A STONE WAS CUT OUT OF A MOUNTAIN WITHOUT HANDS: and it struck the statue upon the feet thereof that were of iron and clay, and broke them in pieces."
>
> – *Daniel* 2:31-34

Daniel's interpretation of this dream is:

> "God of heaven will set up a kingdom that shall never be destroyed, and his kingdom shall not be delivered up to another people: and it shall break in pieces, and shall consume all these kingdoms: and itself shall stand for ever."
>
> – *Daniel* 2:44

The Tarot cards' pillar could be a symbol for the "stone cut out of a mountain without hands" and promise of the everlasting kingdom. As a check, I read all the biblical references to lions and pillars using a computer concordance. To my dismay, I discovered Samson, strength personified, is also associated with a lion in Judges 14:5, and pillars in Judges 16:23. Perhaps cardmakers were confused about who should be portrayed? On the other hand, the Charles and Washington decks depict robed angels with halos, hardly a fitting portrayal for Samson!

An Old Testament Apocalypse

THERE'S A DEEPER REASON WHY DANIEL IS THE CORRECT IDENTIFICATION. The *Prophecy of Daniel* is to the Old Testament what *Revelation* is to the New – a full blown Apocalypse. Modern scholarship recognizes two books in *Daniel*: the first six chapters recount stories of the Babylonian exile, while Chapter Seven begins the first of three apocalyptic visions.

The first of these visions introduces four great beasts and "one like the Son of man" foreshadowing similar concepts in *Revelation*, while the third vision provides a chronology of future troubles, concluding with the promise of resurrection missing from *Revelation*:

"And many of those that sleep in the dust of the earth, shall awake: some unto life everlasting, and others unto reproach, to see it always."

— *Daniel* 12:2

And, like *Revelation*, there are numbers: 2, 3, 4, 7, 10, 62, and 120 – 1,290 and 1,335 and their difference 45 – 2,200 and 10,000 x 10,000. When Saint Augustine excluded *Revelation* as a fountainhead of answers about the last times, churchmen like St. Jerome went instead to *Daniel* and found enough there to keep all of *Revelation's* prophecies alive – albeit with slightly different numbers.

The Wheel of Fortune Card

AT FIRST ONE DOESN'T KNOW WHAT TO MAKE OF THIS CARD. THERE'S NO Wheel of Fortune in the Bible, though Ancestor illustrates a kind of wheel – a millstone – where:

"...a mighty angel took up a stone, as it were a great millstone, and cast it into the sea,"

— *Revelation* 18:21.

Nevertheless, early Tarot decks portray this card as the familiar medieval Wheel of Fortune with its motto: "I reign, I shall reign, I reigned, I am without reign," (*Regno, Regnabo, Regnavi, Sum sine regno*).

SOME PORTRAYALS, AS ON THE VISCONTI-SFORZA CARD (*right*) ARE MOST ELEGANT,

...WHILE OTHERS LIKE THE BUDAPEST (*right*) ONE ARE UNBELIEVABLY CRUDE.

The wheel as a symbol of fortune and chance is very old. The *Oxford English Dictionary* has a citation for it dating from 888, and wheels appear at the feet, or under the chair of the goddess Fortuna on coins of the Roman emperors Albinus and Gordianus III.

Legendary Art listed two persons linked to wheels: St. Catherine of Alexandria and the prophet Ezechiel. Wheels figure prominently in the the latter's description of the Tetramorph:

> "Now as I beheld the living creatures, there appeared upon the earth by the living creatures one wheel with four faces. And the appearance of the wheels, and the work of them was like the appearance of the sea: and the four had all one likeness: and their appearance and their work was as it were A WHEEL IN THE MIDST OF A WHEEL...
>
> The wheels had also a size, and a height, and a dreadful appearance: and the whole body was full of eyes round about all the four. And, when the living creatures went, the wheels also went together by them: and when the living creatures were lifted up from the earth, the wheels also were lifted up with them.
>
> Withersoever the spirit went, thither as the spirit went the wheels also were lifted up withal, and followed it: for THE SPIRIT OF LIFE WAS IN THE WHEELS ."
>
> — *Ezechiel* 1:15-21

If you look carefully at the illustration of the Tetramorph shown in Chapter Three, you'll see Ezechiel's wheels beneath the figure.

If Strength represented Daniel, then The Wheel of Fortune could represent the prophet Ezechiel. But why not a simple wheel? Probably because the Wheel of Fortune enhances the card's meaning. It signifies change, and makes the promise, "*I shall reign*" – a central message of Tarot's story.

Ezechiel's Legacy for *Revelation*

AFTER THE *Prophecy of Daniel*, THE *Prophecy of Ezechiel* IS THE OLD TESTAMENT BOOK most closely connected with *Revelation.* It is the source of the *river of waters of life* and *tree of life* appearing there:

> "And every living creature that creepeth whithersoever the torrent shall come, shall live: and there shall be fishes in abundance after these waters shall come thither, and they shall be healed, and all things shall live to which the torrent shall come."
>
> – *Ezechiel* 47:9

> "And by the torrent on the banks thereof on both sides shall grow all trees that bear fruit: their leaf shall not fall off, and their fruit shall not fail: every month shall they bring forth firstfruits, because the waters thereof shall issue out of the sanctuary: and the fruits thereof shall be for food, and the leaves thereof for medicine."
>
> – *Ezechiel* 47:12

In addition, Chapter 40 is the source of an important event in *Revelation* illustrated in Ancestor, the measuring of the holy city:

> "And he that spoke with me, had a measure of a reed of gold, to measure the city and the gates thereof, and the wall. And THE CITY LIETH IN A FOURSQUARE, and the length thereof is as great as the breadth: and he measured the city with the

golden reed for twelve thousand furlongs, AND THE LENGTH AND THE HEIGHT AND THE BREADTH THEREOF ARE EQUAL."

– *Revelation* 21:15-16

This description was the inspiration for the poem, the *Pearl*, given in Chapter Six.

Gog and Magog

FINALLY, CHAPTERS 38 AND 39 TELL OF GOG AND HIS PEOPLE MAGOG, who Christ will defeat in a final battle between good and evil preceding the Last Judgment. Their story demonstrates how Biblical and current events were linked in medieval minds.

Alexander the Great's campaigns of conquest had led him through the Hindu Kush mountains of Afghanistan, into Turkestan, and across the Oxus river into Samarkand deep within central Asia. There he captured the Scythian chief Oxartes and married the chief's daughter Roxana – the stuff of which romantic legends are made. Reports circulated that Alexander had constructed a huge iron gate in a mountain pass in the Caucasus to exclude from the civilized world wild barbarian tribes he found there. Supposedly, this barrier would stand closed "until the end of times cometh," when Gog and his people Magog would breach it and descended upon Israel, obeying God's commandment:

"...thou [Gog] shalt come out of thy place from the northern parts, thou and many people with thee, all of them riding upon horses, a great company and a mighty army. And thou shalt come upon my people of Israel like a cloud, to cover the earth. Thou shalt be in the latter days, and I will bring thee upon my land: that the nations may know me, when I shall be sanctified in thee, O Gog, before their eyes."

– Ezechiel 38:15-16

The Middle Ages identified these wild tribes with the Mongols, then called Tartars. According to Roger Bacon:

> "Aethicus the philosopher in his Cosmography expressly says that the race shut up within the Caspian Gates will rush out into the world, meet the Antichrist, and call him 'God of gods.' Without doubt, the Tartars were within these Gates and issued forth. We know for certain that the Gates are already broken..."
>
> – *Opus Majus*

The events he's referring to occurred in 1222. Ghengis Khan, campaigning with his sons Ogodei, Toluy and Jaghatay, overran Turkestan, Transoxiana and Afghanistan and penetrated the gorges of the Caucasus. Ghengis returned home to Mongolia the next year, leaving his sons and the greater part of his nomadic armies in Persia (modern Iran) and the Caucasus.

From there they entered European Russia, destroying everything before them as far as the Dnieper. Then for a few years their onslaught halted while Ghengis attacked the Chin empire in northern China. But in 1236-37, Prince Batu, under Ogodei, a new Great Khan, led his Golden Horde into Bulgaria and southern Russia, where he massacred the population of Kiev and captured (Russian) Prince Dmitry, who told him of the rich lands of Hungary to the west.

Mongols appeared in Poland in 1240, penetrated Germany, and by the summer of the next year were on the plain of Hungary collecting their forces for a more extensive attack. That winter they crossed the frozen Danube and destroyed the city of Gran near Budapest. Only Ogodei's death, interpreted in Europe as God's divine wrath, halted the invasion as Mongol princes hurried home to their capital of Karakorum to dispute the succession for Great Khan.

The Islamic world fared even worse. In 1258 Prince Hulegu, under Mongke, the new Great Khan, occupied Persia and captured Baghdad, killing between 80,000 and 2,000,000 inhabitants – virtually extinguishing the Abbasid empire. The country's extensive irrigation system, built up and maintained for over 2,000 years was allowed to silt up, and famine and disease ravaged the population so severely that the area has scarcely recovered the prosperity of ancient times today. Hulegu then attacked

Damascus, where Christians cheered on his army from a mosque hastily converted into a church.

This time God's divine wrath was on the Moslem side. Hulegu withdrew to Azerbaijan on news of Mongke's death, leaving his column commander Ket Buqa to subdue Egypt. The Mameluke slave-king Baybars crushed their army at Ain Jalut in 1260, defeating the "invincible" Mongols and saving the civilized world from barbarism.

As the Damascus incident illustrates, the Christian attitude towards Mongols was mixed. On one hand they were Gog and Magog of *Ezechiel*, poised to destroy Christendom. But on the other hand, they were also agents for the destruction of Islam, Christianity's mortal enemy. Europeans took heart that Nestorian Christians were especially powerful at Mongke's court. Both Mongke and Kublai had Christian mothers, and Hulegu had a Christian wife. Popes and kings sent emissaries to the Great Khans to learn of their intentions. Roger Bacon tell us:

> "Franciscans whom Louis, the present king of France, sent forth, passed through the midst of the Gates and went far on into the mountains along with Tartars who had been shut up there."
>
> — *Opus Majus*

Marco Polo would visit Kublai Khan's court in China twenty-five years later.

The Hermit Card

IF THE LAST TWO CARDS REPRESENTED AUTHORS OF BOOKS CONNECTED WITH *Revelation*, then The Hermit card might portray its author, the Apostle John. According to my *Legendary Art* book:

> "St. John is represented in art as an evangelist, an apostle, and a prophet. The Greeks represented him, whether apostle or evangelist, as an old, gray-bearded man....

in Western art... As a prophet, and the author of the *Revelation*, he is an aged man, with flowing beard."

ANCESTOR'S CARD (*right*) PORTRAYS ST. JOHN AS AN AGED MAN WITH FLOWING BEARD EATING HIS BOOK.

This is not as silly as it sounds; the book in question is filled with divine prophecy:

> "And I [John] took the book from the hand of the angel, and ate it up: and it was in my mouth, sweet as honey: and when I had eaten it, my belly was bitter. And he [God] said to me: THOU MUST PROPHESY AGAIN TO MANY NATIONS, AND PEOPLES, AND TONGUES, AND KINGS."
>
> – *Revelation* 10:10-11

By eating the book, John becomes a prophet himself. The *Oxford English Dictionary* gives as one of the definitions of prophecy:

> The foretelling of future events; orig. as an inspired action.

Foretelling connotes knowledge and wisdom, while *future* implies time. These relations help us to see how The Hermit card, like The Popess earlier, uses symbol substitution in its representations.

ANCESTOR'S FULL SCENE SHOWS JOHN WRITING, AND EATING THE BOOK, AND PROPHESYING TO MANY NATIONS.

THE LANTERN ON THE BUDAPEST (*right*), CATELIN GEOFROY, AND MARSEILLES CARDS SUGGEST KNOWLEDGE, WISDOM AND DIOGENES THE CYNIC, WHO LIT A LAMP IN BROAD DAYLIGHT AND WENT LOOKING FOR A "TRUE" MAN,

...WHILE THE HOURGLASS ON THE VISCONTI-SFORZA AND CHARLES VI (*left*) CARDS SYMBOLIZES TIME,

...AS DO THE CRUTCHES ON THE PARIS AND WASHINGTON (*right*) CARDS.

The latter is a Renaissance convention, mostly forgotten today.

Thus, John's book was subsequently transformed into a lantern, hourglass and crutches, and again, Ancestor anticipates all the representations of the early Tarot decks, confirming The Hermit as the Apostle John.

Bibliography

Roger Bacon, J. H. Bridges, ed, *The Opus Majus of Roger Bacon* (Oxford: Clarendon Press, 1897), 1:363-5.

Clara Erskine Clement, "St. John the Evangelist." In *Legendary and Mythological Art*, reprint: (Bracken Books, 1994).

Manuel Komroff, ed, "The Journey of Friar John of Pian de Carpini, & The Journal of Friar William of Rubruck." In *Contemporaries of Marco Polo*, (Dorsett Press, 1989).

Bernard McGinn, "The Legend of Alexander, & Moslems, Mongols, and the Last Days." In *Visions of the End: Apocalyptic Traditions in the Middle Ages,* (Columbia UP, 1979).

Internet

Note: There's no need to type this yourself. Current links to these and future sites, as they become available, can be found at: http://tarot-cards.com

Book of Daniel
http://www.knight.org/advent/cathen/04621b.htm

Ezekiel
http://www.knight.org/advent/cathen/05737b.htm

Gog and Magog
http://www.knight.org/advent/cathen/06628a.htm

HOLY BIBLE
http://www.cybercomm.net/~dcon/drbible.html

Holy Bible: Douay Rheims Version
http://davinci.marc.gatech.edu/catholic/scriptures/douay.htm

St. John the Evangelist
http://www.knight.org/advent/cathen/08492a.htm

Marco Polo: *On the Tartars*
http://www.fordham.edu/halsall/source/mpolo44-46.html

Chapter Nine

Joachim of Fiore

ST. AUGUSTINE'S MILLENNIAL DOCTRINE WAS SUPERSEDED IN THE LATER MIDDLE AGES, when, after about 1200, the *Book of Revelation* began to be interpreted more literally than before. This shouldn't be surprising. St. Augustine finished his *City of God* in 426 AD. The Sixth Age, which had begun with Christ, hadn't progressed very far along by then. But by the twelfth century it had grown long in the tooth. To fill in the period from the time of Christ to the present, religious thinkers went back to *Revelation* and began to interpret the opening of its Seven Seals as separate periods within St. Augustine's Sixth Age.

They were attempting to explain Church history, some of which had already occurred but more was yet to come. This guaranteed that the enterprise short on facts and mostly "qualitative." Thinkers identified the First Seal with the early Apostolic Church, the Second with persecutions of the Roman emperors, and the Third with Christian heresies of the fourth and fifth centuries. They said the Fourth Seal represented a time of false Christians and hypocrites which was redeemed by a Fifth of martyred Christians. The opening of the Sixth Seal and the appearance of the Antichrist would close the Sixth Age which had begun with Christ. His Second Coming would open the Seventh Age.

Scientific Exegesis

At the end of the twelfth century, Joachim of Fiore, the founder of the Florensian religious order in southern Italy, discovered how to make these ideas "scientific." His methods profoundly influenced religious thinking for the next 400 years and have earned him a reputation as a philosopher of history.

Despite his obscurity today, in his own time Joachim was on intimate terms with three popes, and kings and queens sought out his advice. Dante thought so highly of him he placed him in Paradise at the side of St. Bonaventure in his *Divine Comedy*:

> "Here is Rabanus, and beside me here
> Shines the Calabrian Abbot Joachim,
> He with the spirit of prophecy endowed."
> — Canto XII

Tradition states that King Richard the Lionheart (*Coeur de Lion*) of England, stopped to visit Joachim on his way to the third crusade. Their conversation was preserved, and went something like this:

Concerning the Apostle John's vision of the seven-headed dragon in Revelation 12 and 17...

Joachim: The heads are seven kings, five have died, one is, and the last has not yet come. The five are Herod, Nero, Constantius, Mohammed, and Melsemoth [a North African leader].

The one who now is, is Saladin, who presently oppresses God's Church and holds it captive along with the Lord's sepulcher, the holy city Jerusalem, and the land where the Lord walked. But he will soon lose it.

Richard: When will this be?
Joachim: When seven years have passed since the day of Jerusalem's capture [October, 1194].

Richard: Why then have we come thus far so quickly?
Joachim: Your coming was most necessary, because the Lord will give you victory over your enemies, and will exalt your name over all the princes of the earth.

The one [head] not yet come is Antichrist. He is fifteen years old, but not yet come to power.

Richard: Where was he born, and where shall he reign?
Joachim: He has already been born in Rome [*urbe/civitate Romana*] and he will possess the Apostolic See.

Richard: If Antichrist has been born in Rome and will possess the Apostolic See, I know that he is the Clement who is now pope [laughs]. But Antichrist is suppose to be born in Babylon...

At the very least, Joachim was using good psychology; Saladin: al-Malik al-Nasir Salah al-Din Abu 'l-Muzaffer Yusuf ibu Ayyub ibn Shadi (strong king and preserver, honor of the faith, victorious father, Joseph son of Job son of Shadi), was Richard I's Moslem adversary during the third crusade. More to the point, the interview illustrates Joachim's eagerness to interpret historical events as biblical prophecy and his expectation that the Seventh Age was imminent. He wrote more than once, "Moments and seasons from the year 1200 onwards are suspect to me."[1]

Joachim can be difficult reading but his redeeming feature is a fondness for diagrams (*figurae*). The most famous of which concerns the seven tribulations of the Church and portrays the seven-headed dragon he and Richard spoke about. It shows a serpent with seven heads, the first sometimes larger than the others. Each head is labeled with the name of a type of antichrist from the past or yet to come. The serpent's tail represents the final Antichrist who Christ will cast into the lake of fire.

Many of Joachim's doctrines are summarized by diagrams: three interlocking rings reveal the mystery of the trinity; the letters alpha and omega, the patterns of history; a tree with three trunks, the ages of the Father, Son and Holy Spirit, and so forth.

There's even a diagram based on Ezechiel's wheels. Annotations make each one almost a little treatise unto itself. A group of sixteen appeared together in a *Book of Figures* (*Liber Figurarum*) shortly after his death.

The diagram of Ezechiel's wheels (*opposite page*) deserves a closer look as it confirms some of the conclusions of the last chapter. There's absolutely no doubt it was inspired by the *Prophesy of Ezechiel.* Verses 1:15-16 of that book surround the central word *Love*, and references to Ezechiel's wheels are frequent in Joachim's writings. The four figures of the Tetramorph: Man, Ox, Lion and Eagle occupy its periphery, and the four modes of biblical understanding: Morality, History, Allegory, and Anagogy, with their qualities: Humility, Patience, Faith, and Hope, lie within the spaces between the wheels. From what I've said so far, you should have little trouble understanding the symbolism and appreciating some of its subtleties – like the connection between the Lion and Resurrection.

A new element is the four toils of Christ: Nativity, Passion, Resurrection, and Ascension, which also occupy spaces between the wheels. Christ's toils give the diagram a directional sense very much like a medieval Wheel of Fortune. I've added arrows to emphasize the flow: Nativity –> Passion –> Resurrection –> Ascension, which parallel the secular: I am without reign –> I shall reign –> I reign –> I reigned, of the Wheel of Fortune. Tarot cards surely symbolize a similar progression from abject misery to bliss.

The diagram of Ezechiel's "wheel in the midst of a wheel" was offered as divine proof of the parallel relations between the patterns of four: Lion, Resurrection, Allegory and Faith, and so forth, much as a geometrical diagram might illustrate one of Euclid's theorems in geometry. Such a schematic would be far too theoretical for Ancestor. But it belongs to the same corpus as that work, and, as will become apparent later, was almost certainly known to Tarot's creators.

Joachim's Wheel of Ezechiel Diagram

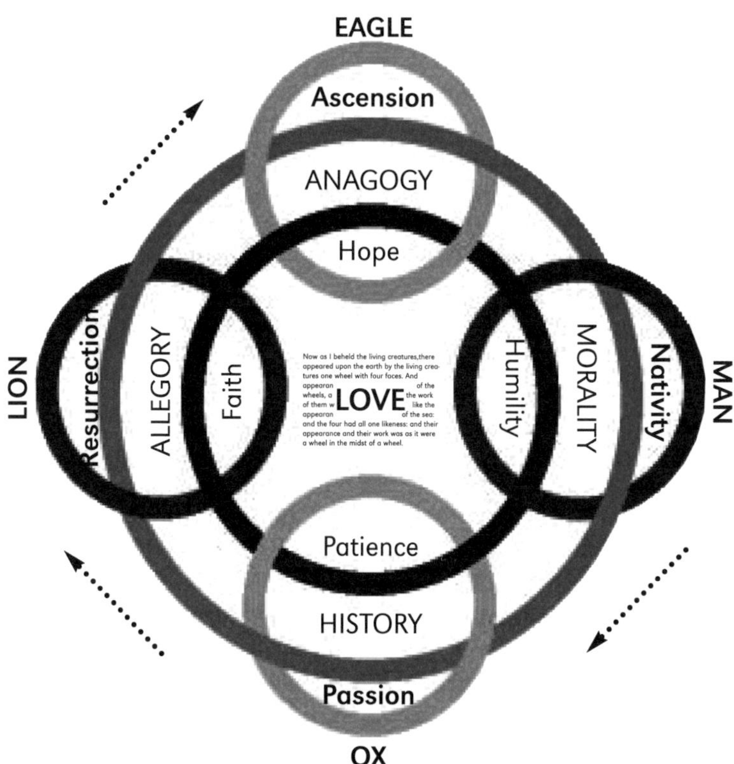

Detail:

Now as I beheld the living creatures, there appeared upon the earth by the living creatures one wheel with four faces. And the appearance of the wheels, and the work of them was like the appearance of the sea: and the four had all one likeness: and their appearance and their work was as it were a wheel in the midst of a wheel.

LOVE

Joachim's Concords

As useful as diagrams are for summarizing Joachim's conclusions, they don't explain his methods. This is only found in his *Book of Concords of the New and Old Testaments* (*Liber de Concordia Noui ac Veteris Testamenti*) where the critical concept of concords is discussed:

> "Therefore in this second way [*concords*] person and person from two Testaments mutually regard one another; and no less city and city, people and people, order and order, war and war, and whatever can be similar, coming together by virtue of their similar affinities; except that the one refers more to the flesh, and the other more to the spirit, although neither that of the spirit nor of the flesh is the more worthy. Not only person to person, but also correct are multitude to multitude relations, as Jerusalem to the Roman (Catholic) Church, Samaria to Constantinople, Babylon to Rome, Egypt to the Byzantine Empire, and so forth." [2]

In the language of mathematical functions:

Old Testament events = flesh (x)
New Testament events = spirit (x)

That is, Old and New Testament events arise from different rules acting on the same underlying stuff – the variable x – so that the New Testament recapitulates, in a way, the Old Testament, just as the Seals, Trumpets and Vials series recapitulate one another in the *Book of Revelation*. And just as *Revelation* has three sequences, a third age of the Holy Spirit with a new rule:

Third Age events = holy spirit (x)

– will recapitulate Old and New Testament events. For Joachim this followed from the nature of the Trinity, a subject he devoted considerable effort to thinking about.

Although to outward appearances, concordant events are dissimilar, their number and types: person-person, city-city, etc. are the same, making it theoretically possible to identify them and work backwards from played-out sequences to discover what lies ahead in others still evolving. Joachim and his followers considered this a real possibility, and exploited it to give detailed predictions of future events. They were so sure of these methods they didn't consider them to be prophecy at all.

Was all this just wishful thinking? It's use in theology is suspect, but science students use a similar idea in their freshman physics courses all the time. I'm talking about the analogies between linear and rotational motion, and electrical circuits:

Freshman Physics Analogies

Linear Motion	Rotations	Elect. Circuits	Elect. Circuits
Mass m	Inertia J	Inductance L	Capacitance C
Force f	Torque T	Voltage V	Current i
Velocity v	Angular Velocity ω	Current i	Voltage V
Damping f/v	Damping T/ω	Resistance R	Conductance 1/R
Power fv	Power Tω	Power vi	Power iv
f = m dv/dt	T = J dw/dt	V = L di/dt	i = C dV/dt

If you can solve a problem in one of these disciplines, you can solve problems in all of them. Because, in Joachim's terminology, they're concordant. Put another way, if you want to solve a problem about electrical circuits, and are a whiz at ordinary mechanics, replace inductance by mass, voltage by force, and current by velocity (the same is true for any pair of columns above) and solve the resulting equations of motion: f = m dv/dt. Then, substitute the original variables back into your answer, i.e., replace mass by inductance, force by current, and velocity by voltage. The solution will be correct.

Had they recognized this earlier, physicists could have developed all of electrical circuit theory from Newton's mechanics by working backwards. Of course it didn't happen that way, but that doesn't mean the principle hasn't been useful. In the early 1900s, telephone signals kept getting weaker and weaker the farther they traveled from their source. An immigrant inventor named Michael Pupin made the substitutions I've described above and recognized the analogous problem of "little balls connected by strings" had been solved by the great French mathematician Lagrange. Pupin replaced Lagrange's variables with the proper electrical ones and collected $1,000,000 from the telephone companies for his solution to their problem.

What I've said only hints at the power and subtlety of these methods. Lagrange's solution comes up again in modern solid state physics, where it's interpreted in yet other ways. Mathematicians speak of theories like this as "elegant" for the almost magical way they connect seemingly unrelated ideas. Joachim and his followers certainly weren't physicists and mathematicians, but their doctrine had all the prerequisites for a similar elegance which must have been every bit as fascinating to them as modern-day scientists find their theories.

Seen in this light, some of the theological precepts Joachim cites in explaining his method echo purely algebraic constraints inherent in its structure. And the diagrams for which he is famous look like attempts to extract variables and relationships from complicated word descriptions – like a high school student with an algebra homework assignment. This was cutting edge stuff then. A half-century later, Raymond Lully first conceived of using symbols as substitutes for complex word descriptions.

Joachim spent the last twenty years of his life setting out his doctrine in four works: 1. the *Book of Concords*, 2. an unfinished *Discourse on the Four Gospels* (*Tractatus super quatuor euangelia*), 3. the *Explanation of the Apocalypse* (*Expositio in Apocalypsim*), and 4. the *Ten-Stringed Harp* (*Psalterium decem chordarum*). The first work is actually two books, Part I explains his methods, and Part II applies them to the Old Testament. Thus the contents of these four works: method, Old Testament, Gospels, and Apocalypse constitute virtually a complete program for "scientifically" interpreting the Bible.

Joachim's Three Ages

YOU CAN GET AN IDEA OF WHAT JOACHIM'S THEORY LOOKED LIKE from another of his diagrams (*following page*). It divides history into three divisions or *status*. The first, an age of the Father, or the Law, was one of fear and servitude. It began with Adam and lasted till Christ's first coming, and represented married men. It was the time of the Jews, and Jacob was their carnal father.

The second division, an age of the Son, or the Gospel, was one of faith and filial submission. It began with Ozias (a king of Juda) and would last till Christ's Second Coming, and represented priests. Joachim thought a certain Moechus from Ozias' time was the father of Romulus and Remus, and thereby of the Roman people and Church. Hence, the unexpected prominence of an otherwise minor king.

The third division, an age of the Holy Spirit, would be a time of love, joy and freedom, when God's secrets would be revealed directly in the hearts of men. It began with St. Benedict (480-540), and represented monks. But it would only come into full flower during the Millennium when:

> "Clearly, just as the letter of the Old Testament was entrusted to the Jews, and the letter of the New to the Roman people, spiritual understanding, which proceeds from both, will be entrusted to spiritual men [Benedict's Sons in Joachim's diagram]." [3]

Each *status* commenced with a period of incubation preparing for critical events to come later. For the first, the critical period was from Abraham to John the Baptist; for the second, from Christ's coming to the present; and for the third, it had just begun. Since the first *status* comprised five of St. Augustine's Ages, and was recapitulated in just the few years of Christ's life, an acceleration of time near the end was a possiblity. The Millennium might be as short as 45 days!

Joachim's Three *Status*

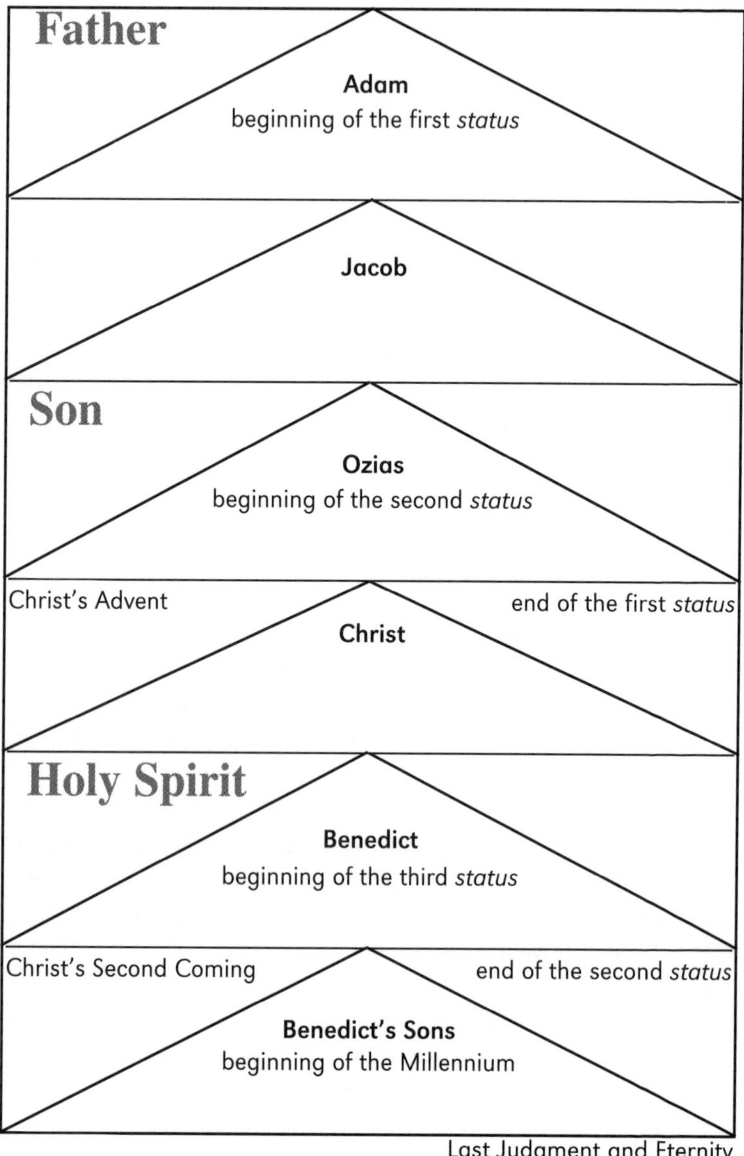

The Trinity

JOACHIM'S LEGACY TO SUCCEEDING GENERATIONS WAS THREE-FOLD: his concept of the Trinity, a suspicion that the time of Antichrist was at hand, and his prediction of two new orders of spiritual men. The first led him to attack the accepted doctrine, Peter Lombard's *Sentences*, for making God:

> "...not so much a Trinity as a quaternity, that is to say three persons and a common essence as if this were a fourth person... such a unity is not true and proper but rather collective and analogous, in the way that many persons are said to be one people and many faithful one church."
>
> – Fourth Lateran Council

He submitted his claims to Pope Innocent III, who stood by Lombard and declared them heretical. This decision, rendered thirteen years after Joachim's death, cast doubts on his entire body of work, since much of it was founded on his ideas about the Trinity. Thus, his followers were at constant risk of floundering on yet undiscovered errors, and some later reacted to this by spreading doubts among the faithful about the authority of the pope and his Church.

The Antichrist

IN HIS OWN TIME JOACHIM WAS MOST IDENTIFIED WITH HIS PREDICTION that Antichrist had already been born and the Second Coming would occur between 1200 and 1260. Robert of Auxerre gives a nice summary of this in a chronicle for the year 1186:

> "In these days, out of Calabria from the region of the papal city of Verone, comes a certain abbot named Joachim, about whom it is reported, though known to only a few and not the multitude, that he received the gift of divine understanding to such a degree he can brilliantly clarify and elucidate difficulties of scriptural interpretation. Accordingly,

they say that the mysteries of *Revelation*, hitherto concealed, were in this way revealed by him through spiritual prophecy, so from the small work which he wrote they may be clearly read.

Indeed, he says that just as the scripture of the Old Testament contains five spiritual ages of ongoing history, from Adam until Christ; likewise the *Book of Revelation* explains that within the Sixth Age beginning with Christ, that selfsame Sixth Age is divided into six smaller separate and equal periods in a corresponding arrangement. He says likewise, the present was revealed to be at the end of the fifth period, soon to be followed by a sixth, in which changing troubles and multiple afflictions will emerge, clearly manifest in the opening of the Sixth Seal, and when during the sixth period the destruction of Babylon occurs.

In truth, in his little book, he remarks that for the future he suspects the world will end inside of two generations, which makes it close to 60 years when he judges the reign of Antichrist will come to pass." [4]

New Orders of Monks

AT FIRST, JOACHIM'S PREDICTIONS OF A COMING AGE OF THE HOLY SPIRIT and new orders of spiritual men passed unnoticed. This changed in 1254 when a young Franciscan, Gerardo di Borgo San Donnino, published his own introduction and gloss to Joachim's work. Unfortunately, he got it wrong. In addition to the principle of threes described above, Joachim also formulated a principle of twos. Knowing when to use which kept his own writings safely orthodox. But in his enthusiasm, Gerardo confused them and announced that the Old and New Testaments would be replaced by a new *Eternal Gospel* (*Evangelium aeternum*) in the coming third age, and other nonsense.

This was all the opening Dominicans at the University of Paris needed. Eager to settle old grudges with their Franciscan rivals, they attacked Gerardo and his order. Condemned by the pope, Gerardo spent the remaining eighteen years of his life in ecclesiastical prisons, and the minister general of the Franciscan order, a follower of Joachim, was forced to resign.

Gerardo's biggest mistake was to say what others were thinking. At one time or another, practically every religious order speculated about their role as Joachim's monks of the last times. Cistertians, Dominicans, Spiritual and Observante Franciscans, Augustinians and Jesuits all carefully examined Joachim's writings for clues about their place in the divine plan and frequently altered his texts to suit their own tastes. Franciscans and Dominicans, especially, interpreted his words:

> "In the future there will be two orders, like the raven and the dove, the one all black and the other spotted."[5]

– as referring to the garments of their own religious orders.

This brings us to a paradox. Much of Joachim's fame rests on manuscripts he never wrote. There were no book reviews, testimonials or celebrity endorsements in the Middle Ages. By publishing under the pseudonym of a famous person, unknown authors could get their ideas read and accepted as genuine, even when they contradicted the original author's authentic writings. Thoth, or Hermes Trismegistus, cited in Court de Gébelin's oeuvre is a case in point. Numerous works on magic, astrology, and alchemy (hence Trismegistus, thrice-greatest) circulated under this name from the first century on. All of them pseudonymous. In Joachim's instance, the list of works attributed to him is longer than that of his genuine writings.

One of these is important for Tarot. The *Commentary on Jeremiah* (*Super Hieremiam*) takes its title from the fact that in Joachim's scheme, events in Italy after 1200 were supposedly concordant with Israel's history in the time of Jeremiah (not a good omen). Parts written in the 1240's, long after his death, impugn the pope, Church and emperor, while extolling the new order of monks; a story that I'll recount in the next chapter.

Bibliography

Dante Alighieri, "Paradiso, Canto XII." In *The Divine Comedy*, William Wordsworth Longfellow tr., 1895.

J. R. Barker, "Analogies" in *Mechanical and Elecrical Vibrations*, (Methuen's Monographs, 1964).

E. Randolph Daniel, *Abbot Joachim of Fiore: Liber de Concordia Noui ac Veteris Testamenti*, (Philadelphia: Transactions of the American Philosophical Society, 1983).

_____, "Joachim of Fiore: Patterns of History in the Apocalypse," In *The Apocalypse in the Middle Ages*, (Cornell UP, 1992).

Bernard McGinn, "Joachim of Fiore, & The Joachite Movement Before 1260." In *Visions of the End: Apocalyptic Traditions in the Middle Ages*, (Columbia UP, 1979).

_____, "Part III: Joachim od Fiore." In *Apocalyptic Spirituality,* (Paulist Press, 1979).

_____, *The Calabrian Abbot: Joachim of Fiore in the History of Western Thought*, (Macmillan, 1985).

Robert Moynihan, "The Development of the 'Pseudo-Joachim' Commentary 'Super Hieremiam': New Manuscript Evidence," *Mélanges de l'école française de Rome. Moyen Âge, Temps Modernes*, Vol 98, 1986, pp 109-42.

Michael Pupin, *From Immigrant to Inventor*, (Charles Scribner's Sons, 1925).

Marjorie Reeves, "Part One: The Reputation of the Abbot Joachim, & Part Two: The New Spiritual Men," In *The Influence of Prophecy in the Later Middle Ages: A Study in Joachimism*, reprint: (U. Notre Dame Pr., 1993).

Marjorie Reeves, Beatrice Hirsch-Reich, "The Rotae Based on Ezekiel I." In *The Figurae of Joachim of Fiore*, (Oxford UP, 1972).

Internet

Note: There's no need to type this yourself. Current links to these and future sites, as they become available, can be found at: http://tarot-cards.com

Blessed Trinity
http://www.knight.org/advent/cathen/15047a.htm
Fourth Lateran Council - 1215 A.D. "On the Error of Abbot Joachim"
http://www.ewtn.com/library/COUNCILS/4LATERAN.txt
Fourth Lateran Council
http://www.knight.org/advent/cathen/09018a.htm
Hermeneutics
http://www.knight.org/advent/cathen/07271a.htm

Translations

1. ab anno 1200 et ultra michi suspecta sunt tempora et momenta.

2. Igitur secundum hunc modum persone et persone duorum testamentorum mutuis se vultibus intuentur; et nichilominus urbs et urbs, populus et populus, ordo et ordo, bellum et bellum, et siqua esse possunt similia, que sibi affinitate similitudinum pari causa rationis conveniant; excepto quod illa magis ad carnem, hec magis ad spiritum referuntur, licet nec ibi quod ad spiritum nec hic deesse valeat quod ad carnem. Igitur non solum persona personam verum etiam multitudo multitudinem respicit ut est Jerusalem Romanam ecclesiam, Samaria Constantinopolitanam, Babylon Romam, Egyptus imperium Constantinopolitanum, et hiis similia.

3. Et sciendum quod littera veteris testamenti commissa fuit

populo Judeorum, littera noui populo Romano, spiritualibus autem viris spiritualis intelligentia que ex utraque procedit.

4. Per hos dies venit ex Calabria partibus ad Urbanum papam Verone morantem quidam abbas nomine Joachim, de quo ferebant, quia, cum prius non plurimum didicisset, divinitus acceperit intelligentie donum, adoe ut facunde diserteque enodaret difficultates quaslibet scripturarum. Hic itaque dicebat, quedam Apocalypsis mysteria hactenus latuisse, sed modo per eum clarescere in spiritu prophetiae, sicut ex opusculo quod conscripsit legentibus liquet. Dicit enim, quia, sicut scripturae veteris Testamenti quinque etatum seculi ab Adam usque ad Christum decursarum hystoriam continent, sic liber Apocalypsis etatis sexte a Christo inchoate cursum exponit, ipsamque etatem sextam in sex etatulas dispertitam earumque singulas singulis huius libri periodis satis congrue designatis. Dicit quoque, haec revelata fuisse in fine etatulae quintae, atque in proximo succedere sextam, in qua tribulationes varias multiplicesque pressuras perhibet emersuras, sicut in apertione sigilli sexti et in sexta libri perioda, ubi de ruina Babylonis agitur, patenter ostenditur. Id vero in libello eius pre ceteris notabile ac suspectum habetur, quod mundi diffinit terminum, et infra duas generationes, quae iuxta ipsum annos faciunt 60, arbitratur implendum quicquid de Antichristo legitur eventurum.

5. Duo sunt ordines affuturi, in corvo et columba, quia ille totus niger et illa varia.

Chapter Ten

Emperor and Antichrist

FREDERICK II HOHENSTAUFEN, "WONDER OF THE WORLD AND ADMIRABLE INNOVATOR"[1] came from a long line of illustrious kings. For brevity, I'll begin with his father, Henry VI. Henry is the reason why Richard the Lionheart shows up so late in Hollywood's Robin Hood movies. Were it not for him, Richard would have been home two years earlier!

In 1192, rumors of troubles in England forced Richard to negotiate a hasty end to the third crusade and depart for home. His ship was wrecked in the Adriatic, and as he attempted to cross Germany in disguise, Duke Leopold of Austria, who he had personally insulted while on crusade, tracked him down and had him imprisoned. When Henry, the Holy Roman Emperor (called King of the Romans then) learned of this, he demanded Richard be surrendered to him.

Richard and Henry negotiated a ransom of 150,000 Cologne marks of silver, amounting to two years of revenue from the English Crown. When news reached England that the king was prisoner somewhere in Germany, Prince John declared Richard dead and claimed the crown for himself. Later, when official word arrived that he was alive, John slipped off to France and joined another of Richard's fellow crusaders and enemies, French

King Philip II Augustus. The two offered to pay Henry 1,500 marks for every month he kept his prisoner, or 150,000 marks to turn him over to them. But a bargain was a bargain, and Henry stuck by Richard.

After three attempts at raising the ransom from England and Normandy, just over 23 tons of silver ingots were collected in London and shipped up the Rhine to Henry. This only amounted to 100,000 marks, but Richard was released on his promise to pay the rest later. He reached London on March 16, 1194, put down another of John's rebellions, raised money and arms, and set off to defend his French possessions. In all, he'd spent a total of five months in England during his ten year reign.

But our story is with the ransom. That same year Henry used Richard's 100,000 marks with some of his own money to invade the Kingdom of Sicily, to which his wife was the lawful heir. In those days, Sicily included the island we know by that name, and southern Italy to within a hundred miles of Rome. After the Hohenstaufens, the mainland became the Kingdom of Naples. But later, the two were reunited again as the Kingdom of the Two Sicilies, which lasted until Garibaldi annexed it to Italy in 1861.

The prize was well worth the price. The yearly revenue from its capital of Palermo alone was more than Richard's revenues from all of England. In Roman times, Egypt, North Africa and Sicily were the bread baskets of the empire; now much of North Africa was no longer safe for farming and a major importer of hard Sicilian wheat. Genoese, Pisans and Venetians shipped it all over the Mediterranean. Sicily was an important producer of cotton, skins and silk too.

To consolidate his conquest, Henry installed loyal German barons throughout his new territories, and as King of the Romans, he commanded the allegiance of Germany north of the Alps. It was beginning to look like the unification of Italy might occur in the Middle Ages under the Hohenstaufens. Especially when his wife, at age 42, gave birth to an heir, Frederick Roger, and Henry had the child elected King of the Romans at the diet of Ratisbon.

Two obstacles stood in the way. First, the papacy controlled the bordering states north of Sicily. While never a large holding in area, extending from Rome to Ravenna, and unruly, more than once its populace forced the pope to flee from Rome, nevertheless these lands made the pope a "player" in the politics of the day. Indeed, the papacy was the most potent force in medieval politics, with the power to make and unmake kings and emperors.

The second obstacle lay north of the Papal States and south of the Alps, the northern Italian cities of Genoa, Pisa, Florence, Venice, Milan and others, the economic powerhouses of their time. Nominally part of the empire owing allegiance to Henry, in fact, these city-states were out for themselves, engaging in almost constant turf battles for territory and trading privileges. Occasionally, they could forget their differences and combine into leagues for mutual defense. But usually they played both ends against the middle, either as Guelfs supporting the papacy or Ghibellines loyal to the empire. And since cities often harbored members of both factions, a swift, violent revolution could quickly turn them from one side to the other.

A conflict seemed inevitable when Henry died. Four-year-old Frederick scarcely had time to be crowned King of Sicily when his mother, Constanza, died too. Her will named pope Innocent III as the child's guardian. That didn't stop his father's barons from using young Frederick and the Kingdom of Sicily for their own ends – something he never forgot. His position in Germany fared even worse. The pope set aside his election on the technicality he wasn't baptized, while two contenders, his uncle Philip of Swabia, and newcomer Otto IV of Brunswick, vied to become emperor.

Medieval Politics

OTTO WASN'T POPULAR WITH THE GERMANS; HIS CHIEF SUPPORTER WAS RICHARD THE LIONHEART! Other than the ignominy of his ransom, there were more substantial reasons for Richard's interest. Otto was a chip off the old Plantagenet block, a favorite of his, whom he had made Earl of York, and later La Marche. Furthermore, with a friendly Roman emperor, Richard would have his old enemy Philip II Augustus of France in a medieval squeeze play between England and Germany.

As today, the campaign for emperor was a contest of money. Richard, and later King John, poured more than 1,000,000 short-cross silver pennies – still being recovered in medieval coin hoards today – into the pockets of German nobles. Both candidates petitioned for papal confirmation. Innocent was rid of one Hohenstaufen and didn't need another. After extracting promises from Otto to confirm and extend the territories of the Papal States, he proclaimed him emperor and excommunicated Philip and his supporters, plunging Germany into civil war.

Otto rapidly lost ground in the contest and was driven back to England, but his luck changed when Philip was murdered over an unrelated matter. Recalled and re-elected, the pope crowned Otto King of the Romans in St. Peter's in 1209. The very next year he foiled Innocent's Hohenstaufen policy by invading Sicily himself. The pope excommunicated him and waited. Expecting the worst, Frederick II had a ship in waiting ready to ferry him to Africa, while Otto awaited naval aid from Pisa for a final assault on Palermo.

It was French King Philip II Augustus who saw the handwriting on the wall and acted. This monarch, who had supported his uncle Philip, now threw his support to Frederick and stirred up revolt in Germany, seconded by Innocent's call to the German princes to elect a Hohenstaufen: "as young in years as old in wisdom." Frederick slipped out of Sicily, and headed for Germany. Threatened at home, Otto did likewise.

Again it was a contest of money, Frederick backed by 20,000 marks from Philip, and Otto by further subsidies from England's King John. In 1214, John and Otto planned a joint attack on Philip, the author of their woes. It was a fatal mistake. Philip's forces routed first the English and then the German armies on the field of Bouvines – Frederick wasn't even there – all but deciding the contest for emperor. Even in defeat Otto refused to give up, nevertheless he was formally deposed, and Frederick made emperor by Innocent III at the Fourth Lateran Council in 1215.

Two events important for the future occurred at this time. First, in consideration for Innocent's support, Frederick swore he would cede Sicily to his own son Henry VII, which would be forever divided from the Empire and Italy – Innocent's solution of the Hohenstaufen problem:

> "Desiring to provide for the welfare of both the Roman church and the Kingdom of Sicily, we firmly promise that as soon as we shall be crowned emperor, we will release from paternal authority our son Henry, whom we, at your command, have crowned king, and we will entirely relinquish all the Kingdom of Sicily...
>
> We do this because, if we should become emperor and at the same time be King of Sicily, it might be inferred that the Kingdom of Sicily belonged to the empire. And such an inference would do injury to the Roman church..."
>
> – *Empire and Papacy*

But later he pulled a switch. After Innocent died, he arranged for Henry's election as emperor and appointed himself regent for Sicily, reversing their roles. Second, at his coronation, after mass was ended, Frederick took the crusader's cross and vows, urging his followers to do the same. The next day, a Sunday, he listened to crusade sermons in the cathedral from dawn to dusk.

Reluctant Crusader

THE OBJECT OF THE FIFTH CRUSADE WAS THE MOSLEM CITY OF DAMIETTA on the Nile delta. At first, the campaign was successful; the crusaders took the city and were offered Jerusalem and their former Latin Kingdom in exchange for its return, but they held out for more. Now they were being besieged by the armies of the Sultan of Egypt, al-Malik al-Kamil, and their situation was desperate. Reminding Frederick of his crusading vows, Pope Honorius III threatened him with excommunication if he didn't do something.

Finally, forty galleys of crusaders, without Frederick, set sail in 1221 for the relief of Damietta, only to arrive hours after the city had fallen. Frederick promised to begin a new crusade before 1225, began preparing a fleet, and then asked for a delay. He was given till the autumn of 1227 and required to put up 100,000 ounces of gold against forfeiture. This time, despite heat and malaria, he set sail with 40,000 crusaders but was forced by illness to send them ahead while he recovered at Pozzouli near Naples. Pope Gregory IX, "forceful in word and deed" (he instituted the Inquisition) would have none of it and excommunicated him.

Frederick sent letters to the kings of Europe complaining of his treatment and in mid 1228 resumed his crusade. The pope was furious. Frederick had turned the expedition into an anti-crusade lead by an excommunicate. Any gains won would be in defiance of the Church! A lesson was in order – Gregory decided to deprive Frederick of his kingdom. In the spring of 1229 a papal army entered Sicily and routed its defenders, while monks spread the rumor that emperor Frederick had died on crusade.

Meanwhile, anxious about events at home, Frederick pressed hard in negotiations with al-Kamil. Three years before, worried about the intentions of his brother the governor of Damascus, al-Kamil had sent an emissary to Frederick suggesting an alliance and offering to surrender Jerusalem as a sign of good faith. Now, Frederick tried to revive that offer. But the brother had died and al-Kamil was now secure in Egypt.

On the other hand, Frederick's army, followed by an army of Hospitaller and Templar knights, was marching down the Syrian coast – the latter a day's journey behind lest they appear to be under the command of an excommunicate. And Frederick worked hard to impress al-Kamil with his learning and the "political necessity" of accomplishing something tangible. Finally, al-Kamil gave in and surrendered Jerusalem with an access corridor to the sea for ten years and ten months, the maximum duration for a truce with an infidel. But portions of the city holy to Islam were retained, the city was not to be fortified, and surrounding settlements remained under Moslem control. As al-Kamil predicted, Jerusalem was easily retaken after the treaty expired.

On March 17, 1229 Frederick, followed by a crowd of pilgrims, entered Jerusalem in triumph. His host, the Qadi of Nablus Shams later related:

"I went with him into al-Aqsa [mosque], whose construction he admired, as he did that of the Dome of the Rock. When we came to the *mihrab* [indicating the direction of Mecca] he admired its beauty, and commended the pulpit, which he climbed to the top. When he descended he took my hand and we went out in the direction of al-Aqsa.

There he found a priest, with the Testament in his hand, about to enter al-Aqsa. The emperor called out to him: 'What has brought you here? By God, if one of you comes here again without permission I shall have his eyes put out! We are the slaves and servants of al-Malik al-Kamil. He has handed over this church to me and you as a gracious gift. I do not want any of you exceeding your duties' The priest made off, quaking with fear...

I recommended the *muezzins* not to give the call to prayer that night, out of respect for the king. In the morning I went to him, and he said: 'O Qadi, why did the *muezzins* not give the call to prayer last night in the usual way?' 'This humble slave,' I replied, 'prevented them out of regard and respect for Your Majesty.' 'You did wrong to do that,' he said; 'my chief aim in passing the night in Jerusalem was to hear the call to prayer given by the *muezzins*, and their cries of praise to God during the night.'"

When the time came for the midday prayer and the *muezzin's* cry rang out, all his pages and valets rose, as well as his tutor, a Sicilian with whom he was reading Aristotle's Logic in all its chapters, and offered the canonic prayer, for they were all Muslims."

– *Arab Historians of the Crusades*

This remarkable tolerance, real, or feigned, served him badly. Moslems believed each religion should observe its prescribed principles correctly and summed him up thusly:

"The emperor... had a red skin, and was bald and short sighted. Had he been a slave he would not have been worth

> two hundred *dirham*. It was clear from what he said that he was a materialist and that his Christianity was simply a game to him."
>
> – *Ibid*

This feeling wasn't confined to Moslems. The chronicler Matthew Paris wrote that Frederick:

> "...questioned the Catholic faith and that he had made statements that showed not only he was weak in faith, but that he was indeed a heretic and a blasphemer. It is not right even to repeat such things, but it is reported that he said there were three impostors who had deceived the people of their time for the purpose of gaining control of the world, Moses, Jesus, and Mohammed."
>
> – *Empire and Papacy*

On his third day in Jerusalem, the Archbishop of Caesarea imposed an interdict on the city, prohibiting church services and disappointing hundreds of pilgrims. Frederick had enough, and left the city the same day. Both the Christian and Moslem worlds saw the treaty with al-Kamil as a betrayal on the part of their leaders. As Frederick departed from the Holy Land on May 1, 1229 he passed by the butcher's quarter on the way to his galley. Recognizing him, the furious butchers pelted him with offal as he boarded his ship to leave.

The Wonder of the World

FREDERICK PROBABLY COMMUNICATED WITH HIS HOSTS IN JERUSALEM IN ARABIC. He was fluent in nine languages, and wrote seven - some, exceedingly well. It was at his court, as Dante points out, that Italian poetry had its birth. This was the era of troubadours and courtly love in literature. Frederick's own court knew and enjoyed the genre, and transplanted it to Sicily. Frederick, his sons, and his ministers all wrote lyrics that still charm readers today.

In addition, he attracted scholars to Sicily to translate Greek and Arabic texts into Latin. Members of the ibn Tibbon family translated the *Commentaries of Averroës* and Ptolemy's *Almagest*. Maimonides *Guide for the Perplexed* was translated in Naples, and Michael Scot translated works of Avicenna and Aristotle's *History of Animals* for the emperor himself.

Frederick corresponded with Jews in Spain and Moslems as far off as Egypt, Morocco and Yemen. After Jerusalem, he maintained contact with al-Kamil, inquiring about philosophy: how was Aristotle able to demonstrate the eternity of matter? And geometry and optics: why does a stick partly immersed in water appear to be bent? Al-Kamil sent an astronomer to instruct him. At his own court, Michael Scot was tasked with providing, "a description of the universe, from its foundations to the uppermost reaches of heaven."

Frederick wrote a book of his own: *On the Art of Hunting with Birds* (*De Arte Venandi cum Avibus*) which is both hunting manual and a scientific description of falcons and their prey. It cites widely, especially Aristotle. But when the philosopher contradicted Frederick's own observations, he was corrected – a rare occurrence in medieval times. There were even experiments: to see if vultures operate by sight or smell Frederick had their eyes seeled and showed they operated by sight.

Astrology

FOR ALL HIS LEARNING, FREDERICK STILL USED ASTROLOGERS TO CAST his children's horoscopes and predict the outcomes of his ventures. It was rumored he even waited to consummate his marriage until his astrologers announced the best time for doing so. Michael Scot, whose early career was devoted to natural science, entered Frederick's service principally as an astrologer. According to Salimbene:

> "...being one day in his palace, he [Frederick] asked Michael Scot the astrologer how far he was from the sky, and Michael having answered as it seemed to him, the emperor

took him to other parts of his kingdom as if for a journey of pleasure, and kept him there several months, bidding meanwhile his architects and carpenters secretly to lower the whole of his palace hall.

Many days afterwards, standing in that same palace with Michael, he asked of him, as if by the way, whether he were indeed so far from the sky as he had before said. Whereupon he made his calculations, and made answer that certainly either the sky had been raised or the earth lowered; and then the emperor knew that he spake truth."

– *The Chronicle of Salimbene*

There are several versions of this story. The emperor is always the skeptic, and Scott is always proven correct in spite of attempts to thwart him.

The First Medieval State

FREDERICK TRANSFORMED SICILY INTO THE FIRST MODERN STATE OF MEDIEVAL EUROPE. His first task after his coronation was to secure the kingdom that his father's barons had despoiled for twenty years. The Assizes of Capua, were statutes that compelled them to submit their charters for re-evaluation and adjustment, revoked local autonomy, and centralized government under his firm hand.

To administer his state, he created a loyal civil service. At Naples, he founded the only secular medieval university outside of Moslem Spain – ironically, its most famous alumnus is St. Thomas Aquinas. Professors earned top salaries and enrollment was guaranteed by forbidding study outside the kingdom. Even poor students were admitted, and graduates were funneled into his elite corps of state clerks and magistrates. He also recognized the need for economic investment. He strengthened the fleet, built a system of state agricultural warehouses, encouraged immigration, and established state monopolies on salt and minerals.

After his return from crusade and subsequent expulsion of the invading papal army from Sicily, he issued the Constitutions of

Melfi; over 200 laws and proclamations which re-introduced something like the old Roman law codes into western government. Not surprisingly, they identify Frederick as "Augustus" and postulate a monarchy based on man, God, and the emperor – without aid or intervention from the pope. To commemorate this event, he minted a gold Augustale coin in 1231, featuring his idealized profile as a Roman emperor, with a finely designed eagle on its reverse. It is the first of only a handful of portrait coins issued before the Renaissance and predates the influential gold trade coins of Florence and Genoa by two decades.

Leisure

FREDERICK WASN'T ALL WORK AND NO PLAY. AFTER FALCONRY, HE ENJOYED ENTERTAINMENT and kept a large troop of singers, dancers, and acrobats, many of them Saracen. He also kept a menagerie of wild beasts, including: giraffe, elephants, camels, lions, leopards, birds, apes and bears. Like most medieval kings, he was constantly traveling throughout his kingdom, with occasional stopovers at hunting lodges. His entertainers, bodyguard, and numerous animals, together with his crown jewels and part of his library, made up a traveling court – they must have presented quite a spectacle. Even his enemies couldn't help being impressed by him. One relates:

> "...he was crafty, wily, avaricious, lustful, malicious, wrathful; and yet a gallant man at times, when he would show his kindness or courtesy; full of solace jocund, delightful, fertile in devices. He knew how to read, write, and sing, to make songs and music."
>
> – *Ibid*

Emperor Frederick was a Renaissance man 200 before the Renaissance.

War With the Papacy

ALL OF THIS IS A PRELUDE TO ONE OF THE MOST UNUSUAL CAREERS any man or emperor can have, as the Antichrist:

> "Opinions as to the nature of Antichrist were divided. Some held he was to be a devil in phantom body... Others again believed that he would be an incarnate demon, true man and true devil... A third view was that HE WOULD BE MERELY A DESPERATELY WICKED MAN, ACTING UPON DIABOLIC INSPIRATIONS, just as the saints act upon divine ones.
>
> Antichrist could have many forerunners, and so St. Jerome and St. Augustine saw an Antichrist in Nero, not the Antichrist, but one of those of whom the Apostle speaks "Even now are there many Antichrists" (1 John 2:18). Thus every enemy of the faith has been regarded as a precursor of the Archpersecutor, who was expected to sum up in himself the cruelty of a Nero or Diocletian... or the spiritual pride of a Mohammed.
>
> In the time of Antichrist... THE CHURCH WILL BE DIVIDED: one portion will hold to the world-power, the other will seek the old paths, and cling to the true Guide. The high places will be filled with unbelievers, and THE CHURCH WILL BE IN A CONDITION OF THE UTMOST SPIRITUAL DEGRADATION, BUT ENJOYING THE HIGHEST STATE PATRONAGE....
>
> He [Antichrist] will inaugurate an awful persecution, which will last for three years and a half, and exceed in horror all persecutions that have gone before... But the Church will remain unwrecked, she will weather the storm... till CHRIST WILL DESCEND TO AVENGE THE BLOOD OF THE SAINTS, BY DESTROYING ANTICHRIST AND THE WORLD POWER."
>
> – *Curious Myths of the Middle Ages*

Events conspired to make it obvious to everyone that Frederick was the Antichrist foretold above. His son Henry's rebellion in Germany precipitated the crisis. The insurrection was easily put down and Henry imprisoned, but afterwards Frederick decided to punish the northern Italian states who had encouraged and supported Henry. The pope came to their aid, and in 1239 Frederick found himself an excommunicate again.

After that, the world just seemed to fall apart. In 1241 Frederick's forces captured a group of cardinals and bishops on their way to a Church council sailing under the banner of the crusader's cross. Contrary to custom they were imprisoned and their case became a *cause célèbre*. Next year, Batu's Mongols – Gog and Magog of the last times – ravaged Hungary and threatened Germany. And Innocent IV, even more hostile than Gregory, was elected pope. Finally, in 1244, Jerusalem fell to the Khwarizmian Turks. During all this, Frederick and the papacy went at it tooth and claw. Chronicles of the day are filled with their diatribes:

"Emperor to the pope:

The fates warn, stars teach, and likewise the flights of birds, that I will soon be the hammer of the world. Rome, a long time wavering, having committed a multitude of errors, will collapse and cease to be the leader of the world."

"Pope to the emperor:

Your reputation relates, Scripture teaches, and your sins announce, that you will have a short life and eternal punishment." [2]

Increasingly, their accusations took on apocalyptic tones. Frederick became the beast from the sea and the great dragon, while Innocent was made out as Satan when his number was reckoned as 666.

Finally, at the Council of Lyon, Innocent IV unmade the emperor Innocent III had made, declaring:

"We mark him out as bound by his sins, an outcast and deprived by our Lord of every honor and dignity; and we deprive him of them by our sentence. We absolve from their oath for ever all those who are bound to him by an oath of

> loyalty, firmly FORBIDDING BY OUR APOSTOLIC AUTHORITY ANYONE IN THE FUTURE TO OBEY OR HEED HIM AS EMPEROR OR KING, and decreeing that anyone who henceforth offers advice, help or favor to him as to an emperor or king, automatically incurs excommunication.
>
> – *First Council of Lyon*

In his place, Innocent installed an anti-emperor, Henry Raspe, and after Raspe's death, William of Holland.

For his part, Frederick was furious:

> "When Frederick heard that the pope had deposed him, he was terribly enraged, and could scarcely contain himself for his wrath. Looking fiercely on those who sat around him, he thundered forth: 'That pope has deposed me in his synod and has taken away my crown. Was there ever such audacity; was there ever such presumption? Where are the chests that contain my treasure?'
>
> And when these were brought and opened before him at his command, he said: 'See now whether my crowns are lost.' Then taking one of them and putting it on his head, he stood up, with a threatening look, and spoke out in a terrible voice from the bitterness of his heart: 'I have not yet lost my crown, nor shall the pope and all his synod take it from me without a bloody struggle. And has his presumption been so boundless that he has dared to depose me from the empire, me, a great prince, who have no superior, indeed no equal?'"
>
> – *Empire and Papacy*

In such a state, even people close to Frederick weren't sure of what he might do:

> "It was feared by some wise and thoughtful men that Frederick in his wrath might turn apostate, or call in to his aid the Tartars from Russia, or give the Sultan of Babylon, with whom he was on the most friendly terms, the chance to

overrun the empire with his pagan hosts, to the destruction of all Christendom..."

– Ibid

Scourge of the Church

IN THIS, WHAT SEEMED TO BE THE PRELUDE TO THE LAST TIMES, THE *Commentary on Jeremiah* was born. It purported to be Joachim of Fiore's prophecy for Henry VI and his descendants. When Henry invaded Sicily for the first time, Joachim foretold his failure and success on a later attempt – which came to pass. So in 1194, this report from Cremona seemed plausible:

> "In these times, a certain exegete, abbot Joachim of Apulia, who possesses the gift of prophecy, foretells the death of Emperor Henry [VI], the future desolation of the Kingdom of Sicily, and weakness in the Roman empire. This declaration is absolutely clear. For the kingdom of Sicily will be thrown into confusion for a long time, and the empire will be divided by schism."[3]

– making Joachim the author of a second prophecy about Henry. Actually, it's the work of his followers, at least in later versions where Frederick is identified as the Antichrist:

> "...KING FREDERICK, and the seed of this Henry and his clan, either the ancestor or the progeny following, WHOSE HEARTS ARE SET UPON THE PUNISHMENT OF THE CHURCH, AND THE DESTRUCTION OF THE CHRISTIAN PEOPLE..."[4]

But that's only part of it. Consistent with the last times, the pope and Church too, are denounced as corrupt! Only a handful of the faithful, Joachim's new order of monks, would remain untainted. Frederick II, heretical sects, and Moslems would become scourges of the Church and the unwitting deliverers of these persecuted monks. All of this would happen in 1260, Joachim's date for Christ's Second Coming.

Then in December 1250 – ten years early – Frederick died. He had suffered from intestinal fevers for some time. After a violent attack of dysentery he made out his will, and robed as a Cistercian monk, renounced his earthly possessions and left the world as a poor penitent. Joachim's followers were stunned at the news their arch-villain was gone.

But an anxious world wouldn't let him rest, "he lived and he lived not." In Sicily a monk saw him descend into the crater of Mount Etna (thought to be the entrance to hell) as a fiery army of his knights rode into the hissing sea. Germans thought he was: "...still alive and will remain alive until the end of the world; there has been and shall be no proper emperor but he." And his legend merged with that of his grandfather Frederick I Barbarossa (Red Beard), sleeping in a cave under Kyffhäuser mountain in Thuringia, awaiting the moment when he would return to redeem Christendom. So strong was this belief that in 1284, when an impostor claimed to be the reincarnated Frederick, he was accepted in the German city of Neuss, and several Italian towns sent ambassadors to look into the situation.

Similar prophecies continued for a decade after his death. The *Commentary on Isaiah* (*Super Esaiam*) transferred his apocalyptic role to his sons, the "seed of Frederick." And one of Joachim's reputed diagrams from this time, the *Premises* (*Praemissiones*), makes the sixth head of the dragon Saladin's, and the seventh, Frederick's – both joined together at the neck!

With the passage of time, flesh and blood Hohenstaufens were replaced by a mythical "Third Frederick" or "Frederick who is to come." In both Italy and Germany it was believed that a future Frederick would someday become the scourge of the Church, either to destroy or renew it. An Aragonese Frederick II, on the throne of Sicily from 1272 to 1337, and Frederick III, King of the Romans from 1415 to 1493, both were candidates for the role.

The Emperor Card

THE EMPEROR APPEARS IN ANCESTOR SEATED NEXT TO THE POPE (*opposite page*).

The commentary there identifies him as Lothar III, and the pope as Innocent II, together at the Concordat of Worms in 1137. I'll show later that these men have no relevance for Tarot.

A feature which might help to identify Tarot's Emperor as Frederick II is the eagle of the Holy Roman Empire which is frequently on his hat, breastplate or shield. Unfortunately, the case for the Visconti-Modrone and Visconti-Sforza decks is ambiguous in this regard. In 1395, Gian Galeazzo Visconti paid the Holy Roman Emperor Wenceslaus, King of Bohemia, 100,000 gold *florins* to make him Duke of Milan. This permitted Gian Galeazzo to quarter a single-headed imperial eagle with the Visconti viper on his coat-of-arms. Thus, the eagle on Visconti cards could be fortuitous.

THE SINGLE-HEADED EAGLE ON THE NEW HAVEN EMPEROR (*right*) AND EMPRESS CARDS IS MORE CLEAR ON THIS POINT.

It's described in the Codex Manesse (*circa* 1300) and is also found on Frederick II's gold *tareni* coins.

Some time during his reign the emblem was changed to a two-headed eagle illustrated by Matthew Paris in 1250.

THIS APPEARS ON THE BUDAPEST EMPEROR AND EMPRESS (*left*) CARDS.

EAGLES ARE ABSENT, HOWEVER, FROM THE WASHINGTON AND CHARLES VI (*right*) CARDS,

...AND THEY CAN BE FOUND ON NUMEROUS ORDINARY CARDS LIKE THIS FRENCH JULIUS CAESAR (*KING OF DIAMONDS*) CARD (*left*).

The German imperial eagle was even occasionally used as a suit mark!

The Empress

TRADITION IDENTIFIES THE EMPRESS AS THE EMPEROR'S CONSORT AND QUEEN. Certainly none of Frederick's wives qualify. All three were chosen for political considerations, and it's rumored he treated them rather shabbily, secluding them in Oriental fashion.

Revelation AND ANCESTOR (*left and opposite page*) PROVIDE THE REAL ANSWER. Just as The Popess represents an institution – the Church – The Empress represents the State, symbolized by:

"Babylon the great, the mother of the fornications, and the abominations of the earth... the woman which thou sawest, is the great city, which hath kingdom over the kings of the earth."

– *Revelation* 17:5 & 17:18

In the final days, she will be utterly destroyed:

> "And a mighty angel took up a stone, as it were a great millstone, and cast it into the sea, saying: With such violence as this shall Babylon, that great city, be thrown down, and shall be found no more at all."
>
> – *Revelation* 18:21

THE WHORE OF BABYLON SITTING ON THE BEAST

The Emperor and Empress cards of the early Tarot decks are stylistically similar.

If he is turned and has an eagle, as in the New Haven deck, she does likewise (*right*),

...and when he is shown face-on without the eagle, as in the Washington deck, so does she(*left*).

The final verdict as to the identities of the Empress and Emperor comes from Tarot's story. For now, at least none of the early Tarot decks contradict the interpretation of The Empress as the Church and Frederic II as The Emperor.

Bibliography

David Abulafia, *Frederick II: A Medieval Emperor*, (Oxford UP, 1988).

Sabine Baring-Gould, "Antichrist and Pope Joan." In *Curious Myths of the Middle Ages*, (London: Longmans, Green & Co., 1894), abridgement: Edward Hardy, ed. (Barnes & Noble, 1994).

Norman Cohn, "The Emperor Frederick as Messiah." In *The Pursuit of the Millenium: Revolutionary Millenarians and Mystical Anarchists of the Middle Ages*, (Oxford UP, 1970).

C. C. Coulton, "The Chronicle of Salimbene, Thirteenth-century Italian Franciscan." In *St. Francis to Dante*, (London: David Nutt, 1906).

Francesco Gabrieli, "Jerusalem Is Handed Over to the Franks, & Muslim Grief in Damascus, Frederick in Jerusalem." In *Arab Historians of the Crusades*, trans E.J. Costello, (Dorsett Pr., 1989).

Philip Grierson, "The Thirteenth Century: The Early Gros and Florin." In *The Coins of Medieval Europe*, (Seaby, 1991).

O Holder-Egger, "Italienishe Prophetien des 13. Jahrhunderts." In *Neues Archiv der Gesellshaft für altere deutsche Geschichtskunde*, xxx (1904-5), pp 323-86.

Robert E. Lerner, "Frederick II, Alive, Aloft, and Allayed, in Franciscan-Joachite Eschatology." In *The Use and Abuse of Eshatologyin the Middle Ages*, ed. D. Verhelst et al. (Leiden, 1988).

Bernard McGinn, "Frederick II Versus the Papacy." In *Visions of the End: Apocalyptic Traditions in the Middle Ages*, (Columbia UP, 1979).

_____, *Antichrist: Two Thousand Years of the Human Fascination With Evil*, (Harper Collins, 1996).

Robert Moynihan, "The Development of the 'Pseudo-Joachim' Commentary 'Super Hieremiam': New Manuscript Evidence." In *Mélanges de l'école française de Rome. Moyen Âge, Temps Modernes*, Vol 98, 1986, pp 109-42.

Marjorie Reeves, “The Worst Antichrist and the Last Emperor.” In *The Influence of Prophecy in the Later Middle Ages: A Study in Joachimism*, (U. Notre Dame Pr.,1993).

Peter Spufford, “The Balance of Payments and the Movement of Silver.” In *Money and its Use in Medieval Europe*, (Cambridge UP, 1988).

Oliver J. Thatcher & Edgar H. McNeal, “Empire and Papacy, 1073-1250.” In *A Source Book for Medieval History*, reprint: (AMS Press, 1971).

Richard Vaughan, *The Illustrated Chronicles of Matthew Paris: Observations of Thirteenth-Century Life*, (Alan Sutton Pub, 1993).

Internet

Note: There’s no need to type this yourself. Current links to these and future sites, as they become available, can be found at: http://tarot-cards.com

Antichrist
http://www.knight.org/advent/cathen/01559a.htm

First Council of Lyons - 1245 A.D. "Bull Deposing The Emperor Frederick II"
http://www.ewtn.com/library/COUNCILS/1LYONS.TXT

Pope Gregory IX
http://www.knight.org/advent/Popes/ppgr09.htm

Pope Honorius III
http://www.knight.org/advent/Popes/pphn03.htm

Pope Innocent III
http://www.knight.org/advent/Popes/ppin03.htm

Pope Innocent IV
http://www.knight.org/advent/Popes/ppin04.htm

Interdict
http://www.knight.org/advent/cathen/08073a.htm

Knights Hospitaller
http://www.knight.org/advent/cathen/07477a.htm

Knights Templar
http://www.knight.org/advent/cathen/14493a.htm
Latin Kingdom of Jerusalem
http://www.knight.org/advent/cathen/08361a.htm
Matthew Paris
http://www.knight.org/advent/cathen/11499a.htm
Salimbene on Frederick II, 13th Century
http://www.fordham.edu/halsall/source/salimbene1.html

Translations

1. stupor mundi et immutator mirabilis

2. Imperator ad papam: Fata moment, stelleque docent, aviumque volatus: Totius subito malleus orbis ero. Roma diu titubans, variis erroribus acta, Concidet et mundi desinet esse caput.

Papa ad imperatorem: Fama refert, scriptura docet, peccata loquuntur, Ouod tibi vita brevis, pena perhennis erit.

3. His temporibus quidam exitit Joachim Appulus abbas, qui spiritum habuit prophetandi, et prophetavit de morte imperatoris Henrici et futura desolatione Siculi regni et defectu Romani imperii. Quod manifestissime declaratum est. Nam regnum Sicilie multo tempore est perturbatum et imperium per scisma divisum.

4. De quo regulus Federicus, et semen eius Henricus et caeteri, qui de sua progenie vel propagatione succedent: quorum cor erit ad affligendum ecclesiam, et delendum populum Christianum...

Chapter Eleven

Romantic Trio

TRADITIONALLY, THE NEXT THREE CARDS ARE ASSOCIATED WITH magic, love and war, ageless themes of stories from ancient myths to modern novels. I'll show that conventional wisdom is mostly correct, but in a way which scarcely could be guessed.

The Magician Card

EL *Bagatella*, AN EARLY NAME FOR THE MAGICIAN, IS RELATED TO THE ENGLISH WORD *bagatelle* meaning trifle. Presumably, because it's the lowest value card in the Tarot deck. It's identification with a juggler – the conjuring kind, not the one who tosses balls in the air – is old too.

Illustrations in the *Book of the Seven Planets,* from the fifteenth century on, show what this fellow looked like. We owe this good fortune to the fact that in medieval astrology: "The moon's children are fishermen, barbers and fowlers, millers, JUGGLERS and messengers," each of whom, as can be seen in the illustration of Chapter Three, was portrayed somewhere on Luna, the moon's, accompaning picture.

Comparing the astrological illustrations (*opposite page*) with the Budapest (*right*) and Washington (*bottom right*) cards leaves no doubt The Magician card depicts a juggler.

The Catelin Geofroy and D'Este (*below*) cards even show a classic Ball and Cups sleight-of-hand in progress:

> "One thing I remember, and I gape with astonishment at it now, and am almost struck dumb. A certain man stepped into the midst, and placed on a three-legged table three small cups, under which he concealed some little white round pebbles such are found on the banks of rivers; these he placed one by one under the cups, and then, I don't know how, made them appear under another cup and showed them in his mouth. Then, when he had swallowed them, he brought them from the nose, another from the ear, and another from the head of those standing near him; last, he made them disappear from before the eyes of all..."
>
> – *Conjurers*

This account is by a second-century Greek writer. Romans called the magician pebble-man (*calcularius)* or bottle-man (*acetabularius)* after this trick. Another name was bag-man (*saccularius)* from his way of hiding objects in his pocket or bag.

The medieval juggler was recognizable by his three chief props: table, magic wand and bag (*gibecière*). Although clearly shown in *Book of the Seven Planets* pictures, early Tarot cards mostly omit the bag.

ONE IS BARELY VISIBLE ON THE NEW HAVEN (*left*) CARD AND IS ALMOST CERTAINLY THE MYSTERIOUS OBJECT BELOW THE MAGICIAN'S RIGHT HAND ON THE VISCONTI-SFORZA (*opposite page*) CARD.

In the Middle Ages a wand or divining rod was believed to be capable of opening the ground and cleaving rocks to reveal hidden treasure, veins of precious metals and springs of water. Even more miraculously, it could point out thieves and murderers. Some of these properties still survive in its cousin the dowsing rod. To make a wand, first a rod (ash was a favorite choice) four cubits (72 inches) long was cut while repeating the Lord's Prayer. It was then split, and two men held the two halves apart at the ends. While making the sign of the cross, one of them repeated the following incantation (every vowel is pronounced):

> *"Ellum super ellam sedebat et virgam viridem in manu. tenebat et dicebat, 'Virgam viridis reunitere in simul.'"*

– together with the Lord's Prayer until the two split halves bent together in the middle.

This sounds impressive until you know he was merely saying:

> He sat on She and held a green rod in his hand and said, "Green rod reunite again."

Furthermore, the rod is almost guaranteed to bend. Since very little force is required, and two people are involved, the inevitable slight imbalance in forces gives the desired effect.

The man then seized the ends in his fist at the junction point and cut off the rest. The magic resided within the section remaining in his grasp.

Tricks mentioned in twelfth and thirteenth-century minstrel's tales suggest possible identities for the objects pictured on the magician's table:

> "Well know I the cork ball [and cups],
> And how to make the beetle come alive,
> And dancing on the table.
> And so I know many a fair table game,
> The result of dexterity and magic.
> I know how to play with the cudgels,
> And also know how to play with the cutlasses,
> And with the cord and rope."
>
> — *Conjurers*

A purely modern convention is to place an object from each of the four Tarot suits: Swords, Wands, Cups and Coins, on the table. Unfortunately, this misses the point of what the scene represents.

Dice are plainly visible on the Budapest card. They were used for divination. Three were rolled at a time and used to select from fifty-six possible fortunes. Throwing a 5-4-3 combination elicited the following warning in one medieval English poem:

> "You that have cast five, four, and trey,
> Be not displeased with what I shall say.
> You love where no love is,
> For where you can't love, there love is." [3]

Similar French and German poems survive from medieval and Renaissance times.

Why a Magician?

WHAT does THE MAGICIAN CARD MEAN? IT'S NOT HARD TO GUESS why he begins the Tarot deck. The critical clue is sequence. The Magician is the first card of Tarot's story, and The World card the last. If the World card represents resolution: "And they lived happily ever after..." then The Magician must be an introduction: "Once upon a time..." and establish the setting for what's to come. In fact it does more, it also states the problem to be resolved.

Prestidigitation or juggling contrasts *par excellence* the difference between appearance and reality. In the Middle Ages what you saw was *not* what you got. It didn't matter that Frederick II was a king and emperor, he and many others chose to face God and judgment as a penitent monk. Earthly life was fickle and transitory, the next life serious business – and for keeps. The juggler signals that the theme to follow has more than a surface meaning and is to be understood anagogically. That, I believe, is the purpose of the card.

Revelation confirms this. In its last chapter John's message to the seven Churches is summed up in two lines:

> "Blessed are THEY THAT WASH THEIR ROBES IN THE BLOOD OF THE LAMB: that they may have a right to the tree of life, AND MAY ENTER IN BY THE GATES INTO THE CITY. Without are dogs, and SORCERERS, and unchaste, and murderers, and servers of idols, AND EVERY ONE THAT LOVETH AND MAKETH A LIE."
>
> – *Revelation* 22:14-15

In Chapter Thirteen I'll show that: "they that wash their robes..." are The Hanged Man. You've seen that "The city" is the new Jerusalem, represented by The World. Here "sorcerers" and "every one that loveth and maketh a lie" are The Magician. Just as the above lines summarize John's message, The Magician, Hanged Man and World cards encapsulate Tarot's story, but in opposite order:

- Lies and errors [The Magician] are everywhere.
- But the Hanged Man will be saved,
- He will inherit The World.

I remarked in Chapter Three how the Tarot of Marseilles connects these three cards: The Magician's wand is repeated on The World card, as are the The Hanged Man's crossed legs. This is the reason why.

The Lovers Card

THE LOVERS CARD TRADITIONALLY SIGNIFIES LOVE AND MARRIAGE. ON THE EARLY DECKS, LIKE THE WASHINGTON (*left*) AND CHARLES VI (*right*) COUPLES PLEDGE THEIR LOVE BEFORE A MEDIEVAL CUPID.

Similar scenes with cupids derive from classical models and appear on fourth-century Christian gilded-glass medallions from the Roman catacombs.

On many cards, like the Visconti-Modrone one in Chapter Five, marriage is conveyed through the gestures of the hands. In medieval Christian marriages the bride dropped her father's hand and took her husband's, which survives in our expression to "give one's hand in marriage." This handclasp marriage goes back to the handshake (*dextrarum junctio)* appearing on Roman coins and tombstones, and occasionally in medieval images of the Marriage of the Virgin. Although a priest was the principal witness to the marriage ceremony, he didn't necessarily join the couple's hands until after the Council of Trent in 1546. Hence a priest doesn't appear on the earliest Tarot decks but figures prominently on the Tarot of Marseilles card.

Offhand, The Lovers card would seem to contradict any connection with Ancestor and *Revelation,* inasmuch as:

> "The children of this world marry, and are given in marriage: But they that shall be accounted worthy of that world, and of the resurrection from the dead, shall neither be married, nor take wives. Neither can they die any more: for they are equal to the angels, and are the children of God, being the children of the resurrection."
>
> – *Luke* 20:34

The key to understanding The Lovers card is the marriage of the Lamb allegory from *Revelation*:

> "Let us be glad and rejoice, and give glory to him; for THE MARRIAGE OF THE LAMB IS COME, and his wife hath prepared herself.... And he [an angel] said to me: Write: Blessed are they that are called to THE MARRIAGE SUPPER OF THE LAMB..."
>
> – *Revelation* 19:7-9

– which is not at all what one expects:

> "And I [John] saw heaven opened, and beheld a white horse; and he that sat upon him was called faithful and true, and with justice doth he judge and fight. And his eyes were as a flame of fire... And he was clothed with a garment sprinkled with blood; and his name is called, The Word of God. And the armies that are in heaven followed him on white horses, clothed in fine linen, white and clean. And out of his mouth proceedeth a sharp two edged sword; that with it he may strike the nations..."
>
> – *Revelation* 19:11-15

> "And I saw the beast, and the kings of the earth, and their armies gathered together to make war with him that sat upon the horse, and with his army. And the beast was taken, and with him the false prophet, who wrought signs before him, wherewith he seduced them who received the character of the beast, and who adored his image. These two were cast alive into the pool of fire, burning with brimstone. And the rest were slain by the sword of him that sitteth upon the horse."
>
> – *Revelation* 19:19-21

The allegory between marriage and horses, armies, and war is clarified by a portion I skipped over:

> "Come, gather yourselves together to THE GREAT SUPPER OF GOD: That you may EAT THE FLESH OF KINGS, and the flesh of tribunes, and the flesh of mighty men, and the flesh of horses, and of them that sit on them, and the flesh of all freemen and bondmen, and of little and of great."
>
> – *Revelation* 19:17-18

These words are spoken by an angel to the "birds that did fly" mentioned in the discussion of The Star card. They show "the marriage of the Lamb" is a euphemism for Christ's (him that sitteth upon the white horse) battle and victory over Satan and his forces – the ultimate triumph of good over evil.

THIS CONFLICT IS PORTRAYED IN ANCESTOR (*opposite page*), HOWEVER, SEVERAL ILLUSTRATIONS ARE REQUIRED TO DO IT.

The Lover's card captures the same idea in a single scene by depicting the euphemism – a distinct advantage for a playing card. By the same token, the card's real message is not marriage, but the triumph over evil which it stands for.

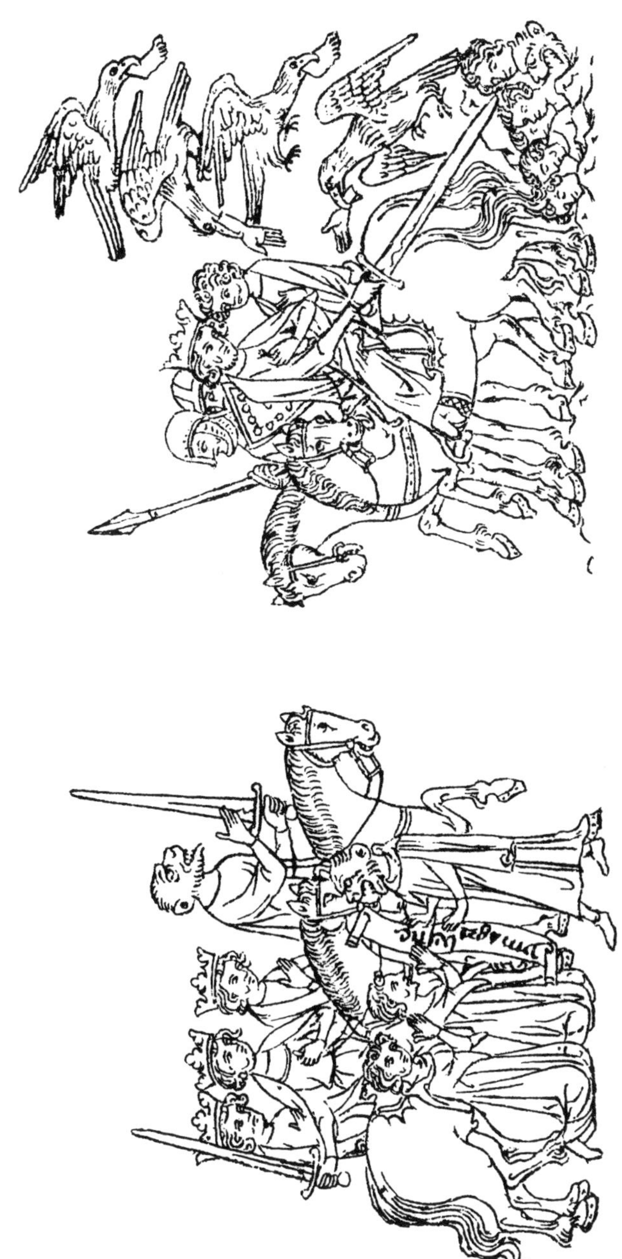

Most *Revelation* illustrations depict the marriage supper allegory as a feast scene around a table. On the contrary, Ancestor (*below*) portrays the marriage itself, with similar hand gestures as on Lovers cards.

The angel on Ancestor's card (*below*) may have even become tarot's Cupid. But what's really striking is that Christ is portrayed as a lamb! Actually, Ancestor's rendition is fairly attractive – more literal ones, like Albrecht Dürer's (*opposite page*) accurately depict his seven horns and seven eyes!

Real Medieval Battles

ON NOVEMBER 27, 1237, FREDERICK II WAS CAMPAIGNING WITH HIS ARMIES in northern Italy. Winter had made fighting nearly impossible, so caution was less than usual. Near Cortenuova a detachment of reconnoitering troops surprised an enemy squadron and a battle began. The early fighting was in Frederick's favor, but bogged down around Milan's *carroccio,* where the enemy made a desperate stand. Only nightfall and rain halted the carnage.

Every important medieval Italian city-state had its *carroccio,* usually a cart pulled by oxen and decked with symbols of the city's power: banners, statues and saint's relics. Milan's was dedicated to St. Ambrose, who opposed the Arian heresy, became Bishop of Milan, and was the city's patron saint. *Carroccios* were solemnly drawn into battle, manned by the most valorous soldiers and guarded to the death. They were symbols of divine protection and a source of morale for the troops. Capture by opposing forces was an admission of military and political defeat.

The battle was expected to be decided the next day, but in the early dawn the opposition began to melt away. In vain, they struggled to carry off the relics and cross from the *carroccio*, but even these were left behind when their wagons became stuck in the mud. They'd suffered a humiliating defeat, which Frederick underscored by having the sad and broken and *carroccio* dragged through the streets of Cremona, Milan's rival.

In a triumphal procession rivaling those of ancient Rome, it was drawn by an an elephant from his menagerie outfitted with a wooden tower bearing Frederick's pennant, and followed by a great procession of captives in chains. Prominent among them was Pietro Tieplolo, podestà of Milan and the doge's son (later put to death). Chroniclers as far away as the Rhineland recorded the event, and Frederick's propagandists gloated over how Caesar Frederick had left the enemy dead in piles.

As a final gesture, the *carroccio* was sent to the popular commune of Rome and displayed on the Campidoglio, bearing the inscription: "This commemorates Caesar's triumph,"[2] where the pope, who supported his enemies, was sure to see it.

Renaissance Triumphs

SIMILAR PROCESSIONS, CALLED *Trionfi*, WERE POPULAR IN RENAISSANCE TIMES. One for Alfonso the Great in Naples, in 1443:

> "...was a strange mixture of antique, allegorical, and purely comic elements. The car, drawn by four white horses, on which he sat enthroned, was lofty and covered with gilding; twenty patricians carried the poles of the canopy of cloth of gold which shaded his head. The part of the procession which the Florentines then present in Naples had undertaken was composed of elegant young cavaliers, skillfully brandishing their lances, of a chariot with the figure of Fortune, and of seven Virtues on horseback.
>
> The goddess herself, in accordance with the inexorable logic of allegory to which even the painters at that time conformed, wore hair only on the front part of her head, while the back part was bald, and the genius who sat on the lower steps of the car, and who symbolized the furtive character of fortune, had his feet immersed in a basin of water. Last of all came a gigantic tower, the door guarded by an angel with a drawn sword; on it stood the four virtues, who each addressed the king with a song."
>
> – *Society and Festivals*

VEHICLES ON MANY CHARIOT CARDS, LIKE THE CHARLES VI (*right*), LOOK LIKE *carroccios*,

...OR *Trionfi* CARS, LIKE THIS ONE FROM A 1465 *Book of the Seven Planets* (*below*).

The name *Trionfi* and other circumstances lead Gertrude Moakley to base her interpretation of Tarot upon Petrarch's poem *I Trionfi,* which describes such a procession. But I think this goes too far. If Tarot's Chariot card portrays a triumph, then what victory or event does it commemorate?

The Last World Emperor

WHEN *Revelation* WAS WRITTEN, ROME MADE WAR ON CHRISTENDOM and Nero was the Antichrist. With the granting of religious toleration by the Edict of Milan in 313 AD and closing of the pagan temples in 356, this changed completely. Thereafter, the Roman Empire was as Christian a nation as any today – something we tend to forget. A new literature began to interpret the, now beneficent, role of the emperor.

The earliest tracts tell about Constantine the Great and his son Constans (his other son Constantius supported the Arian heresy, thereby earning himself a head on Joachim's dragon). Constans was murdered but legend brought him back. Some time around the sixth century, a Last Emperor named Constans was added to the fourth-century *Tiburtine Sibyl* (*Tiburtina*), and by the seventh century he also appears in the so-called *Pseudo-Methodius.* Both accounts originated in the Eastern (Byzantine) empire, which unlike the West, survived the dark ages intact.

The idea passed to the West as manuscripts were loaned and copied from one religious center to another, becoming thoroughly westernized in the process. By the tenth century a *Letter on the Origin and Life of the Antichrist* pitted the King of the Franks against the Antichrist. And in 1146 a Last Emperor prophesy about King Louis VII circulated in France. Anonymous Last Emperors appear in the *Erythraean Sibyl,* and in thirteenth-century prophecies about Frederick II. In the mid-fourteenth century John of Rupescissa a.k.a. Jean de Roquetaillade brought the legends up to date. Between 1345 and 1356 he wrote several manuscripts about a new Frederick who would attack the church and be opposed by a French king. This was during the "Babylonian Captivity" of the popes in Avignon, when France was very much on the minds of Italians. According to John, Antichrist would be destroyed, and the whole world united in a peace presided over by the pope, true Franciscans, and the French monarchy (I'll have more to say about this later). His writings enjoyed great popularity in Italy, France, England, Germany and his homeland of Catalonia.

John's success encouraged Telesphorus of Cosenza to reiterate the theme sometime between 1378 and 1390 during the great schism of the Catholic church. Telesphorus says in his introduction:

> "Here begins the little book of brother Telesphorus, priest and hermit, following original prophetic writings and true accounts, of the cause, status, and result of the present schism and of future tribulations, particularly of the coming time of an eagle-king calling himself Frederick III, through the future time of a pope called the angelic shepherd, and Charles King of France, the future emperor after Frederick III." [3]

This work was even more popular than John's. Numerous copies of the manuscript, some of them illustrated, are found in the libraries of Italy, France, Austria and Germany. His work was translated into French and German and a Latin edition published in Venice in 1516. French editions were printed in Rouen and Lyon as late as 1565 and 1572. Frequently found together with Telesphorus' work is the Second Charlemagne prophecy, another Last Emperor legend, and the most widely disseminated oracle for the next two centuries

What did all these prophecies say? There are too many to consider individually, so I've made up a kind of composite which captures their flavor. In my summary (*opposite page*), each legend is given a code or ID and the Last Emperor's career is divided into eight phases. When a legend explicitly mentions a phase, its ID is listed there. Different options within a phase are indicated by braces: < >.

The composite picture reveals an emperor-hero arising in a time of troubles to conquer the enemies of his people, purify the world for Christianity, and bring forth a golden age. His tasks accomplished, the emperor-messiah returns to Jerusalem to surrender the fruits of victory to Christ, the true messiah, who alone can defeat the last Antichrist in the tail of Joachim's dragon.

The Chariot Card

THE CHARIOT CARD PORTRAYS THE LAST EMPEROR IN HIS TRIUMPHAL ENTRY into Jerusalem on his way to the Mount of Olives. There, where the Apostles watched as Christ, "was raised up: and a cloud received him out of their sight," – *Acts* 1:9, he will give thanks to God, and, in the midst of a great earthquake and signs and wonders, remove the crown from his head and surrender it to Christ.

Summary of the Last Emperor's Career

1. In a time of troubles, – PM, LA, L, ES, F, JR, TC, SC

2. A <Roman – TS, PM> <German – LA>
   <French – L, JR, TC, SC> <anonymous – ES, F> king,

3. Lays waste to and conquers lands and cities of foreigners,
   – TS, PM, L, ES ,F, JR, TC, SC

4. Converts <Jews – TS, JR> <Moslems – F, JR, TC, SC>
   to Christianity,

5. And punishes unfaithful Christians. – PM ,F, JR, TC, SC

6. After a reign of peace and plenty, – TS, LA, L

7. He journeys to Jerusalem and surrenders his crown on
   <Golgotha – TS, PM, TC> <the Mount of Olives – LA, SC>.

8. Antichrist's reign begins. It is brought to an end by
   <Archangel Michael – TS, LA> <Christ – PM, LA, ES>
   <the Last Emperor – JR, TC>

<u>Legend Codes</u>

TS: *Tiburtine Sibyl*
LA: *Life of the Antichrist*
ES: *Erythraean Sibyl*
JR: John of Rupescissa
SC: *Second Charles prophecy*
PM: *Pseudo-Methodius*
L: *Louis VII prophesy*
F: *Frederick II prophecy*
TC: Telesphorus of Cosenza

THIS SCENE IS OBVIOUSLY NEITHER IN *Revelation* NOR ANCESTOR, BUT MAY BE PORTRAYED ON THE VISCONTI-MODRONE WORLD CARD (*right*).

There, a hero on a charger holding a banner occupies the center stage of – perhaps an earthly, rather than the heavenly – Jerusalem, while an angel in the clouds above holds the staff and crown he has just surrendered.

THE VISCONTI-MODRONE, VISCONTI-SFORZA, PARIS AND WASHINGTON (*left*) CARDS ALL PORTRAY CHARIOTEERS WITH CROWNS, ORBS, OR BOTH, CONFIRMING HIS IMPERIAL STATUS,

...ONLY THE FRAGMENTARY BUDAPEST (*right*) AND TAROT OF MARSEILLES CHARIOT CARDS ARE WITHOUT THEM.

Bibliography

Sabine Baring-Gould, “The Divining Rod.” In *Curious Myths of the Middle Ages*, (London: Longmans, Green & Co., 1894), abridgement: Edward Hardy, ed. (Barnes & Noble, 1994).

W. L. Braekman, "Fortune-Telling by the Casting of Dice: a Middle English Poem and Its Background." In *Studia Neophilologica*, 52 (1980), 3-29.

Jocob Burckhardt, “Society and Festivals.” In *The Civilization of the Renaissance in Italy*, reprint: (Barns & Noble, 1992).

Georges Duby, “The Aristocratic Households of Feudal France: Christian Marriages.” In *A History of Private Life: Revelations of the Medieval World*, tr. Arthur Goldhammer, (Harvard UP, 1988), pp 124-36.

John Fiske, “The Descent of Fire.” In *Myths and Myth Makers*, reprint: (Random House, 1996).

Stuart R. Kaplan, “A Poet, a Scribe, a Condottiere, and a Lady.” In *The Enclycopedia of Tarot*, (U.S. Games Sytsems Inc, 1994), Vol II.

Heinrich Keller, *Mittelalteriches Hausbuch: Bilderhandschift des 15. Jahrhunderts mit vollstandigen Tert und facsimilierten ubbilddungen*, reprint: (George Olms Verlag, 1986).

Ernst Kitzinger, “The Late Antique and Early Christian Period.” In *Early Medieval Art*, (Indiana UP, 1983), p 14 & plate I.

F. Lippmann, *The Seven Planets*, trans. F. Simmons, (London: International Chalcographical Society, 1895).

Bernard McGinn, *Visions of the End: Apocalyptic Traditions in the Middle Ages*, (Columbia UP, 1979).

Gertrude Moakley, “The Tarot Trumps and Petrarch’s *Trionfi*.” In *Bulletin of The New York Public Library*, Vol 60, No 2, Feb. 1956, pp 55-69.

_____, *The Tarot Cards Painted by Bonifacio Bembo for the Visconti-Sforza Family: An Iconographic and Historical Study*, (New York Public Library, 1966).

Marjorie Reeves, “Part III: Antichrist and the Last World Emperor.” In *The Influence of Prophecy in the Later Middle Ages: A Study of Joachimism*, (Oxford UP, 1969).

Bill Tarr, "Cups and Balls, & A Cups and Balls Routine." In Now You See It, Now You Don't! Lessons in Sleight of Hand, (Vintage Books: 1976).

Lynn Thorndike, "Medicine to the Twelfth Century." In *A History of Magic and Experimental Science*, (Columbia University Press, 1923), vol 1.

Kurt Volkmann, *The Oldest Deception: Cups and Balls in the 15th and 16th Centuries*, trans Barrows Mussey (Minneapolis: Jones, 1956)

Arthur Watson, "Conjurers." In *The Reliquary and Illustrated Archaeologist*, New Series, Vol XI, London 1909, pp 81-100 and pp 176-191.

Internet

Note: There's no need to type this yourself. Current links to these and future sites, as they become available, can be found at: http://tarot-cards.com

Council of Trent: Session Twenty-Four on Matrimony
http://www.ewtn.com/library/COUNCILS/TRENT24.TXT

Council of Trent
http://www.knight.org/advent/cathen/15030c.htm

Great Schism of the West
http://www.truecatholic.org/greatschism.htm

Lamb in Early Christian Symbolism
http://www.knight.org/advent/cathen/08755b.htm

Mystical Marriage
http://www.knight.org/advent/cathen/09703a.htm

The Civilization of the Renaissance in Italy: Festivals
http://www.idbsu.edu/courses/hy309/docs/burckhardt/5-9.html

The Planets and Their Children
http://www.englib.cornell.edu/mhh4/planets/planets.html

Telesphorus of Cozenza
http://www.knight.org/advent/cathen/14477c.htm

Translations

1. You yat as castyn synk, quarter, tray,
be not displessid [y]at i sal say,
you loues qwer no loue is,
for you can [not] loue yher loue is.

2. triumphos Caesaris ut referat.

3. Incipit libellus fratris Thelofori presbyteri ac heremite secundum auctoritates prescriptorum prophetarum et verarum cronicarum de causia, statu, cognitione ac fine instantis scismatis et tribulationum futurarum, maxime tempore futuri regis aquilonis vocantis se Fredericum imperatorem III usque ad tempora futuri pape vocati angelici pastoris et Karoli regis Francie, futuri imperatoris post Fredericum III supradictum.

Chapter Twelve

Poverty and the Popes

IN 1170, UPON HEARING A TROUBADOUR RECITING THE *Legend of Saint Alexis* in the street, a rich businessman of Lyons, France invited the man home to learn more. Next morning, worried for his soul, he visited the local school of theology and was admonished:

> "If thou wilt be perfect, go sell what thou hast, and give to the poor, and thou shalt have treasure in heaven: and come follow me."
>
> – *Matthew* 19:21

So, after dividing his wealth between his wife and the poor, he and a band of followers wandered the countryside preaching a doctrine of poverty. Dressed like monks, they went barefoot, lived in chastity, and shared their meager earnings equally with one another. Before long, they ran afoul of their archbishop, and petitioned the pope in Rome for a license to preach. At length their request was granted upon the condition the archbishop would supervise their efforts.

A generation later in 1209, a different petitioner and his band solicited another pope to approve their rule (laws and regulations of a religious order):

> "This is the brothers' way of life: to live in obedience, in chastity, without anything of their own and to follow the doctrine and footsteps of our Lord Jesus Christ."

– and were promptly shown the door.

In the twelfth and thirteenth centuries religiously inclined men and women increasingly found monastic life unsatisfying. Instead, they sought a more personal commitment centered about *evangelical poverty*: imitation of Christ's and his disciple's poverty, and *apostolic preaching*: ceaseless religious activity to attract new converts to God. This new thinking threatened to substitute individual choice for Church authority and spread heresy throughout Christendom.

As legend has it, Pope Innocent III saw in a dream the Lateran basilica (the medieval predecessor of the Vatican) tipped to one side and about to topple. Then, the petitioner he'd thrown out that day put his shoulder to a corner and held it up. The next day he had the man recalled, gave him words of encouragement and invited him to return when the number of brothers had increased – a shaky start – but official sanction nevertheless, for St. Francis of Assisi and his Friars Minor (*Fratres minores*).

As for the earlier petitioners, the Poor Men of Lyons or Waldenses, as they came to be known, continued to preach in defiance of their archbishop and were branded heretics. Innocent received some back into the Church but the rest hardened in their opposition to his authority, comparing churchmen with the persecutors of Christ:

> "...all vices and sins are in the Church, and they [Waldenses] alone live righteously... the Pope is the head of all errors... the Prelates are Scribes; and the Monks, Pharisees."
>
> — *Of the Sects of Modern Heretics*

Even more dangerous sects flourished. Cathars, or Patarenes as they were called in Italy, lived side by side with Waldensians in southern France and northern Italy. Their beliefs perpetuated old

Manichean heresies from the fourth century. Innocent fought both groups, no holds barred. He declared that heretics were traitors to God and authorized the confiscation of their property. And he instituted the Albigensian crusade against them in southern France, granting participants the same indulgences as for taking the cross for Palestine. Once begun, the action proved impossible to control, and tens of thousands of innocents were burned at the stake and massacred in their cities in thirty years of warfare, strife and devastation.

The most effective crusaders in this conflict proved to be the mendicant orders, Dominicans and Franciscans:

> "Very sparing in food and raiment, possessing neither gold not silver nor anything of their own, they went through cities, town, and villages, preaching the Gospel ... thinking not of the morrow, nor keeping anything for the next morning....
>
> Whatsoever was left over from their table of the alms given them, this they gave to the poor. They went shod only with the Gospel, they slept in their clothes on mats, and laid stones for pillows under their heads."
>
> – *Matthew Paris*

Without resort to physical force, the mendicants conquered by their exemplary lives, winning back souls for the Church. But their victory was not without its price. So many Dominicans became inquisitors they earned the nickname hunting dogs of the Lord (*Domini canes*). And one day zealous Franciscans would themselves be declared heretics. But all this lay far in the future when St. Francis and his eleven followers departed from their papal audience.

St. Francis' Poverty

ST. FRANCIS OF ASSISI HAS BEEN POPULAR WITH EVERY AGE. HIS LOVE for all God's creation, heartfelt affection for birds and animals and artless poetry, make him alive for us while his contemporaries remain lifeless biographies. But his peers saw and admired much more than this in the man.

Christ's poverty was central to St. Francis' life. He carried poverty, humility, and renunciation to lengths considered nearly impossible in the Middle Ages, and which we can scarcely imagine today – interpreting literally the biblical admonition:

> "Do not possess gold, nor silver, nor money in your purses: Nor scrip for your journey, nor two coats, nor shoes, nor a staff..."
>
> – *Matthew* 10:9-11

Poverty was the cornerstone of his Rule, moderated only slightly at papal insistence:

> "I STRICTLY FORBID THE BROTHERS TO RECEIVE MONEY IN ANY FORM either directly or through an intermediary... those who have already promised obedience MAY HAVE ONE TUNIC WITH A HOOD, AND, IF THEY WISH, ANOTHER WITHOUT A HOOD. AND THOSE WHO ARE FORCED BY NECESSITY MAY WEAR SHOES. And let all the brothers wear poor clothes, and let them mend them with pieces of sackcloth or other material, with the blessing of God..."
>
> – *Franciscan Rule* of 1223

The Friars Minor were to serve God, and trust in Him for their well-being, working without a safety net:

> "The brothers shall not acquire anything as their own, neither a house nor a place nor anything at all. Instead, as pilgrims and strangers in this world who serve the Lord in poverty and humility, let them go begging for alms with full trust...."
>
> – *Ibid*

Shortly before his death, St. Francis dictated his Testament, clarifying his thoughts in light of experience. Apparently even then poverty was under assault, for he wrote:

"Let the brothers take great care not to accept churches, habitations, or any buildings erected for them unless as in accordance with the holy poverty which we have vowed in the Rule; and let them not live in them except as strangers and pilgrims...."

— *St. Francis' Testament*

For Francis, it was impossible to compromise the Rule on this point, for poverty was the road to salvation and Christ:

"...when his brethren once asked him in conclave, by which virtue we become dearest to Christ, he, as if opening to them the secret of his heart replied: 'KNOW, MY BRETHREN, THAT POVERTY IS THE SPECIAL WAY TO SALVATION; for it is the special food of humility, and the root of perfection, whose fruits, although hidden are manifold... he who would attain to this height of perfection must lay aside not only worldly prudence, but even all knowledge of letters, that thus stripped of all things he may come to see what is the power of the Lord....'"

— *Legenda Sancti Francisci*

While such ideals might befit a small monastic order, they were becoming harder and harder for the Order of Friars Minor to keep. From eleven original followers, it had grown to over 5,000 by the time of Francis' death, and 30,000 by mid century, spreading into Hungary, Germany, England, France and Spain.

As Francis feared, poverty was relaxed. His Rule denied property not only to individuals, but to the order itself as well. Popes resolved this difficulty by assuming ownership of everything donated to the order, granting the brothers its use but not its control, and the floodgates were opened. By the late fourteenth century chroniclers were complaining:

"The friars, unmindful of their profession, have forgotten to what end their orders were instituted; for the holy men their law-givers desired them to be poor and free of all kind of temporal possessions, that they should not have anything which they might fear to lose on account of saying the truth.

> But now they are envious of possessors, approve the crimes of the great, induce the commonality into error, and praise the sins of both."
>
> – *Wandering Preachers And Friars*

More specifically, the charges included:

> "Thei techen lordis and namely ladies that if they dyen in Fraunceys habite, thei schul nevere cum in helle for vertu therof... Freris bylden mony grete chirchis and costily waste housis, and cloystris as hit were castels, and that without nede... Grete housis make not men holy, and onely by holynesse is God wel served...."
>
> – *Ibid*

While much of this is sour grapes from rival religious factions, it's also eloquent testimony of Friars Minor's success proselytizing the secular world. That, with poverty, was their major claim to distinction. St. Francis himself was enormously successful in this endeavor, whole cities came out to hear him preach. And afterwards:

> "Francis, the herald of the truth, cast forth devils, healed the sick, and, what is more, by the efficacy of his word softened the most hardened hearts and brought them into penance..."
>
> – *Legenda Sancti Francisci*

This has somewhat of the atmosphere of a modern revival meeting about it, suggesting how revolutionary Franciscans were in their early days. Very soon the Friars Minors became a career path for aspiring young men. While some new converts remained simple itinerant preachers, others became teachers, pastors, bishops, cardinals – and even inquisitors. Kings and municipalities sought them out as administrators. The first Franciscan pope, Nicholas IV, was elected in 1288. No monastic wallflowers, they were very much a part of the world of their time.

Franciscan Spirituals

NOT EVERY FRANCISCAN WELCOMED THIS CHANGE. A SPIRITUAL faction deplored the relaxation of poverty, but as long as they were free to maintain their own stricter standards there was little trouble. However, this changed too. Gradually, the power to interpret Francis' Rule was taken away from the brothers and vested in the order's minister generals. By the last quarter of the thirteenth century, successive Papal Bulls had fragmented the Rule's sweeping general principles into a morass of clarifying paragraphs and clauses. Too late, the Spirituals began to object. Their chief theorist was Petrus Johannis Olivi, a first rate mind and ardent student of Joachim of Fiore, who fired their imaginations with statements like:

> "I believe and know the Rule and lesser regulations of St. Francis to be the true Gospels, Epistles, and apex of all else, in which observances Christ's work will be completed - just as in the labor and rest of the sixth and seventh days." [1]

For Spirituals, the Rule, or parts of it at least, were beyond the authority of even the pope to modify. It was a Franciscan's personal covenant with God, and brothers had a duty to disobey anyone who attempted to interfere with that sacred promise. Now that poverty was being compromised, what was to be done?

Olivi developed a doctrine of "poor and scanty use" (*usus pauper et tenuis*). It wasn't enough that Friars Minor didn't own property, they should only use of it what was absolutely required. Excessive use (*usus dives*) of any property – two dishes of food when one sufficed – was contrary to their vows and a sin. Critics argued this was a recipe for disaster, requiring brothers to be perpetually on the verge of starvation and collapse or risk eternal damnation. Olivi replied that a vast gulf separated excessive from what sufficed, and errors in judging the latter were merely venial (pardonable) and not mortal sins.

In 1283, Olivi was censured for his writings on poor use and other questions and in 1285 he was accused of being the head of a superstitious sect in Provence, France. A charismatic man, he and his fellow Franciscans had found eager converts in the local population. Too valuable to waste, he was quietly rehabilitated in a series of re-assignments to Florence, Montpellier and eventually Narbonne, France. His career in tatters, and with only a few years to live, his most influential work still lay before him.

In 1298, he began his *Popular Commentary on the Apocalypse* (*Postilla super Apocalypsim*). It used Joachim's concords, and the division of the Sixth Age into seven periods, to break new ground – explicitly writing St. Francis and his Rule into Joachim of Fiore's scenario. This kind of thinking was probably a generation old when Olivi wrote, but no one had dared to openly defend it before. According to Olivi, Spirituals were Joachim's new order of monks, and change was eminent:

> "Indeed, even as in the sixth age, worldly Judaism and the old ways of prior generations were cast aside when a new man, Christ, came with a new law, eternal life and the cross; SO IN THE SIXTH *status*, THE WORLDLY CHURCH AND THE OLD WAYS OF PRIOR GENERATIONS WILL BE CAST ASIDE, AND CHRIST'S LAW, ETERNAL LIFE, AND THE CROSS WILL BE RESTORED." [2]

On the subject of St. Francis, Olivi again went beyond traditional faith, suggesting:

> "...he [unidentified source] understood concerning St. Francis, that in the oppression of the Babylonian temptation when Francis' reputation and the Rule will be crucified in the place of Christ himself, FRANCIS WILL GLORIOUSLY RISE AGAIN, SO JUST AS IN HIS LIFE AND THE STIGMATA OF THE CROSS HE SINGULARLY IMITATED CHRIST, SO WILL HE WILL BE MADE LIKE CHRIST IN A RESURRECTION NECESSARY FOR CONFIRMING AND INFORMING HIS DISCIPLES, just as Christ's resurrection was necessary to confirm the apostles and inform them about the foundation and governance of the future church.." [3]

In his *Commentary*, Olivi distinguished between the worldly or carnal Church (*carnali ecclesia*) and the true spiritual one. Out of the former would come the mystical Antichrist, a false pope and enemy of poverty who would attack the Rule and lead a life of opulence and indulgence. In turn, he would be succeeded by the great or open Antichrist foretold in *Revelation*. Spiritual Franciscans could expect merciless persecution for their allegiance to poverty and the Rule.

This was strong stuff. After his death, Olivi's writings were condemned at the General Chapter of Lyons and their possession forbidden upon pain of excommunication. The persecution he predicted had begun.

Celestine V, the Angelic Pope

EARLIER IN 1294, IT LOOKED LIKE EVENTS MIGHT GO THE OTHER WAY when Pietro di Morrone, a hermit from the province of Calabria, became Pope Celestine V. A very different kind of man from his predecessors and distinguished for his holiness, many expected him to steer the Church from its worldly course. He embraced poverty so ardently it was reported he slept in a little hut he built for himself inside the papal palace! But, desperately unhappy after only five months in office, and realizing how unequal he was to the task expected of him, Celestine abdicated.

Spirituals were stunned and furious. Some had received his permission to found a new group strictly observing the Rule, and had expressed their gratitude by enshrining him as the Angelic Pope (*pastor angelicus*). This was an idea inspired by the Byzantine *Leo Oracles* of the eighth century, which the Spirituals picked up in Armenia where they had found temporary refuge from their enemies. Now they found themselves thrown to the wolves when Celestine's acts were nullified by his successor Boniface VIII. Spirituals argued that the vicar of Christ had no right to step down. And their outrage only increased, when, to make sure Celestine wouldn't change his mind, Boniface held the holy man under guard in an out-of-the-way castle until his death two years later. Olivi saw all of this, and argued Celestine's abdication was permissible, but possibly he foresaw the mystical Antichrist in the treatment meted out to the unfortunate Celestine.

Pope John XXII Outlaws the Spirituals

ONE LAST EFFORT WAS MADE TO SETTLE THE ISSUE OF POOR USE AFTER OLIVI'S DEATH. In a papal bull (*Exivi de paradiso*) Pope Clement V attempted a compromise:

> "Some of the friars believe and say that, just as they are vowed to a very strict renunciation of ownership, THEY ARE ALSO ENJOINED THE GREATEST RESTRAINT IN THE USE OF THINGS... we declare that the Friars Minor in professing their rule are ONLY OBLIGED TO THE STRICT AND RESTRAINED USE EXPRESSED IN THE RULE. To say, however, as some are said to assert, that it is heretical to hold that a restricted use of things is or is not included in the vow of evangelical poverty, this we judge to be presumptuous and rash."
>
> – Council of Vienne, 1311-12

Then, in 1316, Pope John XXII settled the question once and for all, with the justification: "Poverty is indeed great, but integrity is greater, and obedience is the greatest good of all." [4] He issued his own bull (*Quorundum exigit*) nullifying clauses on granaries and cellars and wearing poor clothing in Clement's earlier compromise. These issues, trivial as they sound today, penetrated to the heart of poor use. By laying up supplies for the future, the order was not trusting in the Lord to provide and deliberately using more than strictly required for sustenance. Furthermore, some Spirituals deliberately wore scandalously short, skimpy, and tattered rags as an insignia of their commitment to poverty. By John's decree, granaries were in, and short habits out, if the order's minister generals decided so.

The purpose of John's bull was to separate the sheep from the goats. Spiritual leaders were summoned to Avignon, brought before an inquisition, and asked if they would obey the bull, and if the pope had the authority to command what it said. Twenty-five answered no, but after several months of persuasion their number dwindled to five. One was imprisoned, and the other four burnt at the stake as heretics in Marseilles in 1318. Later, some of the original twenty-five recanted their recantations.

Not satisfied, in 1323 John delivered the knockout punch. A second bull (*Cum inter nonnullos*) declared:

> "...to affirm pertinaciously, that Our Redeemer and Lord Jesus Christ and His Apostles did not have anything individually, not even in common, is to be censured as heretical..."
>
> — *Cum inter nonnullos*

It was now forbidden to even bring the subject of poverty up – the Spirituals were total outcasts! Not surprisingly this drew more fire; amazingly from some of the same men who'd helped John bring the Spirituals down in the first place. His new critics fled to the protection of William of Bavaria's court in Germany, where many now found themselves in agreement with their former adversaries. For Spirituals and their sympathizers everywhere, Pope John XXII was Olivi's promised mystical Antichrist. Boniface was just a rehearsal; John had betrayed poverty, the Rule, and St. Francis – the Sixth Seal had surely been opened.

A Future Angelic Pope

AS THE REALITY OF THE MYSTICAL ANTICHRIST GREW APPARENT, SO DID THAT OF HIS ANTITHESIS, the Angelic Pope. It received tangible form in a series of captioned portraits of historical popes, followed by additional ones of angelic popes to come.

In one such series, the *Prophecy of the Last Pontiffs* (*Vaticinia de Summis Pontificibus*), Celestine V's caption reads: "Elevation of OBEDIENCE, POVERTY, CHASTITY, temperance and destroyer of hypocrisy."[5] Significantly, the capitalized qualities are St. Francis' virtues. Captions for future angelic popes include: "Good grace – simony ceases, Good prayer, Good intentions – love abounds,"[6] while Boniface VIII's caption reads: "Rent by detestable hypocrisy"[7] After 1350 the number of portraits was doubled to thirty in the *Prophecy of Anselm* (*Vaticinia de Anselmi*). Here, Celestine V is the only angelic pope. The very last portrait of the series, showing a beast, is Antichrist, whose caption reads: "You are terrible, who can resist you?"[8]

Another manuscript of this time (*Liber de Flore*) said there would be four angelic popes: The first, a poor monk, with the help of a king descended from heaven, would rectify the world and end the schism between the East and West. The emperor-king would become a Franciscan, and war would be abolished. The second, a Frenchman, would heal the division between France and Germany. The third, an Italian Spiritual, would reform the religious orders and distribute the wealth of the Church to the poor. The fourth, a Gascon, would receive the homage of Gog and Magog and unify the world. After these four, the great Antichrist would begin his reign – the prelude to Christ's Second Coming.

It's important to remember that all this was about individuals, not the institution. Spirituals didn't deny the authority of the Church or even of the papacy; they sought to replace the bad with the good, to regenerate the Church, not destroy it. But in their zeal they lost all perspective and brought about their own destruction.

The Pope (Hierophant) Card

THERE'S NO DOUBT ABOUT THE POPE CARD OF THE EARLY TAROT DECKS. HE MAY HOLD THE KEYS OF ST. PETER AS ON THE CHARLES VI (*left*) CARD, OR A PAPAL STAFF AS ON THE BUDAPEST (*right*) CARD.

And he almost always wears a triple crown or tiara – making his identification virtually certain. But since good Catholics, and others, have frequently objected to this conclusion, the card is often given another name. The Hierophant is a modern favorite. Usually, two prelates, identified by tonsures or cardinals hats, are at his side.

Popes don't ordinarily occur in *Revelation* pictures. After all, there's no mention of the pope in the Bible. But they're plentiful in Ancestor, frequently appearing as one head of a two-headed figure. Ancestor is even more explicit.

ONE ILLUSTRATION THERE (*right*) SHOWS INNOCENT II, WHO REIGNED FROM 1130 TO 1147, WEARING THE PREDECESSOR OF THE TRIPLE CROWN, LOOKING REMARKABLY LIKE THE POPE CARD OF THE WASHINGTON DECK (*below*).

Bibliography

St. Bonaventure, *The Life of St. Francis of Assisi: From the Legenda Sancti Francisci*, reprint: (Tan Books, 1988).

David Burr, *Olivi and Franciscan Poverty: the Origins of the Usus Pauper Controversy*, (U. Penn Pr., 1989).

_____, "Mendicant Readings of the Apocalypse." In *The Apocalypse in the Middle Ages*, R. K. Emmerson, B. McGinn, eds., (Cornell UP, 1992).

_____, *Olivi's Peaceable Kingdom: A Reading of the Apocalypse Commentary*, (U. Penn Pr., 1993).

G. G. Coulton, "Matthew Paris." In *Five Centuries of Religion*, (Cambridge UP, 1923).

Herbert Grundmann, "The Religious Movement in the Twelfth Century: Apostolic Life and Christian Poverty." In *Religious Movements in the Middle Ages*, trans Steven Rowan, (U. Notre Dame Pr., 1995).

J. J. Jusserand, "Wandering Preachers And Friars." In *English Wayfaring Life in the Middle Ages*, trans Lucy Toulmin Smith, reprint: (Corner House Pub, 1974).

Malcolm Lambert, "Spiritual Franciscans and Heretical Joachimite." In *Medieval Heresy: Popular Movements From the Gregorian Reform to the Reformation*, (Blackwell Pub, 1992).

Bernard McGinn, "The Angelic Pope, & The Franciscan Spirituals." In *Visions of the End: Traditions in the Middle Ages*, (Columbia UP, 1979).

Marjorie Reeves, "Part Four: Angelic Pope and Renovatio Mund." In *The Influence of Prophecy in the Later Middle Ages*, (U. Notre Dame Pr., 1993).

Jacobus de Voragine, "Saint Alexis." In *The Golden Legend: Readings on the Saints*, William Granger Ryan trans., (Princeton UP, 1993), vol 1.

Internet

Note: There's no need to type this yourself. Current links to these and future sites, as they become available, can be found at: http://tarot-cards.com

Albigenses
http://www.knight.org/advent/cathen/01267e.htm
Pope Boniface VIII
http://www.knight.org/advent/Popes/ppbo08.htm
Bulls and Briefs
http://www.knight.org/advent/cathen/03052b.htm
Cathars
http://www.knight.org/advent/cathen/03435a.htm
Pope St. Celestine V
http://www.knight.org/advent/Popes/ppce05.htm
Pope Clement V
http://www.knight.org/advent/Popes/ppcl05.htm
Conversion of Peter Waldo
http://www.fordham.edu/halsall/source/waldo1.html
Council of Vienne 1311-12 A.D.
http://www.ewtn.com/library/COUNCILS/VIENNE.TXT
Crosier
http://www.knight.org/advent/cathen/04515c.htm
Cum Inter Nonnullos
http://www.ici.net/cust_pages/panther/francis/qinn-e.html
Exivi de Paradiso
http://www.ici.net/cust_pages/panther/francis/exivi-e.html
St. Francis' *Rule of 1221* (*Regula non Bullata*)
http://www.ici.net/customers/panther/francis/regnon-e.html
St. Francis' *Rule of 1223* (*Regula Bullata*)
http://www.ici.net/cust_pages/panther/francis/opuscule.html#RegulaBullata
St. Francis' *Rule of 1223*
http://www.fordham.edu/halsall/source/stfran-rule.html

St. Francis' *Testament*
http://www.ici.net/cust_pages/panther/francis/opuscule.html#Testamentum
St. Francis' *Testament*
http://www.fordham.edu/halsall/source/stfran-test.html
Franciscan Archive
http://www.ici.net/cust_pages/panther/francis/noframes.html
Pope John XXII
http://www.knight.org/advent/Popes/ppjo22.htm
Of the Sects of Modern Heretics
http://www.fordham.edu/halsall/source/waldo2.html
Order of Friars Minor
http://www.knight.org/advent/cathen/06281a.htm
Pope
http://www.knight.org/advent/cathen/12260a.htm
Power of the Keys
http://www.knight.org/advent/cathen/08631b.htm
Quia Quorundam
http://www.ici.net/cust_pages/panther/francis/qquor-e.html
Selections from the Olivi's *Apocalypse Commentary*
http://www.fordham.edu/halsall/source/olivi.html
Ubertino of Casale
http://www.knight.org/advent/cathen/15116a.htm
Waldenses
http://www.knight.org/advent/cathen/15527b.htm

Translations

1. ...teneo et scio regulam S. Francisci statumque minorum esse vere evangelicum et apostolicum et finem omnium aliorum, in quo et per quem sollemniora suorum operum consummaturus est Christus tanquam in opere et requie sexte et septime diei.

2. Sicut etiam in sexta aetate, reiecto carnali Judaismo et vetustate prioris seculi, venit novus homo Christus cum nova lege et

vita et cruce, sic in sexto statu, reiecta carnali Eccesia et vetustate prioris seculi, renovabitur Christi lex et vita et crux.

3. ...percepterat Franciscum in illa pressura temptationis babilonice, in qua eius status et regula quasi instar Christi crucifigetur, resurget gloriousus, ut sicut in vita et in crucis stigmatibus est Christo singulariter assimilatus, sic et in resurrectione Christo assimiletur, necessaria tunc suis discipulis confirmandis et informandis, sicut Christi resurrectio fuit necessaria appostolis confirmandis et super fundatione et gubernatione future ecclesie informandis.

4. Magna quidem pauperas, sed maior integritas; bonum est obedienctia maximum.

5. Elatio, Obedientia, Paupertas, Castitas, Temperantia, Ypoccrisorum Destructor.

6. Bona gratia Simonia cessabit; Bona oratio; Bona intentio caritas abondabit.

7. Incisio hypocrisis in abominatione erit.

8. Terribilis es, quis resistet tibi?

Chapter Thirteen

Crimes and Punishments

An anonymous diary from Florence, Italy reads:

> "Today, October 13, 1377, they began a fresco on the facade of the palace where the podestà lives, depicting the face and person of the traitor Messer Ridolfo da Camerino, traitor to the Holy Mother Church, the people of the Commune of Florence and the League and all its members.... He is on a gallows, tied at the top and suspended [upside down] by his left foot. On his left hand side there is a siren, and on his right a basilisk. On his head at the bottom is a large mitra. To the side and tied to his neck is a devil. His arms are spread out, and with both right and left hands he gives the finger to the Church and the Commune of Florence, as he betrays the Commune to the Pope."[1]

Ridolfo da Camerino was a condottiere who deserted to the pope's side during the War of Eight Saints (*otto dei preti*) named after eight Florentine citizens appointed to confiscate papal property. An outlaw, his defaming portrait (*pitture infamanti*) was ordered painted. That wasn't unusual. Records from more than two dozen northern Italian communities between the fourteenth and sixteenth centuries contain similar orders. What's unique is the description of the painting itself. Placed on the walls of public buildings, all traces of defaming portraits have long-since vanished.

ONE CAN'T HELP NOTICE THE SIMILARITY BETWEEN THE DIARY'S DESCRIPTION AND THE WASHINGTON DECK'S HANGED MAN TAROT CARD (*right*).

What did hanging upside down signify? One theory is that defaming portraits were "in absentia" punishments, and hanging upside down meant the perpetrator was still at large. Another theory suggests it was a stock representation for all traitors. I believe that, more specifically, it meant "turncoat," which many traitors were, and the symbolism of the Florentine painting is a list of Ridolfo's crimes and the punishment he could expect when apprehended.

The mythical siren had the power of charming with her song, and the basilisk killed with its breath. These and the finger gestures speak of honeyed lies and premeditated deceit. The mitra, which looks like a dunce cap, was worn by heretics about to be burned at the stake. Together with the devil tied to his neck, it must surely mean this turncoat could expect to go straight to hell when justice caught up with him.

Critical evidence for deciding between these theories comes from pictures showing some men hung by their necks while others are suspended by one foot. Two descriptions of pictures like this exist. In the first, Sandro Botticelli:

"...painted in 1478 on the wall where the jail above the Doghana once was, Messers Jacopo, Francesco, and Renato de'Pazzi; Messer Francesco Salviati, the archbishop of Pisa; the two Jacopo Salviatis, one the brother and the other a relative of Messer Francesco; and Bernardo Bandini, all hanged by the neck. And Napoleone Francese hung by one foot. Because they were involved in the conspiracy against Giuliano and Lorenzo de'Medici, and for whom Lorenzo composed epitaphs at the foot of each one. Below the others, that for Bernardo Bandini says in this manner:

> I am Bernardo Bandini newly judged,
> A deadly traitor to the Church.
> A rebel, I await a death even more harsh." [2]

Napoleone Francese was the only conspirator never caught and is painted upside down. But when Botticelli painted the picture, Bandini was still at large too, as his epitaph makes clear. If the "in absentia" hypothesis is correct, then Bandini's original (upside down) portrait was redone after his capture and execution a year later – before the eye-witness description of the painting was written. But in that case the epitaph should have been changed too. Furthermore, the malefactors were both corporally punished and defamed after their deaths.

A second example contradicts the traitor hypothesis:

"On Easter morning it was discovered that three citizens were painted on facade of the palace of the podestà: Alessandro di Gherardo Corsini in a long coat and hood, Taddeo di Guiducci, blind in one eye and similarly dressed, and Pierfrancesco di Giorgio Ridolfi, hung by one foot. Each of whom had written at his feet, his name, family's name, and an inscription in large letters, saying: FOR THE TRAITOR TO HIS COUNTRY." [3]

Here, all are branded traitors, but only one is hung upside down. So the third man must have been a different kind of traitor than the others. Like the portrait described at the beginning of this chapter, their clothing and postures seem to be saying something about the nature of their crimes. Amazingly, seven preliminary studies for the hanging man, by artist Andrea del Sarto have survived and can be seen today.

Evidence for the true meaning of hanging upside down comes from a 1393 decree for Milan and Lombardy:

> "Let him be drug on a [wooden] plank at a horse's tail to the place of execution, and there be suspended by one foot to the gallows, and be left there until he is dead. As long as he lives let him be given food and drink." [4]

This is one of the Visconti's torture-punishments, of which the forty-day execution (*quarantena*) for high treason was the most cruel and infamous. Illustrations from the sixteenth and seventeenth centuries show hanging by one foot as a preliminary to both decapitation and drowning. Clark's Martyrologia (1677) shows one with the caption: "Som were hanged up by one Foote, their heads and brests in the water."

Records point to the conclusion that hanging upside down by one foot was a real punishment for specific crimes, as well as a form of humiliation and disgrace. The combination of punishment, death and disgrace suggests a connection with *Revelation*, and a meaning for The Hanged Man card – the martyr:

> "THE SOULS OF THEM THAT WERE BEHEADED for the testimony of Jesus, and for the word of God, and who had not adored the beast nor his image, nor received his character on their foreheads, or in their hands; and THEY LIVED AND REIGNED WITH CHRIST A THOUSAND YEARS."
>
> – *Revelation* 20:4

Humiliated in the eyes of the world, the martyr conquers in the end, recalling the words of The Wheel of Fortune: "I shall reign" (*Regnabo*). As such The Hanged Man is the hero of Tarot's story. He will inherit the Millennium.

The Third Order

IN 1317 JOHN XXII BROADENED HIS ATTACK AGAINST THE SPIRITUALS to include: "certain impious rabble commonly called fraticelli, or brothers-of-the-poor-life, Bizochi or Beguines or other names." [5] He probably didn't know exactly who they were, nor do we nowadays, other than they were lay men and women, sympathetic with Spiritual and sometimes more radical ideas.

The Franciscan Order, to this day, is composed of three groups: the Friars Minor, Poor Clares for women, and the Third Order – laypersons who wish to dedicate themselves to a more spiritual life while remaining in the world. All three were created by St. Francis, and are testimony to his commitment to apostolic preaching. Dominicans too, fostered religious lay communities, especially for German women.

Although conversion of Jews and Saracens got a lot of talk, the truth was that mendicant's major gains were made at home among the faithful who were barely included in the Church's traditional rituals. Charismatic men like Johannes Peter Olivi found disciples eager to recapture the zeal of early Christianity in their lives. The enormity of mendicant influence can be seen in the explosion of vernacular religious literature at this time.

For most of the Middle Ages all religious writing was in Latin. Ecclesiastics had no reason to desire anything else, and the documents I've cited so far were part of a professional literature common people knew little about. Everyday language was only used for simple sermons which no one cared to write down. By the fourteenth century, a vast literature of sermons, prayers, religious meditations, theological discussions, narratives and visions existed in vernaculars. How did this come about?

One possibility is that itinerant preachers created it. But although these men preached in vernaculars, even Waldensians, who learned their theology from translations, wrote what they needed in Latin. Evidence suggests that this religious literature was created in the mid-thirteenth century by the mendicant orders to instruct their lay communities. These people had the interest, but not the training, especially in Latin, to delve into religious subjects.

There are records of Church decrees forbidding friars from translating sermons and other religious writings, and translations were universally condemned wherever found, because once shown the basics, lay-authors, often women, elaborated them with new ideas of their own. From the springboard of mendicant idealism, amateurs forged a full-blown mysticism with little regarded for Church authority.

The Beguines of Provence

MANY LAY GROUPS WERE LOYAL TO SPIRITUALS. AFTER HIS DEATH in 1298, a thriving Olivi cult sprang up around his grave at Narbonne, France. Pilgrims included not only the laity but clergy too – even cardinals. On the anniversary of his death it drew crowds almost as large as St. Francis' gravesite at Assisi. The situation grew so critical that, as a precaution, in 1318 Olivi's tomb was destroyed and his remains quietly reburied in an unknown spot. And after the four Spirituals were burnt at the stake in Marseilles, crowds collected and treasured their ashes as precious relics.

Beguines in Provence claimed to be members of the Third Order, called themselves poor brothers and sisters of penitence, and lived communally in houses called Homes of Poverty, often supporting themselves by manual labor or begging. For laymen, they had a sophisticated understanding of Spiritual issues and doctrine. Inquisition records record:

> "Likewise they said they suspected lord Pope John [XXII] was a heretic and the mystic Antichrist and blamed him for the four Spirituals condemned and burnt at Marseilles, who he prosecuted for seeking to strictly observe their vows, and because the lord Pope issued a papal decree on their possessing granaries and cellars and forbidding their habits." [6]

Olivi's *Popular Commentary* was translated into the vernacular and became the handbook of their movement. One man said:

> "Of that *Commentary,* which he himself heard in the vernacular in many places and more than 30 times, he heard and remembered in particular, that brother Petrus Johannis espoused in said *Commentary* that the Roman Church was the great Whore of Babylon."[7]

There's no doubt the Beguines of Provence were the remnant of Olivi's disciples, members testified:

> "That Elias was St. Francis, and that Enoch was the holy father, brother Petrus Johannis... Thus, plainly, as St. Francis was the witness to the evangelical poverty which Christ began, brother Petrus Johannis was witness to the divinity of Holy Scripture." [8]

Elias and Enoch are the two witnesses portrayed in Ancestor and described in *Revelation*:

> "And I will give unto my two witnesses, and they shall prophesy a thousand two hundred sixty days, clothed in sackcloth.... These have power to shut heaven, that it rain not in the days of their prophecy: and they have power over waters to turn them into blood, and to strike the earth with all plagues as often as they will.
>
> And when they shall have finished their testimony, the beast, that ascendeth out of the abyss, shall make war against them, and shall overcome them, and kill them."
>
> – *Revelation* 11:3-7

This Inquisition testimony, when interpreted literally, is heavy with anagogical meaning. On the subject of Olivi himself, Beguines went even further, claiming:

> "Likewise all the teachings of brother Petrus Johannis Olivi are true and orthodox, and were revealed to him by illumination from the Holy Spirit, by which he learned the truth of

> the Gospels and Rule of St. Francis. They [Beguines] call Olivi a holy father and great doctor, who is the angel described in *Revelation* whose face is like the sun, and who holds an open book in his hand, and to whom the future is clearly revealed, and that he ought to be counted for all time as the holiest of all the doctors." [9]

The angel mentioned here is the one who gives St. John the Apostle the book which he eats. As will become apparent from a few more citations, these biblical allusions were more than mere metaphor.

Beguines of Provence believed the carnal church would shortly be destroyed by Frederick II of Sicily, namesake of Frederick II Hohenstaufen:

> "Likewise they preach that the carnal church, plainly the Roman (Catholic) Church, will be destroyed before the advent of Antichrist, in a war against that Frederick, King of Sicily, who now reigns." [10]

They believed that the Second Coming was eminent; one man reported:

> "Likewise he said he believed that before the year which he reckoned as 1330 AD, the great Antichrist would be incarnated, have run his course, and be dead." [11]

There were several candidates for this lessor, mystic Antichrist:

> "...as for who they say is the Antichrist, some assert he will be an apostate Franciscan who holds a high position within the Church, suggesting brother Angelo [of Clareno, a Spiritual!] who is an apostate from the Order of Friars Minor. Others claim that lord Philip of Majorca is the Antichrist. Still more say Frederick [of Aragon], king of Sicily, will become emperor and persecutor of the Roman (Catholic) Church, and will be the predicted Antichrist who everyone will worship." [12]

This composite testimony, from records of the Inquisition which eradicated their movement by 1330, describes only one group. Others, called fraticelli, existed in Italy, Germany and the Low Countries. How much did all these groups have in common? Though historians disagree, Beguines themselves denied any connection. And angry over what they perceived as betrayal, they denied any ties to Franciscans as well, describing them as Friars Minor:

> "...if they can be called that, who are certainly not Minor in humility and simplicity, but Major in arrogance, cunning, ambition and deception, as is manifest to the whole world."[13]

Fraticelli in Northern Italy?

HISTORY SAYS SPIRITUALS AND THEIR LAY GROUPS WERE FINISHED. That only a few struggled on till 1466 in scattered dissident groups in Germany and southern and central Italy, dwindling into anti-papalism and triviality. This assertion merits a closer look.

In southern Italy, Spirituals at first found a stronghold in Sicily with the Aragonese King Frederick II. But after he made up his differences with John XXII, most then sought refuge in Naples with Robert the Wise. Naples became an asylum for malcontents, refugee Beguines from Provence and fraticelli from Tuscany and even Germany. They were still there as late as 1362.

Perugia, midway between Rome and Florence, was another of their strongholds. In 1374 faithful Catholics petitioned the Observanti Franciscans to settle there to check their spreading influence. And a fraticelli letter written from there, claims:

> "...that which is today so lamentable [the Great Schism], was obviously inspired by Pope John XXII and the other successors who followed him, splitting Church unity and doctrine through badly misunderstanding Scripture and opposing the poverty of Christ "[14]

This letter suggests Spiritual ideas were still going strong in the 1380's.

In 1382 fraticelli from Germany were in Florence, the center of resistance against Pope Gregory XI, and a safe haven where many patriotic and influential citizens harbored anti-clerical sentiments. Their influence became so dreaded the commune reenacted 150-year-old heresy laws against them, and an itinerant fraticelli preacher, Michael di Calci, was burnt at the stake there in 1389. The basis for his conviction was his opinion on the poverty of Christ and: "And when he was asked about the most venerable and most holy John XXII," he responded, "He [John] was a heretic."[15] In 1411, another trial was held in nearby Lucca, but the accused, a wine seller and his companions, escaped punishment with a confession and feigned repentance.

Fraticelli were also numerous in the March of Ancona, a base from where they sent out preachers to visit the faithful. In 1429 the Church began an inquisition in that area which lasted until 1466. Far from a minor affair, the Church compared it with the Hussite heresy in Bohemia, while the fraticelli condemned its leader, St. Bernardo of Sienna, as the Antichrist. At the last trial, held in 1466, over half the village of Poli were discovered to be fraticelli, and the lord of the village had given them protection.

Records of fraticelli, often from Inquisitions, are from areas within or on the margin of the Papal States, where ecclesiastical control was strong. Thus, they only provide a rough idea of what was going on, and when. They do, however, establish a fraticelli "signature," viz: 1. the time of Antichrist was near, 2. a Frederick would be his instrument for punishing the Church, and 3. the pope was an enemy of poverty and a heretic. These traits distinguish the fraticelli from Waldensians, mystics, and other dissident religious groups of the time.

We know that fraticelli congregated in areas free from papal control, like Naples, under strong leaders who could protect them. It's reasonable, then, to also expect them in northern Italy and southern Germany, where the Viscontis of Milan had been censured in a papal bull for harboring heretics, and later Louis of Bavaria openly flouted the pope. And, indeed, a faint fraticelli signature is present in these areas.

Petrus Johannis Olivi initiated a new fashion in millinarian predictions. Not even Joachim of Fiore would hazard a guess as to its duration. Olivi confidently calculated the Millennium would last 700 years, more or less. In the 1390's, a German Franciscan, Frederick of Brunswick championed 1,000 years. Other early fifteenth-century estimates include: 1400 years from Turin, Italy in 1400; 890 years from Teramo, Italy in 1410; 500 years from Florence, Italy in 1422; and 6,000 years from Basel, Switzerland in 1446. Thus, certain aspects of Spiritual thinking continued uninterrupted in Italy and Germany well into the fifteenth century.

Stronger evidence comes from St. Bernardino of Siena, complaining in a sermon written some time after 1417:

> "A good many are certainly lead astray, supposing that through the Holy Spirit events occur which were shaped earlier, and whatever spiritual errors are suggested to them. Consequently, we are replete with prophecies all the time, ad nauseam, and imagine the coming of Antichrist; the signs of impending judgment; the persecution and renewal of the Church, and so forth; who are venerable men and the vows, etc., it is proper to trust in; the writings of Joachim and other prophets interpreting diverse mysteries and which of these are true and authentic; finding yet other ways of serving God..." [16]

Franciscans weren't the only ones harboring such thoughts. The celebrated Dominican preacher and missionary St. Vincent Ferrer (1357-1419) traveled throughout Spain, Italy, France and England, preaching the coming of Antichrist and the end of the world in his own generation.

All this hints that a century after their dissolution, Spiritual's ideas were still a force to be reckoned with. That history has confused a lack of data about Spiritual-influenced groups with their extinction. Such a claim might be just an interesting speculation, except for one overlooked piece of evidence – Tarot cards.

John of Rupescissa

TAROT'S STORY BEGINS IN AVIGNON, THE SEAT OF THE PAPACY. THERE in 1349, a young Franciscan, John of Rupescissa, wrote out prophecies of the coming Antichrist from the papal prison while the Black Death raged outside. John was a Catalan from northwestern Spain, and a disciple of Olivi and Arnold of Villanova – physician to the pope, member of the Third Order, and prophet of the last times. Like Olivi, Arnold wrote tracts supporting the Beguines in Provence, but unlike him, he showed little interest in the *Book of Revelation*. Instead, he argued:

> "All now agree that times of future events are revealed by God to the faithful, like the time of Christ's first advent and the time of his crucifixion; and also the time of the Antichrist's coming which is plain from *Daniel* (chapter) IX, and the same is true for (chapter) XII."[17]

Arnold summarized his thoughts in *The Time of Antichrist's Coming* (*De tempore adventus Antichristi*) which was condemned at once by the University of Paris, and only smoothed over after Arnold's private confession – good physicians were hard to find – to the pope himself . Arnold may have been an alchemist too; works on alchemy circulated under his name.

John of Rupescissa certainly was. Furthermore, alchemy was in perfect harmony with his faith. While transforming base metals into gold was strictly forbidden to a Franciscan, whose vows commanded he shun money in all its forms, nothing prohibited finding an elixir of youth. Not to achieve immortality, which was clearly impossible, but to maintain health and vigor for as long as possible – so evangelical men could continue their work into old age. In John's words:

> "Here begins the first book of the *Considerations of the Fifth Essence* (*De Consideratione Quintae Essentiae*) of all things delivered to poor and evangelical men serving Jesus

Christ composed by master John of Rupescissa professor of sacred theology.[18]

Fifth Essence came from the fact, that:

> "It is necessary to seek that substance which possesses with respect to the four humors [blood, phlegm, choler and melancholy] that which heaven possesses with respect to the four elements [earth, air, fire and water], which is called the fifth essence, or heaven, so to speak." [19]

John had a modern advertising executive's way with words – Fifth Essence, today, is the name for a women's perfume. It's to his credit that he found what he was seeking: "I affirm the fifth essence is fire water (*aqua ardens*)."[20] Alcohol! Booze! Strong stuff made by repeated distillation, which could be identified by its marvelous odor. He personally vouched for its efficacy:

> "When my mortal and impious enemies held me in chains in a most harsh and vexing prison workhouse, the suffering was more than could be imagined when my body festered from the awful filth of the cell and my iron fetters. Merciful attendants procured alcohol from a certain holy man and friend of God. And anointing myself with this lotion I was cured in the blink of an eye." [21]

Remember John of Rupescissa the next time a nurse swabs your arm with alcohol before administering your flu shot!

Another of his alchemical treatises, the *Book of Light* (*Liber Lucis*) further expands upon the connection between alchemy, religion and the last times, revealing John's Spiritual sympathies:

> "I Considered the tribulations of the elect prophesied in the (sacred) Holy Gospels by Christ, the worst tribulations to occur in the time of Antichrist in the present age, when many within the sacred Roman Catholic Church will, in turn, be afflicted with doubt and flee to the mountains, and surely the Church will be despoiled all its temporal wealth by

> tyrants. But though tossed by stormy waves, nevertheless, the ship of Saint Peter will be freed in the last days, lord over all.
>
> Therefore to alleviate the pressing needs and poverty of those future holy people and God's elect, with this gift of knowledge of a true mystery without compare, I want to talk of the ultimate philosopher's stone for the moon and for the sun, for the white and for the red..."[22]

John spent much of his life in prisons, but not for his alchemy and prophecy. Indeed, his jailers allowed, and even commanded him to write them down. He mentions being jailed in the years 1345, 1349, and 1356, and some *Fifth Essence* manuscripts refer to a seven year imprisonment. John was a little puzzled as to the reason for these incarcerations; most probably it was for his Spiritualist leanings.

John's *magnum opus* was *Walk With Me in Tribulation* (*Vade Mecum in Tribulatione*) written in 1356, but most of its ideas are foreshadowed in a list of twenty-nine insights or perceptions (*intellectus*) composed in 1349. In the tradition of exegetes like Joachim of Fiore, he claimed to only possess an understanding of the spirit, but not the gift of prophecy, and that his insights clarified secrets others had only partially penetrated.

In a way, this is an accurate assessment. If Joachim was the creator of the age of the Holy Spirit and the two new orders of monks, and Olivi was responsible for writing St. Francis, poverty, and the Spirituals into its scenario, then John of Rupescissa is the great systematizer who assembles everything together. He borrows a little from each author, and adds some of his own, to produce a coherent story consistent with what's gone before.

Here are the opening lines of John's perceptions of 1349, where I've capitalized concepts connected with Tarot. So many of these ideas are depicted on Tarot cards that I believe John has claim to be called the father of Tarot.

"• Perceived in revelation, the parentage and birth of Antichrist and his name, character and whereabouts.

First, I understood that the descendants (seed) of EMPEROR FREDERICK...

• Perceived second, the coming of many Antichrists.

Second, I understood that many Antichrists must arise...

• Perceived third, the fates of Italy and France and their tribulations.

Third, I understood and saw clearly from this prison...

• Perceived fourth, the multitude of remarkable calamities foretold for the time of Antichrist, of which some have happened, while others are yet to occur.

Fourth, I understood there shall be many future disasters from JOHN (*Book of Revelation*)...

[There is no fifth perception]

• Perceived sixth in revelation, secrets in [*The Prophecy of*] DANIEL clarifying the time of Antichrist and when he will arise and acquire power:

Sixth, I understood in the future around the year1366...

• Perceived seventh in revelation, the coming of a FALSE POPE and terrible misfortunes for the Christian Church, the subjugation of the TRUE [Angelic] POPE and the birth of the WHORE OF *Revelation* described in Chapter Seventeen.

Seventh, I understood while pondering in prison...

• Perceived eighth in revelation, the time when ANTICHRIST WILL BE ELECTED EMPEROR and HE WILL BEGIN TO PERSECUTE THE CHURCH – not as Antichrist but as a TYRANT.

Eighth, I understood that around the time of the beginning of the predicted Schism...

- Perceived ninth in revelation, how the Order of Friars Minor will be divided into three parts, of which two will embrace heresy while the third part will remain steadfast to the catholic pontiff of the orthodox faith.

  Ninth, I understood that in those times the Order of Friars Minor...

- Perceived tenth in revelation, the peril of heresy to the mendicant orders and their apostasy, except for the MENDICANT [Spiritual] PORTION of the Friars Minor, and how the whore [of Babylon] will be slain.

  Tenth, I understood that in the future there will exist an order of monks...

- Perceived eleventh in revelation, the transformations of the MONARCHY under Antichrist and what his law of heresy will accomplish and how under him good-for-nothings will be united.

  Eleventh, I understood that the impact of the WHORE foretold...

- Perceived twelfth in revelation, the final conflict of the Church with the coming Antichrist and how the elect will rebel.

  Twelfth, I understood that the conflict of the Holy Roman (Catholic) Church...

- Perceived 13th in revelation, the war of the prince of the faith against the wickedness of Antichrist.

  Thirteenth, I understood that this general wickedness...

- Perceived 14th in revelation, the manner and order of how the coming Antichrist will subdue the secular world.

  Fourteenth, I understood that the manner and process by which...

- Perceived 15th in revelation, secrets of the [Hundred Years] war between the kings of France and England and how agreements between those princes, which are very troublesome for the Church, shall arise before the time of the spiteful Antichrist.

Fifteenth, I understood that contrary to the opinion of the multitude...

- Perceived 16th in revelation, what will eventually befall lord Pope Clement VI.

  Sixteenth, I understood that in the year 1345...

- Perceived 17th in revelation, the eventual futures of the FOUR FINAL [Angelic] POPES who will follow, in order.

  Seventeenth, I understood about the first of the final popes...

- Perceived 18th in revelation, two omens before the time of Antichrist to be fulfilled by both the kings of France and England after Antichrist is elected emperor.

  Eighteenth, I understood that in the future two signs...

- Perceived 19th in revelation, the murder of Antichrist and victory of the Holy Roman (Catholic) Church and explanation of puzzles hidden in Scripture.

  Nineteenth, I understood that the Holy Church so bravely...

- Perceived 20th in revelation, the mystery of 1,000 YEARS OF SUNLIGHT [the Millennium] which will endure in the world after Antichrist's coming and how this is proved by Scripture.

  Twentieth, I understood that 1,000 years of sunlight must remain...

- Perceived 21st in revelation, the three persons of the Trinity and the three remarkable resurrections (sic) of the saints.

  Twenty-first, I understood that three bodily advents...

- Perceived 22nd in revelation, THE DEATH OF THE WICKED AND IMPIOUS who cannot enjoy the future mystery but blaspheme the Bible.

  Twenty-second, I understood that all the carnal multitude...

- Perceived 23rd in revelation, of future heretics before the interval of the 1,000 YEARS OF SUNLIGHT [Millennium] who will perish after Antichrist and how this is proven by Scripture.

  Twenty-third, I understood that from the fleeting hours of the 1,000 years...

- Perceived 24th in revelation, the purpose of the coming Antichrist's mission.

  Twenty-fourth, I understood that amazingly and incomprehensibly...

- Perceived 25th in revelation, the archangel's prophecy in DANIEL of 45 consecutive years of troubles after the future Antichrist.

  Twenty-fifth, I understood that in the future after the death of Antichrist...

- Perceived 26th in revelation, a single, UNIVERSAL CATHOLIC MONARCHY after the future coming Antichrist, with the DESTRUCTION OF THE ROMAN EMPIRE, subjection of the entire secular world and conversion of the Jews to Christianity.

  Twenty-sixth, I understood that after the death of Antichrist...

- Perceived 27th in revelation, the movement of the seat of the Roman Catholic Church to the CITY OF JERUSALEM and evidence of Scripture about the renewal of this city and its glory and majesty.

  Twenty-seventh, I understood that in the future the city...

- Perceived 28th in revelation, the efforts of the prophets concerning the peace lasting 1,000 years, beginning a little after the coming Antichrist dominates the Church.
  Twenty-eighth, I understood that peace of the future Church...

- Perceived 29th in revelation, the chronology of future events for 1,000 years from the disposition of the earth to the end of the universe.
  Twenty-ninth, I understood that the Holy Spirit possesses such plenitude...

- Last of its kind, and perceived 30th in revelation, the birth of Gog, his coming and destruction, and disclosure of a secret in *The Prophecy of* EZECHIEL of the CONVERSION OF THE ENTIRE EARTH IN THE LAST GENERATION.
  Thirtieth and last, I understood that at the end of the predicted 1,000...

Thus, most reverend father and lord [Cardinal William Curti], are my prison-inspired perceptions of future events... This was written by me, brother John of Rupescissa, Order of the Friars Minor of the provence of Aquitaine, in the custody of the Ruthenenis convent in Aurillac in the Roman curia of Avignon, from the prison of lord Pope Clement VI, in the eighth year of his pontificate.... The year 1349, from his incarnation, of Our Lord Jesus Christ, in the month of November on Saint Martin's day, to the glory of God, Amen." [23]

John's themes supply the subjects, missing from *Revelation*, found on Tarot cards – like the Frederick, an incarnation of Antichrist, who will be emperor and make war on the Church. Likewise he associates the whore of Babylon with the Holy Roman empire. It will be replaced by a universal Catholic monarchy, founded by a French Last Emperor – thought the text here does not explicitly mention him.

True (Angelic) and false popes are also described, and the elect are identified as persecuted, mendicant [Spiritual] Franciscans. In the last times, the whole world will be converted to Christianity, and impious blasphemers put to death. Finally, John, Daniel, and Ezechiel are explicitly identified with religious doctrine – Ezechiel standing for the conversion of the last generation.

After you've read the next chapter, come back to John of Rupescissa's perceptions and compare the meanings for the Tarot cards with what he has to say. See if you don't agree their messages are similar.

The Hanged Man Card

ANCESTOR (*opposite page*) PORTRAYS MANY MARTYRDOMS, BUT NONE OF THEM resembles The Hanged Man Tarot card. Death is by decapitation in Ancestor. However, given the changes that have occurred on other cards, it's not unthinkable that Tarot's Hanged Man is an updated version of one of Ancestor's illustrations.

Otherwise, all Hanged Man cards from the early decks look much the same.

SOMETIMES HE HAS HIS HANDS TIED BEHIND HIS BACK, OR IS SUSPENDED BY THE RIGHT FOOT RATHER THAN THE LEFT, AS ON THE BUDAPEST CARD (*right*),

...THAT'S ABOUT THE EXTENT OF THEIR DIFFERENCES. CARDS LIKE THE CHARLES VI HANGED MAN (*right*) SIMPLY PERMUTE THESE ELEMENTS.

Now that I've gone through the Tarot deck card by card (except for The Fool), it's time to consider what the deck as a whole is saying. John of Rupescissa's perceptions are a prelude to this program. The new point of view will bring in additional evidence and shore up interpretations which might still seem doubtful.

Bibliography

Rosalind and Christopher Brooke, Popular Religion in the Middle Ages: Western Europe 1000-13000, reprint: (Barns & Noble, 1996).

Samuel Y. Edgerton, Jr., "Effigies of Shame: The Trecento, & The Quattrocento and Cinquecento." In *Pictures and Punishment: Art and Criminal Prosecution During the Florentine Renaissance*, (Ithica, 1985).

D. Douie, "The Fraticelli, & The Béguins of France." In *The Nature and Effect of the Heresy of the Fraticelli*, (Manchester, 1932).

Herbert Grundmann, "The Origins of a Religious Literature in the Vernacular." In *Religious Movements in the Middle Ages*, tr. Stephen Rowan, (U Notre Dame Pr. 1995)

Gordon Leff, "Spirituals, Beguins and Fraticelli." In *Heresy in the Later Middle Ages*, (Manchester, 1967).

Robert E. Lerner, "The Medieval Return to the Thousand-Year Sabbath." In *The Apocalypse in the Middle Ages*, Richard K. Emmerson & Bernard McGinn eds., (Cornell UP, 1992).

George March, "The Enemies in Angelo Clareno's History of the Franciscan Order." In *The Use and Abuse of Eshatologyin the Middle Ages*, ed. D. Verhelst et al. (Leiden, 1988).

Bernard McGinn, "Arnold of Villanova, John of Rupescissa, & The Fraticelli." In *Visions of the End, Apocalyptic Traditions in the Middle Ages*, (Columbia UP, 1979).

Lionello Puppi, *Torment in Art: Pain, Violence and Martyrdom*, (Rizzoli, 1991)

Marjorie Reeves, "Spiritual Franciscans and Fraticelli, & Observantine Franciscans." In *The Influence of Prophecy in the Later Middle Ages: A Study in Joachimism*, (U. Notre Dame Pr., 1993).

Gerorge Ridley Scott, "Figure: Various Ancient Tortures." In *A History of Torture*, reprint: (Studio Editions Ltd, 1995), p 8-9.

Lynn Thorndike, "John of Rupescissa: Chemist and Prophet, & Appendices 21-24." In *A History of Magic and Experimental Science* (Columbia UP, 1934), Vol III.

Internet

Note: There's no need to type this yourself. Current links to these and future sites, as they become available, can be found at: http://tarot-cards.com

Avignon
http://www.knight.org/advent/cathen/02158a.htm
Beguines & Beghards
http://www.knight.org/advent/cathen/02389c.htm
Andrea del Sarto
http://ubmail.ubalt.edu/~pfitz/ART/REN/vasari17.htm
St. Vincent Ferrer
http://www.knight.org/advent/cathen/15437a.htm
Franciscan Order
http://www.knight.org/advent/cathen/06217a.htm
Bernard Gui: *Inquisitorial Technique*
http://www.fordham.edu/halsall/source/heresy2.html
Bernard Gui: *Inquisitor's Manual*
http://www.fordham.edu/halsall/source/bernardgui-inq.html
Case of Na Prous, a Beguine
http://www.fordham.edu/halsall/source/naprous.html
Filippo Lippi and Boticelli
http://ubmail.ubalt.edu/~pfitz/ART/REN/vasari9.htm
Introduction to Inquisition Documents
http://www.fordham.edu/halsall/source/inquisition1.html

Translations

1. Oggi, a'di 13 d'ottobre anno 1377, si comminciò a intonicare nella faccia del palagio dove str messer lo Podestà, e dipigniere la faccia e la persona del traditore di messer Ridolfo da Camerino, traditore della Santa Madre Chiesa e del popolo e del Comune di Firenze, e della Lega e di tutti collegati. E simile si si dipigne nella faccia del Palagio, sopra la Condotta, cosi dipinto.

Egli e in su'n uno paio di forche, di sopra, legato lo piè manco, impiccato, e da lato, dalla man manca, à una sirene e dal lato ritto un bavilischio; ed à in capo di sotto una gran mitra; e dal lato a lui è legato pella gola da un diavolo; ed egli à dispartite le braccia da ma'ritta e da man nanca, e fa le fica alla Chiesa e al Commune di Firenze, com'egli tradito il Papa e'l Comune di Firenze.

2. Dipinse nel 1478 nella facciata dove gia era il bargiello sopra la doghana, Messer Jacopo, Franco. et Rinato de Pazzi, et Messer Franco. Salviata archiveschovo di Pisa, et dui Jacopi Salviati, luno fratello et l'altro affine di detto Messer Franco., et Bernardo Bandidi, impicchati per la gola, et Napoleone Franzesi impicchato per uno pie, che sitronorono nella congiura contro a Giuliano et Lorenzo de Medici, alli quali Lorenzo poi fece ai piedi li epitaffi, et infra l'altri a Bernardo Bandino che in questo modo diceva: "Son Bernardo Bandini un nuovo Giuda / Traditore micidiale in chiesa io fui / Ribello per aspettare morte più cruda."

3. La mattina della pasqua di Resurresso si scoprirono tre cittadini dipinti nella facciata del palagio del potestà: Alessandro di Gherardo Corsini in mantello e cappuccio, Taddeo di Francesco Guiducci, cieco da un occhio nel medesimo abito, e Pierfrancesco di Giorgio Ridolfi impiccato per un piè, ognuno de'quali aveva scritto a piè il nome e casato suo in un breve, il quale diceva a lettere da speziali: PER TRADITORE DELLA PATRIA.

4. Straxinetur ad caudam equi cum asside ad locum iustitie et ibidem per pedem furcis suspendatur, et ibi tantum teneatur quod a se ipso moriatur; detur tamen ei de cibo et de cibo et potu donec vivit.

5. nonnulli tamen profanae multitudinis viri, qui vulgariter 'fraticelli' seu 'frates de paupere vita', aut 'bizzochi', sive 'beghini' vel aliis nominibus nuncupantur.

6. Item habebant dictum dominum lohannem papem suspectum quod esset hereticus et misticus Antichristus pro eo quod condamnaverat quattor minores Massilie condemnatos et combustos, vel quia fecit eos condemnari, pro quod petebant puram observationem vortorum suorum et quia dominus papa fecerat decretalem super granariis et celariis habendis per eos et disposuerat de eorum habititibus.

7. De qua postilla audivit ipse pluries legi etiam plus quam xxx vicibus in vulgari, et plura se audivisse et retinuisse recognovit, et specialiter quod frater Petrus Johannis exponit in dicta postilla Romanorum ecclesiam esse illam babilonem magnum meretricem.

8. quod ille Elias fuit sanctus Francis, et ille Enoch fuit sanctus pater, frater Petrus Johannis... Ita videlicet quod sanctus Franciscus portavit testimonium pauperis vitae quam Christus incepit, et frater Petrus Johannis tulit testamonium divinitatis in sancta scriptura.

9. Item quod tota doctrina fratris Petri Johannis Olivi est vera et catholica, et habuit eam per illuminacionem spiritus scanti, per quam cognovit veritatem evangelicam et regule sancti Francisci, quem vocant sanctum patrem et magnum doctorem, et quod est ille angelus de quo scribitur in Apocalpsi, quod facies eius erat ut sol, et habebat librum apertum in manu sua, et quod illi clarius fuit revelatum tempus futurum, et illa que debent contingere pro tempore futuro, quam alicui alii doctori.

10. Item, dogmatizant quod ecclesia carnalis, videlicet Romana ecclesia, ante predicationem Anti-Christi est destruenda per bella que contra ipsam faciet Fridericus, rex Sicilie, qui nunc regnat.

11. Item dixit se credidisse quod infra annum quo computabitur incarnacio domini M ccc xxx Antichristus maior fecerit cursum suum et erit mortatus.

12. Quem antichristum dicunt esse aliquem apostatam ordinis minorum, quia est alcior status ecclesie, ut dicunt, dicentes quod erit frater Angelus qui est aposta ordinis fratrum minorum. Alli dicunt dominum Pillippum de Majoricis esse Antichristum. Dicunt etiam plures ex eis quod Fredericus rex Sicilie erit imperator et persequetur ecclesiam Romanam, et facit quod dictus antichristus ab omnibus adoretur.

13. Si minores possent appellari, quia non sunt Minores, scilicet in humilitate et simplitate, set Maiores in superbia, astucia, ambitione, et abusione, ut est manifestum toti mundo

14. E che questo sia oggi in tra lloro, apare per isperienza evidente che papa Iohanni XXII e gli altri successori si partirono, e partono dalia unione e vera chiesa per lo male intendre la Scriptura inverso la povertà di Xpo.

15. Et quando dicea 'il venerabilissimo et sanctissimo papa Giovanni XXII', rispondea 'ma eretico'.

16. Plerique etiam seducuntur, putantes per Spiritum Sanctum fieri quod ipsi prius finxerunt, vel quod spiritus erroris suggessit eis. Proinde vaticiniis iam usque ad nausaem repleti sumus; ut puta de Antichristi adventu, de signis iudicii propinquantis, de Ecclesiae persecutione et reformatione et similibus, quibus etiam viri graves atque devoti plusquam oportuit creduli exstiterunt, de scripturis Ioachim et aliorum vaticinantium interpretationes varias extrahentes; quae etsi vera et authentica forent; attamen servi Dei plurima alia reperirent, in quibus possent fructuosis occupari...

17. Constat autem quod a deo sunt revelata populo fideli tempora plurium eventuum, sicut tempus primi adventus Christi et tempus passionis ipsius, ut patet Danielis IX, et etiam tempus adventus Antichristi, sicut patet XII eiusdem.

18. Incipit primus liber de consideratione quinte essentie omnium rerum tradendus pauperibus et evangelicis viris servis yesu

christi a magistro Iohanne de Rupescissa sacre theologie professore compositus.

19. oportet rem quaerere que sic se habet respectu quatuor qualitatum sicut se habet celum respectu quatuor elementorum, que res vocatur quinta essentia sicut celum.

20. Ego assero quod quinta essentia est aqua ardens...

21. Cum inimici mi mortales et iniuste contra deum me tenuerunt in vinculis in obdurissimo carceris ergastulo vexatus hiis passionibus supra quam credi potest quia corpus corrumpebatur ex malitia squalorum carceris et ferri ingenio et benignitate servorum habui aquam ardentem a quodam sancto viro amico dei et me ex sola unctione cum ea lotione in ictu oculi sum sanatus.

22. Consideravi tribulationes electorum in (sacro) sancto ewangelio prophetatas a christo maxime tribulationes temporum antichristi instare in annis quibus est sacrosancta ecclesia univeralis romana hoc dubium plurimum affligenda et ad montes fuganda et certe per tyrannos omnibus divitiis temporalibus spoilanda in seccessu temporis. Sed licet jactetur in validis fluctibus Petri navicula est tamen liberanda in fine dierum domina generalis. Quapropter ad sublevandam gravem inopiam et paupertatem futuram populi sancti et electi dei quibus datum est noscere misterium veritatis sine parabolis lapidem maximum philosophorum ad lunam et ad solem, ad album et ad rubeum volo dicere...

23. Intellectus in revelatione patrum et generis antichristi et nominis eius et persone et loci. Primo intellexi quod de semine frederici imperatoris...

Intellectus secundus in adventu multorum anitchristum. Secundo intellexi multos debere fieri antichristos...

Intellectus tertius in extremis ytallorum et gallicorum et in tribulatione eorum. Tertio intellexi in eodem carcere clare et vidi neapolim...

Intellectus quartus in multitudine notabilium cladium preeuntium tempus proximi antichristi quarem quedam sunt facte quedam adhuc facture. Quarto intellexi multas clades futuras erunt in lanius...

Intellectus sextus in revelatione secretorum Danielis super apertione temporis antichristi et quando consurget ad seculum acquirendum. Sexto intellexi esse futurum ut circa annum domini M.ccc.lxvi...

Intellectus septimus in revelatione adventus unius falsi pappe et casus malorum ecclasiaticorum a fide et ab hobediencia veri pappe et de generatione meretrici apocalipsis capitulo xvii descripte. Septimo intellexi sed magis explicite tholoze in carcere...

Intellectus octavus in revelatione temporis in quo eligetur ad imperium antichristus et quando incipet affligere eccesiam non ut antichristus set ut tirannus. Octavo intellexi quod circa tempus introductionis predicte scismatis...

Intellectus nonus in revelatione qualiter ordo fratrum minorum in tres partes dividentur quarum due efficientur heretice et pars tertia adherens catholico pontifici orthodoxe fidei remanebit. Nono intellexi ordinem fratrum minorum in tempore illo...

Intellectus decimus in revelatione casus ordinum mendicorum in heresi et adnichilationis eorum excepta mendica portione fratrum minorum et qualiter meretrix occidetur. Decimo intellexi futuro existere ut ordo heremitarium...

Intellectus undecimus in revelatione transmutationis monarche in antichristum et qualiter eius lex per hereticos conficientur et sub ea reprobi unientur. Undecimo intellexi quod percussa meretrice prescripta...

Intellectus duodecimus in revelatione conflictus ultime eccesie cum proximo antichristo et qualiter rebellabunt ellecti. Duodecimo intellexi conflictum sacrosancte romane ecclesie...

Intellectus xiii in revelatione bellorum principum fidelium contra reprobatorum antichristum. Tertiodecimo intellexi quod ipse generalis reproborum...

Intellectus xiiii in revelatione qualiter proximus antichristus et per quem modum et ordinem subiciet seculum universum. Quartodecimo intellexi modum et processum per quem...

Intellectus xv in revelatione misterii bellorum regum francie et anglicorum et cuisdam concordie principum contra ecclesiam nimis laboriosis que fiet ante tempora antichristi maligni. Quintodecimo intellexi falsam esse opinionem multorum...

Intellectus xvi in revelatione eventuum accidentium sub domino pappa clemente sexto. Sextodecimo intellexi eodem anno M.ccc.xlv...

Intellectus xvii in revelatione eventum futurorum sub quatuor summorum pontificum qui ordinate succedent. Decimoseptimo intellexi sub summo pontifice immediate...

Intellectus xviii in revelatione duorum passagiorum ante tempora antichristi quorum ultimum pariter fiet per reges francie et anglicorum postque eligetur ad imperium antichristus. Decimo octavo intellexi esse futura duo passagia...

Intellectus decimusnonus in revelatione occisionis antichristi et victorie ecclesie sacrosante romane et expositionis quorundam ministrorum occultorum scripture. Decimonono intellexi sanctam ecclesiam tam fortiter...

Intellectus xx in revelatione misterii mille annorum solarium quibus durabit mundus post antichristum proximum et qualiter hoc ex scriptura probatur. Vicessimo intellexi mille annis solaribus debere durare...

Intellectus xxi in revelatione trium personalium adventuum verbi et trium notabilium resurrexionem sanctorum. Vicesimoprimo intellexi tres adventus corporales...

Intellectus xxii in revelationes excecacionis reproborum et quod impii non poterunt capere futurorum misteria sed blafemabunt hunc librum. Vicesimosecundo intellexi totam multitudinem carnalium...

Intellectus xxiii in revelatione hereticorum futurorum infra spatium mille annorum solarium qui fluent post antichristum et quod hoc ex scriptura probatur. Vicesimtertio intellexi ex fluxis horum mille annorum...

Intellectus xxiiii in revelatione utilitatum missionis proximi antichristi. Vicesimoquarto intellexi quod pro maxima et imprehensibill...

Intellectus xxv in revelatione archanorum Danielis prophete super successione xlv annorum larorlosorum post antichristum futurorum. Vicesimoquinto intellexi futuros esse post mortem antichristi...

Intellectus xxvi in revelatione unius generalis catholice monarchie post antichristum proximum affuture cum destructo romano imperio totum seculum subicietur Iudeis tunc conversis ad christum. Vicesimsexto intellexi post mortem antichristi...

Intellectus xxvii in revelatione translationis sedis ecclesie generalis romane in civitatem Iherusalem appertio scripturarum super renovationem illius civitatis et super gloria et magnitude eius. Vicesimoseptimo intellexi futurum esse ut civitas...

Intellectus xxviii in revelationis intentionis prophetarum super pace M annis durature aut quasi post proximum antichristum ecclesie potestatam. Vicesimooctavo intellexi pacem istam futuram ecclesie...

Intellectus xxix in revelatione eventuum futurorum in successione mille annorum et dispositione orbis usque ad finem mondi. Vicesimonono intellexi tantam plenitudinem spiritus sancti...

Intellectus xxx et ultimus huiusmodi libri in revelatione generationis gog et adventus ac destructionis eius et apertionis secretorum ezechielis prophete super conversione totius orbis et in fine seculorum. Trisimo et ultimo intellexi in fine predictorum mille...

Hec ergo, reverendissime pater et domine, sunt per me de futuris eventibus in carceribus intellecta... Scripta sunt hec per me fratem Iohannem de Rupescissa ordinis fratrum minorum provincie Acquitanie custodie Ruthenenius conventus Aurelhiaci in Romana curia in Avinione in carcere domini pappe Clementis VI pontifficatus sui anno octavo. Qui carcer vocatur carcer Soldani. Anno ab Incarnatione domini nostri Ihesu christi M.ccc.xlix in mense novembris in die sancti Martini ad gloriam dei, Amen.

Chapter Fourteen

Tarot's Story

SO FAR, EACH CARD HAS BEEN DISSECTED TO YIELD AS MANY CLUES to its identity as possible. However, on a card-by-card basis, many interpretations can be justified; just think of all of the occult meanings that have been suggested. The real test is when you put them together. Then, what seemed compelling about card A's meaning may completely contradict card B's. Or cards C and D, which seemed doubtful when considered alone, may support one another so that the whole becomes greater than the sum of its parts.

Likewise, this is an opportunity to introduce new data. I've asserted there's a story behind Tarot. But so far, no story has been put forth, not even *Revelation's,* which has furnished most of my clues so far. Actually, Tarot portrays two stories. It begins with a French version of the Last Emperor prophecy from the 1380s and finishes with *Revelation*. The former was never illustrated, so *Revelation's* characters were borrowed whenever possible to portray it. *Revelation's* meanings were also retained in the borrowings, so we're able to understand much of what's going on from *Revelation* alone.

These are John of Rupescissa's doctrines, though not his actual writings. So, whenever questions of interpretation arise, I've used his ideas to clarify them. I don't claim that everything you'll read here reproduces Tarot's original meaning with perfect fidelity. Nevertheless it all hangs together and accounts for why each succeeding card triumphs over and captures the one before it.

As a matter of fact, there are three *triumphi* sequences to explain. Tarot decks follow three distinct organizing principles, exemplified by the Budapest, Washington, and Marseilles decks. Far from disproving the story theory, they provide additional confirmation of its correctness.

The First Tarot Story

SO WITHOUT FURTHER DELAY, HERE'S THE FIRST VERSION OF TAROT'S STORY. I've capitalized the meanings of each card for your convenience:

> THERE'S MORE TO LIFE THAN MEETS THE EYE (The Magician). We spend our days laying up worldly treasure, ignoring the treasures of heaven our eyes cannot see.
>
> We obey the EMPIRE (The Empress),
>
> ...neglecting God's kingdom, the CHURCH (The Popess).
>
> In the last times the Church will be persecuted by a cruel emperor, the THIRD FREDERICK (The Emperor).
>
> Wherefore an ANGELIC POPE (The Pope) will arise to lead the Church back to poverty and Christ,
>
> ...and with God's aid PURIFY THE EARTH (Temperance) of the unfaithful.
>
> In those troubled times, a LAST WORLD EMPEROR (The Chariot) will come forth to champion the pope and Church,

...and (The Lovers) TRIUMPH OVER THE EVIL emperor, his empire, and all the nations of the world.

Afterwards, as prophesied in DANIEL (Strength), the great Antichrist will begin his reign in Jerusalem,

...and, as prophesied in EZECHIEL (The Wheel of Fortune), Gog and Magog will join him,

...and, as prophesied in the Apocalypse of JOHN (The Hermit), Christ will destroy them all.

Only MARTYRS (The Hanged Man) persecuted for Christ's sake will inherit the Millennium.

SINNERS WILL PERISH (Death) [Rupescissa's 22nd perception],

... just punishment for the FOLLOWERS OF SATAN (The Devil).

Christ's Second Coming will be preceded by the opening of the Sixth Seal, announced by:

- a great EARTHQUAKE (The Tower),
- STARS falling to earth (The Star),
- The full MOON (The Moon) like blood, and
- The SUN (The Sun) black as sackcloth.

Afterwards, the rest of the dead will RISE FROM THEIR TOMBS (Judgment),

...and ARCHANGEL MICHAEL (Justice) will weigh their souls in his scales,

...admitting the elect to NEW JERUSALEM (The World).

If you've had trouble remembering the sequence of Tarot cards until now, think about the story, and go through it again. You'll find that you can now remember it with few, or no mistakes. Then read this prophecy from the 1380s:

> Charles, the son of Charles, from the most illustrious nation of the Lily [France], will have a lofty forehead, high eyebrows, wide eyes, an aquiline nose and be crowned at about thirteen years of age. In his fourteenth year HE WILL GATHER A GREAT ARMY AND DESTROY ALL THE TYRANTS OF HIS KINGDOM. [He will slay some and force the others to flee to the mountains and hide in caves.]
>
> Like a bride with a bridegroom, justice will accompany him, and until his 24th year he will make war, subjugating English, Spanish, Aragonese, Burgundians, Lombards and Italians. He will destroy Rome and Florence and burn them with fire. [He will cause salt to be sown in the rich earth of their lands, and PUT TO DEATH IMPIOUS PRIESTS WHO USURP THE APOSTOLIC SEE of Peter and Paul. That year,] he will be crowned both king and emperor.
>
> Afterwards he will cross the sea with a great army and invade Greece. He will be called King of the Greeks. He will conquer Syrians, Turks, Hispanos, Barbarians, Palestinians, and Georgians, and COMMAND THAT WHOEVER DOES NOT WORSHIP THE CRUCIFIX WILL DIE. And none will be able to resist him for the arm of God will always be with him and HE WILL POSSESS DOMINION OVER NEARLY ALL THE EARTH.
>
> This accomplished, he will be called Saint of Saints and COME TO HOLY JERUSALEM, ascend the Mount of Olives and pray to the Father, removing the crown from his head. Giving thanks to God, in the midst of a great earthquake, signs and wonders he will give up his spirit in the 31st year of his reign.
>
> He will be crowned by the ANGELIC SHEPHERD [Pope] and will be the first emperor after the THIRD FREDERICK, after the present schism, tribulations, persecutions by false prophets, and the aforesaid FREDERICK."

This prophecy, recorded by Gui de Corsaint in the archives of

Côte-d'Or, France for 1381-2, subsequently became the most widely disseminated prophecy for the next two centuries. It was frequently bundled together with Telesphorus' work, which contains the final paragraph reproduced here, omitted from the Côte-d'Or version.

Compare the cast of characters: the Angelic Pope, Third Frederick, Last World Emperor, and their deeds with the meanings I've suggested for Tarot cards: commanding worship and slaying impious priests (purification of the earth), conquering nations and founding a world monarchy (triumph over evil), the triumphal entry into Jerusalem and surrender of the crown. There's a good match. The major discrepancy is the Last World Emperor, not the Angelic Pope, purifies the earth. In John of Rupescissa's doctrines, however, the (last four) Angelic Popes perform this function.

Thus, after an anagogic introduction by The Magician the French Last Emperor prophecy accounts for the sequence of Tarot cards through The Lovers, and *Revelation* interprets most of the rest, beginning with The Hanged Man. In between, Strength, The Wheel of Fortune, and The Hermit refer to prophetic books of the Bible or events described within them. I've tried to indicate what these events might be by using clues from John of Rupescissa's understandings.

The Other Tarot Stories

THE FIRST TAROT STORY DESCRIBES THE CARD SEQUENCE OF THE BUDAPEST DECK, which is very similar to the order given in the early sermon on Tarot and is probably the original sequence. But we're not finished; there are still sequences for the Washington and Marseilles decks to account for. All other arrangements differ from one of these three by only a transposition of one or two cards.

The first five cards of all three sequences are practically identical, except that The Popess card precedes, rather than follows The Empress in the two new sequences:

Initial Card Sequences

Budapest	**Washington**	**Marseilles**
The Magician	The Magician	The Magician
	The Popess	The Popess
The Empress	The Empress	The Empress
The Popess		
The Emperor	The Emperor	The Emperor
The Pope	The Pope	The Pope
Temperance •		

Thus, the new stories probably begin more like:

> THERE'S MORE TO LIFE THAN MEETS THE EYE (The Magician). We spend our days laying up worldly treasure, ignoring the treasures of heaven our eyes cannot see.
>
> The CHURCH (The Popess) is the key to unlocking these secrets,
>
> ...but in the last times the she will be persecuted by the EMPIRE (The Empress),
>
> ...obeying a cruel emperor, the THIRD FREDERICK (The Emperor).
>
> Wherefore an ANGELIC POPE (The Pope) will arise to lead the Church back to poverty and Christ, etc.

All three sequences are consistent with the persecution of the Church. Either The Empress or Emperor follows (dominates) The Popess (Church) in each case.

At the end of the deck all three sequences are likewise in good agreement:

Final Card Sequences:

All Three

The Devil
The Tower
The Star
The Moon
The Sun

Budapest	Washington	Marseilles
Judgment	The World	Judgment
Justice •		
The World	Judgment	The World

Here, the only difference is the Justice card of the Budapest deck occurs earlier in the other two sequences, and the order of the last two cards of the Washington deck is opposite of that of the other two (the observant reader will have noticed the Washington deck itself is unnumbered after card XII, and what I'm describing here are later decks of the same type). From the standpoint of meaning this transposition is unnerving. Anyone familiar with the Second Coming knows that new Jerusalem (The World) comes after resurrection (Judgment) and not before.

The major difference between sequences occurs in mid-deck:

First Half of the Mid-Card Sequences

Budapest	Washington	Marseilles
The Chariot	The Lovers	The Lovers
	Temperance •	
	Justice •	
	Strength •	
The Lovers	The Chariot	The Chariot
		Justice •

Continuing with the Washington deck, note that its three so-called cardinal virtue cards are grouped together between The Lovers and Chariot cards. To make this easier to see, I've placed a bullet (•) after cardinal virtue cards in the text. This is the tip-off. Together with the reversal of its Judgment and World cards, it indicates that the story line has been lost, and the Washington deck is simply a re-shuffling of the original Tarot sequence based on superficial resemblances. Significantly, the remaining cards seem to have been left where they originally were.

The same cards in the Budapest and Marseilles decks are thoroughly integrated with the others, as one would expect for a story not about cardinal virtues. I've already told the Budapest story, what about the Marseilles? After introducing the Angelic Pope, I believe it focused more on the Last World Emperor's surrender of his crown and subsequent events:

> Wherefore an ANGELIC POPE (The Pope) will arise to lead the Church back to poverty and Christ.
>
> In those troubled times, a hero will come forth to champion the pope and Church and (The Lovers) TRIUMPH OVER THE EVIL emperor, his empire and all the nations of the world.
>
> His tasks finished, the LAST WORLD EMPEROR (The Chariot) will come to Jerusalem, take the crown from his head, and give over his spirit.
>
> After which, ARCHANGEL MICHAEL (Justice) will defeat the dragon in heaven, commencing Antichrist's reign in Jerusalem.

In Chapter Five, one of the *pledge of allegiance* cards had two different interpretations, and consequently, positions within the deck. The Justice card above is another instance of this.

IT'S SECOND MEANING IS ILLUSTRATED IN ANCESTOR (*opposite page*) WHERE ARCHANGEL MICHAEL IS DEPICTED IN HIS *Revelation* ROLE:

> "And THERE WAS A GREAT BATTLE IN HEAVEN, MICHAEL AND HIS ANGELS FOUGHT WITH THE DRAGON, and the dragon fought and his angels: And they prevailed not, neither was their place found any more in heaven. And that great dragon was cast out, that old serpent, who is called the devil and SATAN, WHO SEDUCETH THE WHOLE WORLD; AND HE WAS CAST UNTO THE EARTH, and his angels were thrown down with him."
>
> — *Revelation* 12:7-9

In the Budapest story Michael is the weigher of souls, and in this one the conqueror who casts Satan from heaven. Note that both the Budapest and Marseilles sequences (using different cards) refer to Antichrist at this point.

The next three cards are not that different:

Last Half of the Mid-Card Sequences

Budapest	Washington	Marseilles
Strength •		The Hermit
Wheel of Fortune	Wheel of Fortune	Wheel Fortune
The Hermit	The Hermit	Strength •
Hanged Man	Hanged Man	Hanged Man
Death	Death	Death
		Temperance •

The order of the apocalyptic books: Daniel, Ezechiel and John in the first (and second?) sequence is merely reversed in the third. The fact the cards remain grouped together seems more significant than their change in order. The final difference between the sequences is that Temperance follows Death in the Marseilles story. This is consistent with the following story segment:

> Only the MARTYRS (The Hanged Man) persecuted for Christ sake, will be saved and inherit the Millennium.
>
> SINNERS WILL PERISH (Death),

...PURIFYING THE EARTH (Temperance) for the elect,

... punishment for the FOLLOWERS OF SATAN (The Devil).

Thus, the Marseilles story reaffirms the Budapest theme with a minor change in emphasis. This is especially gratifying since I first used the Marseilles deck to unravel Tarot's meaning.

The Tarot Sermon

THE SERMON AGAINST TAROT IN CHAPTER FIVE USES A SLIGHTLY DIFFERENT VERSION of the Budapest sequence which can't be ignored. Specifically, the order of its first five cards are:

The Magician
The Empress (Empire)
The Emperor
The Popess (Church)
The Pope

Offhand, this looks like medieval politics as usual: empire controls subjects, emperor rules empire, Church controls emperor, pope guides Church. As mentioned earlier, in some versions of the Last World Emperor prophecy, the last paragraph is missing. This eliminates the Angelic Pope and Third Frederick from the story and could explain the sermon's card sequence.

The other difference between the Tarot sermon and Budapest sequences occurs in the next three cards:

Budapest	Sermon
Temperance	Temperance
The Chariot	The Lovers
The Lovers	The Chariot

This makes the purification of the earth, triumph over the forces of evil, and surrender of his crown in Jerusalem all part of the

Last World Emperor's role – in perfect agreement with the French Last World Emperor prophecy, and the only possibility with a missing Angelic Pope.

Lessons From John Ball

WHERE TAROT'S STORY INVOLVES REAL HISTORICAL FIGURES, INTERPRETATIONS can become quite complex. Who might be represented on a card changes over time. Mortals die, but prophecy goes on. This is the phenomenon of Shakespeare combining John Ball with Jack Cade in *Henry VI*. Ball and Wat Tyler created the usurper role, which Cade took over and augmented seventy years later. Shakespeare's character is more than just Cade alone. In the same way Nero was probably the model for Antichrist, which Frederick II Hohenstaufen, and a succession of later Fredericks unwillingly perpetuated in the Middle Ages.

To help keep track of the players I've summarized the actors of these historical dramas in a table (*opposite page*). After each card name and meaning follows a list, arranged from last to earliest known example, of the groups or persons identified with that role. My assessment of the most important ones for Tarot are capitalized. Further information within parenthesis gives the authority for each identification, or the date when it was current. Thus, POPE CELESTINE V (Spirituals) under The Pope, means Celestine was thought to be the Angelic Pope by the Spirituals. A few entries are new or almost so: Charles of Anjou, the brother of a French king, destroyed the Hohenstaufen dynasty in Sicily, Frederick I was Frederick II's famous German grandfather, and Frederick II of Aragon was connected to the Hohenstaufens through marriage.

Lastly, I've identified The Hanged Man as a fraticelli. But these are not the scattered groups known to history. They lived in northern Italy and openly championed Spiritual ideas. Perhaps a different name for them would have been more appropriate.

Card Genealogies

The Pope – Angelic Pope (Tarot):
· four last popes (John of Rupescissa)
· POPE CELESTINE V (Spirituals)
· Eastern Patriarchs (*Leo Oracles*)

The Pope – false pope (fraticelli):
· POPE JOHN XXII (Spirituals)
· mystic Antichrist (Olivi)
· Pope Boniface VIII (Spirituals)

The Emperor – The Third Frederick (Tarot):
· Frederick II of Aragon (John of Rupescissa)
· Hohenstaufen sons (1260)
· FREDERICK II HOHENSTAUFEN (Spirituals)
· Antichrist (Bible)
· Emperor Nero (68 AD)

The Chariot – Last World Emperor (Tarot):
· CHARLES, THE SON OF CHARLES (after 1381-2)
· Charles of Anjou (John of Rupescissa)
· Louis VII (1150)
· King of the Franks (950)
· Constans (*Tiburine Sibyl* & *Pseudo-Methodius*).

The Chariot – Last World Emperor (Karnöffel):
· Frederick II Hohenstaufen (1250)
· FREDERICK I BARBAROSSA (1190)
· King of the Franks (950)...
· Constans (*Tiburine Sibyl* & *Pseudo-Methodius*).

The Hanged Man – fraticelli (Tarot):
· mendicant Franciscans (John of Rupescissa)
· SPIRITUALS (Beguines)
· two new orders of monks (Joachim of Fiore)
·"These that are clothed in white robes." (*Revelation*)

The Earliest Trumps

THE SECOND MEANING OF THE CHARIOT IN THE TABLE REMAINS TO BE ADDRESSED. Although trumps were popularized in Tarot, it's not necessarily the first card game to use them. That distinction may belong to an even older card game, *Karnöffel*, which is still played in Switzerland today as the "Emperor's Game" (*Kaiserspeil*). Like modern games, *Karnöffel* promotes one of the ordinary suits to trump status in the course of play, but in other respects it's hardly conventional.

Originally this game was played with a forty-eight card German deck with no Aces. There's nothing strange about that. Modern thirty-six and thirty-two card German decks still use Johannes von Rheinfelden's King (*König*), Over (*Ober*) and Under (*Unter*) while discarding his Ace through five or six as the case may be.

What is remarkable is that *Karnöffel's* creators decided to use only part of the suit for trumps. Only the 2 through 7 and Under were promoted to trumps. The King, Over, 10, 9, and 8 continued to be played as an ordinary fourth suit. And of the trumps, only the Under (*Karnöffel*), 6 (Pope) , and 2 (Emperor), were full fledged trumps or King-takers. The 3 (Over-taker) wouldn't beat Kings, the 4 (Under-taker) wouldn't beat Kings or Overs, and the 5 (suit-taker) only beat cards below an Under.

Stranger yet was the 7 (Devil or Evil 7). It lost to every card, except when led, when it captured all the cards except the *Karnöffel* (Tarot's Fool is played similarly, except it always loses). While these card capture rules are complicated, nothing too extraordinary occurs following the lead of an ordinary suit card. Upon a lead from the trump suit however, the cards rank in the order:

Under - (7) - 6 - 2 - King - 3 - Over - 4 - 5 - 10 - 9 - 8 - (7)

which appears totally absurd to someone not aware of what's going on. This, coupled with the fact that an Under, not a King, was the highest card or *Karnöffel* earned the game a questionable reputation. It didn't help, either, that the game was mostly played by peasants and soldiers and ignored by the upper classes.

I'm sure the names: Pope, Emperor, and Devil haven't escaped your attention, but there's more. A nineteenth-century description of the Swiss game calls the 7 of trumps the Prophetess (*Sibille*) or Oracle (*Babeli*). And another 1783 description of the Thuringian (German) game calls the then four full-fledged trumps: the Old Beast (*das alte Thier*), Red Beast (*das rothe Their*), Yellow Beast (*das gelbe Thier*), and the Madman (*der Tolle*). The latter is another name for Tarot's Fool. The colors may not be significant. Leaves and Hearts suits in modern German decks are called Greens (*Grün*) and Reds (*Rot*) today. But *Beasts* recall the beasts of the Apocalypse from *Daniel* and *Revelation* suggesting a religious connection. And the Pope, Emperor, Devil, and Madman suggest a connection with Tarot too.

At one time *Karnöffel* may have been known in Italy. On this point, a chronicle from Würzburg, Germany for 1443-1455 mentions: "a certain individual ... playing at cards a game called the Emperor's Game (Ludus Imperatoris)," [2] a literal Latin rendering of *Kaiserspeil.* The same Latin name occurs in records of Ferrara. In 1450, Andrea di Bonsignore was paid two *lire* for painting two decks of Emperor cards (*carte da Imperatori*), and an account book for 1452-7 records two payments at twelve *soldi* per deck for *carte da imperaturi* and *carte de imperatore*. Also, records state that Borso d'Este played at cards: "of the Emperor" (*dell'imperatore*) in Ferrara around 1454.

Early accounts of *Karnöffel* come from Germany: Nördlingen in 1426, Augsburg in 1446, and Balgau in 1448. So it's certainly contemporary with, or earlier than Tarot. And their relationship may be deeper than the idea of trumps. It's possible that *Karnöffel* portrays the career of a German Last World Emperor and was the inspiration for Tarot's Major Arcana cards.

The German Last World Emperor

FREDERICK II WASN'T "ONE OF MANY ANTICHRISTS" EVERYWHERE. North of the Alps in Germany, he was a hero, reincarnated in the (1409 and 1439) Prophecy of Gamelon:

> "Gamelon, a holy man of excellent piety and a relative of saintly Pope Boniface [IX] had a vision about the state of the Church in future times before the last day. And this is what he saw...
>
> A cherub said to Gamelon, 'Look to the South.' An armed man approached, dressed in red garments and wearing a ruby crown. And on the crown was written: 'All kingdoms ought to be beneath my feet, I come from the field of the lily [France].' The armed man bore an apple in his left hand, and in his right a blood-stained sword.
>
> The cherub said, 'The armed man is an emperor who will come from the south, who will begin the evil of the Church and have an evil birth. He will be crowned by the pope, subdue most of Italy, and take power away from the Teutons [Germans]. And the Teutons will chose themselves an emperor from upper Germany, that is, from the Rhine. He will summon a secular council in Aachen and will install a patriarch in Mainz who will be crowned pope. This emperor-elect will attack the other Roman emperor and will slay him. Rome will not be attended to, the Apostolic See will be overwhelmed, and all spiritual authority will pass to Mainz. The Church's possessions will be taken away and the priests slain...
>
> The Frederick who reigned will reign, and will command and will extend his wings to the ends of the earth. He will demolish and disperse those before the time of the last pontiff and clergy."[3]

This German legend foretells the chastisement of the Church by the Last World Emperor, without the complications of poverty and spiritual men. It divides Europe into two powerful camps: a French emperor, Italian pope, and the Church; opposed by the German emperor, his pope, and the German nation. It's not difficult to imagine the former group as *Karnöffel's* partial trumps, the latter as full-fledged ones, while *Karnöffel's* Devil is the Antichrist of the last times.

The idea for a religious allegory using trumps might have occurred first to the creators of *Karnöffel.* Afterwards Italians could have replaced the Teutonic legend with one more palatable to their own taste. Intense national pride lay behind each version, so there's little likelihood Italians would ignore a German challenge. But promoting an ordinary suit wouldn't do for the Italians because their legend was so much more complex. They'd have to make up a special suit for trumps.

If this is so, why did Tarot achieve such popularity, while *Karnöffel* lingered in obscurity? After all, promoting an ordinary suit to trumps is what modern trump games do today. Undoubtedly, some of the blame is due to the complication of only using part of the suit for trumps. *Karnöffel's* creators seemed to go out of their way to introduce complexity – perhaps for religious, rather than entertainment considerations. But the biggest reason must have been in the players. Once Tarot found its way to the courts of northern Italy it was spread throughout Europe with other Italian culture, and the number of Tarot players simply became overwhelming.

Tarot and Religion

WHY WOULD RELIGIOUS IDEAS FIND EXPRESSION IN TAROT AND *Karnöffel*? It wasn't long before cards and religion were at odds, but Johannes von Rheinfelden's 1377 moral treatise is a reminder that card games could be, and once were, viewed as allegories of: "the state of the world, as it is in respect to morals."

There are other plausible explanations for religious ideas on cards. In 1412 a Waldensian, Master Nicholas of Dresden composed his "Tables of Old and New Styles, or Antichrist's Cauldron" (*Tabule veteris et novi coloris seu cortina de Antichristo*). His styles or "colors" contrasted Christ's humility (*Theologus*) with the pope's canonical rules (*Iurista*) to show they were exact opposites, and the pope was Antichrist. This would only be of interest to scholars except that each table was illustrated with pictures: Christ carrying a cross was contrasted with the pope riding a horse, Christ kneeling and washing the disciple's feet was contrasted with the pope sitting on a throne and having his feet kissed, and so forth. Although none survive, eyewitness accounts say Nicholas had the pictures placed on banners or placards and carried though the streets in processions and hung on the walls of Bethlehem chapel in Prague.

A procession through the streets in Italy was a *triumph*, thus the placards might be considered *triumphi* – the same name as early Tarot cards. Such a procession would have familiarized everyone watching with what Tarot's images looked like. This, in turn, could have made them a profitable, low risk item for card makers to reproduce. Remember how the Bologna cardmaker in St. Bernardino's story grew rich reproducing the saint's symbol.

Another possibility is that Tarot cards are an outgrowth s of sets of pictures created as teaching or memory aids. The so-called *tarocchi of Mantegna* cards, which bear such a resemblance to genuine Tarot cards that they're frequently confused for the real thing, may be an example of this.

Court de Gébelin had a different idea. He conjectured that secret wisdom was purposely hidden within the cards:

> "Its time to recover the allegories which it [Tarot] was fated to preserve; and show how among a people most wise, an entire game was based upon allegory; and THOSE SAGES KNEW HOW TO DISGUISE AS AN AMUSEMENT THE MOST USEFUL KNOWLEDGE , and not just make a game." [4]

For occultists ever since, Tarot has been viewed as a veil to preserve and transmit secret knowledge to an elect, while hiding it from the rest of us. This was common enough in the Middle Ages. Alchemists, for instance, wanted credit for their discoveries and to maintain economic control over them. Consequently, they buried their discoveries in impenetrable cant and cryptic anagrams. But this reasoning doesn't hold for Tarot's message. People should have been shouting Christ's Second Coming from the rooftops.

Thus, I have to disagree with occultists on the purpose of Tarot's imagery. Just as emphatically, I disagree with the proponents of the chance hypothesis who say Tarot has no meaning. Everything I've presented contradicts that supposition.

Fifteenth-Century Popular Culture

ALL THIS TALK OF RELIGION AND THE LAST TIMES SEEMS STRANGE today. But in the early fifteenth century it was the rage. The Third Order and other lay groups had brought about a complete change in popular taste. The poetry of the troubadours admired in Frederick II's day was out, and religion was in.

Cheap, mass produced block-books (*following page*) printed at this time reflect this reality. Looking rather like medieval comic books, they were written in vernaculars and profusely illustrated so common people could understand them.

The earliest were printed in Haarlem in the Netherlands perhaps as early as 1420, and they soon spread to Germany. A list of the eight bestselling titles (in no particular order) for 1440 would look like:

1. *Pauper's Bible (Book of the Poor)*
2. *Art of Dying*
3. *Book of Revelation*
4. *Dance of Death*
5. *Book of the Seven Planets*
6. *Story of David*
7. Aesop's Fable of the *Suffering Lion*
8. *Antichrist and the Fifteen Signs of the Last Judgment*[5]

Today this would be considered heavy reading, but not then. Likewise, in the late Middle Ages, a card game based on Christ's Second Coming would have been right in the mainstream of popular culture.

It's impossible to do justice to this topic in a short space. The classic, Huizinga reference in the bibliography should convince doubters of the pervaisivness of religion in everyday life during this era. You'll certainly be surprised at what you find there.

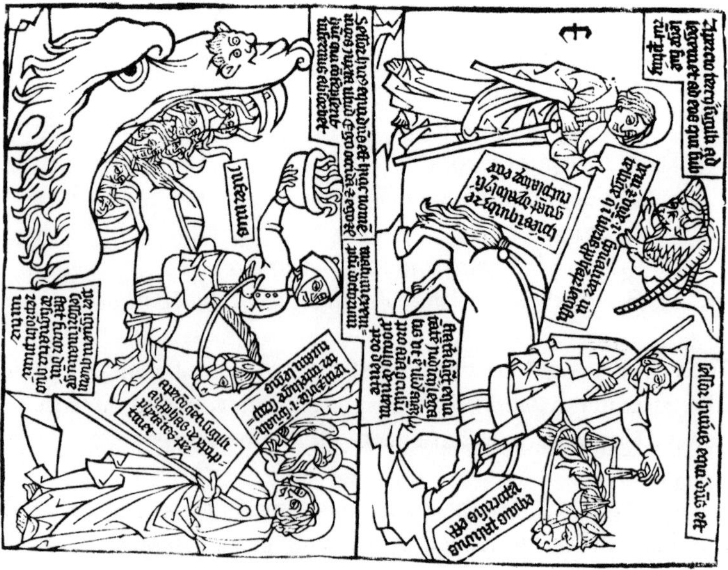

A Block-book depiction of the Four Horsemen of the Apocalypse, looking like a modern comic book.

Bibliography

Gertrude Bing, "The Apocalypse Block-Books and Their Manuscript Models." In *The Journal of the Warburg and Courtauld Institutes*, 30 (1967), pp 104-37; and 31 (1968), pp 103-47.

Maurice Chaume, "Une prophétie relative à Charles VI." In *Revue du Moyen Âge latin*, iii, (1947), p 27-42.

Emil Donkel, "Studien über die Prophezeiung des Fr. Telesforus von Cosenza, O.F. M." In *Archivum Franciscanum Historicum*, (1933) An. xxvi, p 33-49.

Michael Dummett, "History and Mystery." In *The Game of Tarot from Ferrara to Salt Lake City*, (Gerald Duckworth and Co., 1980).

Erwin Herrmann, "'*Veniet Aquila, de cuis volatu delebitur leo*': Zur Gamaleon-Predigt des Johann von Wünschelburg." In K. Schnith, ed., *Festiva Lanx: Studien zum Mittelalterlichen Geisteleben*, (Munich: Salesianische Offizin, 1966), pp 95-117.

Johann Huizinga, "The Vision of Death" & following. In *The Waning of the Middle Ages: A Study of the Forms of Life, Thought, and Art in France and the Netherlands in the XIVth and XVth Centuries*, (London: Edward Arnold, 1963), chapts XI-XVII.

Helga Lengenfelder, *Die lateinisch-deutschen Blockbücher des Berlin-Breslauer Sammelbandes, Staatliche Museen zu Berlin - Preussicher Kulturbesitz, Kupferstichkabinett, Cim 1,2,5,7,9,10,12.*, (München: 1992).

Kaminsky, Bilderback, Boba, Rosenberg, *Master Nicholas of Dresden: The Old Color and the New*, Transactions of the American Philosophical Society, n.s., 55.1 (Philadelphia, 1965).

Bernard McGinn, "Political Prophecies: French Versus German Imperial Legends, & Apocalypticism, the Great Schism, and the Conciliar Movement." In *Visions of the End: Apocalyptic Traditions in the Middle Ages*, (Columbia UP, 1979).

_____, "Portraying Antichrist in the Middle Ages." In *The Use and Abuse of Eshatologyin the Middle Ages*, ed. D. Verhelst et al. (Leiden, 1988).

David Parlett, "Simple Tricksters." In *The Oxford Guide to Card Games*, (Oxford UP, 1990).

Marjorie Reeves, "The Second Charlemagne." In *The Influence of Prophecy in the Later Middle Ages: A Study in Joachism*, (U. Notre Dame Pr., 1993).

Frederick van der Meer, "The First Block-book." In *Apocalypse: Visions From the Book of Revelation in Western Art*, (Alpine Fine Arts, 1978), chapt XVI.

Internet

Note: There's no need to type this yourself. Current links to these and future sites, as they become available, can be found at: http://tarot-cards.com

Biblia Pauperam
http://www.knight.org/advent/cathen/02547a.htm
Book of the Poor
http://www.lang.uiuc.edu/LLL/etexts/bp-eng.html
Dance of Death
http://www.knight.org/advent/cathen/04617a.htm

Translations

1. Karolus filius Karoli, ex natione illustrissimi Lilii habens frontem longam, supercila alta, oculos longos, nasum aquilinum, circa sue etatis annum xiii coronabitur. et in anno xiiii, magnum exercitum congregabit omnesque tirampnos sui regni destruet. [Et morte percuciet eos; fugientes in montibus et cavernis abscondentur a facie ejus.] Nam ut sponsa cum sponso sic erit justicia sociata cum eo; usque ad xxiiii annum suum deducet bella, subjugans Anglicos, Hyspanos, Aragones, Burgales, Lungobardos, Ytalicos; Romam cum Florentia destruet et igne

comburet. [Poteritque sal seminare cum arena habundans super terram illam, pravos clericos qui sedem apostolicam petri et pauli invaserunt morte percuciet eos. Endemque anno,] duplicem coronam obtinebit, postmodum mare transiens cum exercitu magno intrabit Greciam. Et Rex Grecorum nominabitur. Caldeos, Thucenos, Yspanos, Barbaros, Palestinos, Giorgianos subiugabit, faciens edictum et quicunque Crucifixum non adoraverit morte moriatur et non erit qui possit ei resistere, quia divinum brachium semper cum ipso erit et fere dominium universe terre possidebit. His factis sanctus sanctorum vocabitur, veniens ad sanctam Jerusalem et accendens ad montem Oliveti, orans ad ad Patrem deponensque coronam de capite, Deo gratias agens cum magno terremotu, signis et mirabilibus, emittet spiritum suum anno regni xxxi. Hic coronatus erit ab Angelico pastore et primus Imperator post Federicum tercium, post presens scisma et tribulationes et persecutiones pseudo-prophetarum et dicti Federici.

2. unus quidam ... ludens ad cartas ludum vocatum imperatoris.

3. Gamelon, beatus vir et excellentis religionis, consanguineus Bonifacy pape qui sanctus est, habuit quandam visionem de statu ecclesie quem habitura esset futuris temporibus ante diem nouissimim, et est visio talis.... Et dixit masculus ad Gamaleon: Respice ad meridiem. Et accessit vir armatus, qui fuit vestitus rubeis vestimentis, et habuit coronam de rubino. Et in corona eius fuit scriptum: Sub pedibus meis debent esse omnia regna veniam quidem de campo lily. Et vir armatus in sinistra manu habuit pomum, et in dextra gladium cruentatum. Et masculuc dixit: Armatus vir est imperator qui veniet a meridie, qui incipet malum ecclesie et malum habebit ortum. Ille coronabitur a papa, et maiorem Ytaliam sibi subiugabit, et aufert potestatem a Theotonicis. Et hy Theutonici eligent sibi imperatorem de Alamania alta, id est Reno. Et ille faciet in Aquisgrano concilium, et ponet patriarcham in Maguncia qui coronabitur in papam. Et imperator electus inadet alium Romanum imperatorem et occident eum. Et Roma non curabitur, et sedes apostolica cooperietur, et omnis spiritualitos exibit a Maguncia. Et posses-

siones auferuntur ab ecclesia et occidentur sacerdotes... Fridericus, qui regnans regnabit, imperabit extendetque alas suas usque af fines terre. Cuius sub tempore summus pontifex et clerus dilapidabitur et dispergetur.

4. Il étoit tems de retrouver les Allégories qu'il étoit destiné à conserver, & de faire voir que chez le Peuple le plus sage, tout jusqu'aux Jeux, étoit fondé sur l'Allégorie, & que ces Sages savoient changer en amusement les connoissances le plus utiles & n'en faire qu'un Jeu.

5.

1. *Biblia pauperum*
2. *Ars moriendi*
3. *Apocalypse*
4. *Danse macabre*
6. *Historia David*
7. *Fabel vom kranken Lowen*
8. *Der Antichrist und die 15 Zeichen vor dem Jüngsten Gericht.*

Chapter Fifteen

The Fool

ONE CARD REMAINS – THE FOOL. TRADITIONALLY, IT STANDS APART from the rest of the deck, though some modern games make it the twenty-second and highest, trump. Originally it lost to every card, but could be played in place of any one of them. Because of this, another name for The Fool is The Excuse (Italian: *Scusa*, French: *Excuse*, German: *Sküs*). Fool is a poor translation of *El matto,* its name. A better rendering is Madman!

Such a card would seem to have little to do with Christ's Second Coming and the Millennium. But thinking allegorically, if Tarot's ordinary suits represent the secular world, and its trump suit the kingdom of heaven, then The Fool partakes of the properties of both. It's a picture card like a trump, and yet has a low value like a suit card. In the Middle Ages, one man was believed to have achieved this state, evidenced by the signs he bore on his body – St. Francis of Assisi.

> "After having fasted for fifty days in his solitary cell on Mount Alverna, and passed the time in all the fervor of prayer and ecstatic contemplation, transported almost to heaven by the ardor of his desires, then he beheld, as it were, a seraph, with six shining wings, bearing down upon

him from above, and between his wings was the form of a man crucified. By this he understood to be figured a heavenly and immortal intelligence, subject to death and humiliation.

AND IT WAS MANIFESTED TO HIM THAT HE WAS TO BE TRANSFORMED INTO A RESEMBLANCE TO CHRIST, not by the martyrdom of the flesh, but by the might and fire of Divine love. When the vision had disappeared, and he had recovered a little from its effect, IT WAS SEEN THAT IN HIS HANDS, HIS FEET, AND SIDE HE CARRIED THE WOUNDS OF OUR SAVIOR," (*opposite page*).

– *Legenda Sancti Francisci*

To many, St. Francis' stigmata were proof that in his lifetime he had imitated the purity of angels to become the perfect follower of Christ. Some Franciscans went further, believing he was literally *Revelation's* Angel of the Sixth Seal. In 1264, no less than the minister general of their order, St. Bonaventure wrote in his official biography of St. Francis:

"We may also truly say that HE [St. Francis] WAS TRULY SHADOWED FORTH by that other friend of Christ, the Apostle and Evangelist St. John, UNDER THE SIMILITUDE OF THE ANGEL WHOM HE [St. John] SAW ASCENDING FROM THE RISING OF THE SUN, HAVING THE SIGN OF THE LIVING GOD. Under this figure we may assuredly discern Francis, the servant, herald, and messenger of God..."

– *Ibid*

Petrus Johannis Olivi reiterated the assertion in his *Popular Apocalypse Commentary* and was posthumously censured for it. Churchmen ruled that Bonaventure's claim was metaphorical, while Olivi's presumed to be official dogma. To understand what the fuss was about, compare Bonaventure's statement with *Revelation*:

"After these things, I [John] saw four angels standing on the four corners of the earth, holding the four winds of the earth, that they should not blow upon the earth, nor upon

"HE BEHELD, AS IT WERE, A SERAPH, WITH SIX SHINING WINGS, BEARING DOWN UPON HIM FROM ABOVE, AND BETWEEN HIS WINGS WAS THE FORM OF A MAN CRUCIFIED."

> the sea, nor on any tree.
>
> AND I SAW ANOTHER ANGEL ASCENDING FROM THE RISING OF THE SUN, HAVING THE SIGN OF THE LIVING GOD; and he cried with a loud voice to the four angels, to whom it was given to hurt the earth and the sea, Saying: HURT NOT THE EARTH, nor the sea, nor the trees, TILL WE SIGN THE SERVANTS OF OUR GOD in their foreheads."
>
> – *Revelation* 6:12 - 7:3

As the incarnation of the Angel of the Sixth Seal, St. Francis becomes the protector of the servants of God, the inheritors of the Millennium, marking them with the "sign of God" (the Franciscan Rule?). In this capacity he is the both the initiator and witness to Tarot's story.

St. Francis in the *Divine Comedy*

IDENTIFYING ST. FRANCIS AS TAROT'S FOOL SEEMS ALMOST IRREVERENT, if not completely out of character. The Fools on the d'Este and Charles VI cards are court jesters, and those on the Budapest and the Marseilles cards wandering beggars. All wear foolscaps. And religious symbols are completely absent. Where are St. Francis' corded tunic, stigmata, or a bird or lamb, attributes frequently associated with him?

In fact, a completely secular description is perfectly reasonable. Consider, for example, Dante's treatment in Canto XI (*Paradiso*) of the *Divine Comedy.* Dante belonged to the Third Order, so you'd expect his treatment to be both knowledgeable and reverent. It goes:

> From that slope, there, where it breaks most
> In steepness, rose upon the world a sun
> As it does sometimes from over the Ganges.
>
> Thus, let him who speaks of that place
> Say not Assisi, which says little,
> But Orient, if he would speak properly.

He was not yet far distant from his rising
Before he made the earth to take
Some comfort from his mighty virtue.

For a certain Lady, he, in youth his father's
wrath incurred, unto whom, as unto death
The gate of pleasure no one doth unlock.

And before his spiritual court,
Et coram patre was unto her united;
So day by day more fervently he loved her.

She, reft of her first husband, scorned, obscure,
Eleven hundred years and more, had
Waited without a suitor till he came.

Here Dante introduces St. Francis (sun), his vow of poverty (Lady), Christ (husband) and God (*Et coram patre* – "in the Father's presence") without explicitly naming any of them. But he's just warming up. After two obscure stanzas describing poverty's abandonment, he continues:

So that I may not proceed too darkly, take
Francis and Poverty for these lovers
Henceforth in my speech diffuse.

Their concord and their joyous semblances,
Love, and wonder, and sweet regard,
Bringing forth a fount of HOLY thoughts;

True, he uses the word *holy*, but makes up for it with a lovers allegory seemingly mocking Francis' vow of chastity, which is worthy of *Revelation's* Marriage of the Lamb allegory. This is all the more surprising because St. Francis only tolerated two flesh-and-blood women in his life, his mother Pica, and St. Clare, the founder of the Poor Clares. Remarkably, the allegory is not Dante's invention, but St. Francis' own:

> "...he glorified in the privilege of poverty rather than any other thing, being wont to call it, now HIS MOTHER, now HIS SPOUSE, now HIS LADY..."
>
> — *Legenda Sancti Francisci*

Until you know Bernard, Giles, and Sylvester were Francis' first converts, and the Friars Minor went barefoot and tied their tunics with a cord, the next stanzas make little sense:

So much that the venerable Bernard
First bared his feet, and after such great peace
Ran, and running, thought himself too slow.

O wealth unknown! O veritable good!
Giles bares his feet, and bares his feet Sylvester
Chasing after the bridegroom, the bride delights
them so!

Then goes his way that father and master,
With his Lady and with that family
Now girding on the humble cord;

When you do, it's apparent their subject is the Rule, poverty and the order's growth, again without seeming to say so.

The next stanza alludes to an incident I'll take up shortly:

Nor cowardice of heart weighed down his brow
At being the son of Peter Bernardone,
Nor for appearing marvelously scorned;

And while the following lines seem to break the pattern, they're really the exception that proves the rule because they describe lesser-known figures who wouldn't be recognizable without religious symbols:

But regally, his hard conditions he
Disclosed to INNOCENT, and received from him
The first seal upon his ORDER.

After the people of poverty increased
Behind this man, whose admirable life
Were better sung in the GLORY OF HEAVEN,

A second crown from the ETERNAL SPIRIT,
Awarded by HONORIUS. reconfirmed
The HOLY PURPOSE of this CHIEF OF SHEPHERDS.

And afterwards, through thirst of MARTYRDOM,
In the presence of the haughty SULTAN, he
PREACHED CHRIST, and likewise others who
followed him.

When Dante returns to St. Francis, only one further mention of Christ is required to clarify the reference to his stigmata (final seal); his evangelism, humility and *Last Testament* require no religious terms at all:

And, finding the people too unripe for conversion,
And to not tarry there in vain, he
Returned to harvest the Italian fields,

There, on the rude rock 'twixt Tiber and the Arno
From CHRIST he received the final seal,
Which during two whole years his members bore.

When He who destined him to so much good fortune,
Was pleased to draw him up to the reward
That he merited by making himself lowly.

Unto his brothers, as to rightful heirs,
His most dear lady he did recommend
And bade they should love her faithfully;

And from her bosom the illustrious soul
Wished to depart, returning to its kingdom,
And for its body wished no other bier...

This is a remarkable summary of St. Francis' life. It succeeded in Dante's time because St. Francis' biography was known to everyone. For the opposite reason, readers frequently have trouble with it today.

The Madman

WHAT WORKED FOR DANTE, SHOULD ALSO WORK FOR TAROT. SINCE DANTE covered all the bases, one of his stanzas and Tarot's Fool should share the same reference – otherwise Dante missed something important in St. Francis' life. This something is the incident I skipped over about "appearing marvelously scorned." When Francis first summoned the courage to break with his father and follow Christ:

> "...he made his way to Assisi, where, when the citizens saw him, pale and meager in countenance, and changed in mind and character, MANY OF THEM JUDGED HE WAS OUT OF HIS SENSES, and began to throw stones and mud at him and to cry after him as a MADMAN. But the good servant of God, unmoved by all these insults, went on his way as if he heard them not.
>
> These cries soon reached the ears of his father, who ran to the spot, not to deliver him, but rather to oppress him more cruelly: for seizing him without mercy, he dragged him to his house, reproaching and tormenting him with words, blows, and bonds..."
>
> – *Legenda Sancti Francisci*

It took a few more days and incidents before the break with his father was complete, but this event marked a defining moment in Francis' spiritual life. The epitaph "madman" (*pazzus*) stuck. Francis occasionally used it himself when he wanted to make a point. To be called a madman became sort of a badge of honor among early Franciscans, signifying they had grasped St. Francis' teachings. Brother Juniper, of whom St. Francis said: "He would be a good Friar Minor who had overcome the world as perfectly as Brother Juniper," illustrates this:

"He [Juniper] stripped himself of all but his inner garment, and thus, passing through the city of Spoleto, he came to the convent. The brethren, much displeased and scandalized, rebuked him sharply, CALLING HIM A FOOL, A MADMAN, and a disgrace to the Order of St. Francis, and DECLARING THAT HE OUGHT TO BE PUT IN CHAINS AS A MADMAN."

– *The Little Flowers of St. Francis of Assisi*

In modern times, St. Francis has been called God's Fool, alluding to:

"If any man among you seem to be wise in this world, let him become a fool, that he may be wise. For the wisdom of this world is foolishness with God."

– *1 Corinthians* 3:18-19

This misses the point of the medieval stories. According to the *Oxford English Dictionary*, fool can have the two meanings:

1.a. One deficient in judgment or sense, ONE WHO ACTS OR BEHAVES STUPIDLY, a silly person, a simpleton. (In Biblical use applied to vicious or impious persons.)... 1709 POPE Ess. Crit. 625 For Fools rush in where Angels fear to tread...

†4. One who is deficient in, or destitute of reason or intellect; a weak minded or idiotic person. Obsolete except in NATURAL OR BORN FOOL, A BORN IDIOT (now rare except as a mere term of abuse)... 1540 Act 32 Hen. VIII c. 46 Ideottes and fooles natural... 1670 LASSELS Voy. Italy II. 212 THE PAZZORELLA, WHERE THEY KEEP MADMEN AND FOOLES...

Corinthians uses fool in the first sense. In medieval times, the second, almost never encountered today, was more common. In their stories, St. Francis and Brother Juniper are being compared with natural fools. The name for asylum (*pazzorella*), where madmen and fools were kept is comes from the same root as Francis' epitaph (*pazzus*). This is the true meaning behind "marvelously scorned," in Dante.

Medieval and Renaissance Fools

IN ROMAN TIMES, RICH MEN KEPT DWARFS, THE DEFORMED, AND NATURAL FOOLS (*nanus, moriones, stulti*, and *fatui*) as slaves in their households for amusement. Plutarch describes how, in the slave market in Rome, many buyers would pay no attention to the most beautiful girls and boys and would seek out horrible freaks and monstrosities. The greater the deformity, the higher their purchase price, Quintillian adds. This custom was revived in the medieval courts of Europe, lasting till the mid-seventeenth century and even longer in backward countries like Peter the Great's Russia.

There were three classes of fools. The first were dwarfs and the deformed:

> "One day, after the destruction of Victoria by the men of Parma, he [Frederick II Hohenstaufen] SMOTE HIS HAND ON THE HUMP OF A CERTAIN JESTER, saying 'My Lord Dallio, when shall this box be opened?' to whom the other answered, 'Tis odds if it be ever opened now, for I lost the key in Victoria.' The emperor, hearing how this jester recalled his own sorrow and shame, groaned and said, with the Psalmist, 'I was troubled, and I spoke not.'"
>
> – *The Chronicle of Salimbene*

Diego Velázquez's 1656 painting, *Las Meninas* shows the Spanish fool, a dwarf, in the company of the members of the royal family.

The second class of fools were men of sound mind who "acted the fool." One of the most famous of these was the wandering buffoon Gonella:

> "...a clever and industrious man, the inventor of many jests which adorned the histrionic art, and he also performed with wonderful ingenuity many laughable things by way of a joke, FROM WHICH... THERE SPRANG A NUMEROUS RACE OF ACTORS WHO DELIGHTED ITALIAN DESPOTS with their jocular inventions."
>
> – *The Fool*

We find more larceny and malice than humor in his jests today:

> "...he stopped to dine at a place called *Scaricalasino*, and played an odious trick on some peasants who were afflicted with goiter. He dressed up as a physician and persuaded the poor creatures to assemble together in one room and there carry out a prescribed treatment until he returned from Bologna to complete the cure.
>
> Having arrived at his destination he told the magistrate who was inexperienced and ambitious, that if he sent officers to *Scaricalasino* he would be able to arrest some villagers who were coining false money, knowing of course that his 'treatment' had been specially devised to make his 'patients' look as if they were doing so.
>
> When the trick was discovered Gonella was already in Florence, unrecognizable in a new disguise, but the villagers continued to expect the return of the great physician, meanwhile getting more swollen and more stupid every day."
>
> — *Ibid*

Because Gonella and his humor were models for the Italian courts where the game of Tarot was played, he may be the source of the wandering beggar on the Marseilles card (*right*),

...BUT WHAT ABOUT THE COURT JESTERS ON THE D'ESTE AND CHARLES VI (*right*) CARDS?

By far the largest number of fools were natural fools. We know this from descriptions of their exploits, and because many required special keepers to care for them. One of the most beloved was Bernardino, nicknamed "Little Fool" (*Il Matello*), a favorite of Isabella (née d'Este) Gonzaga, the Duchess of Mantua, and her brother Alfonzo d'Este, Duke of Ferrara.

Bernardino was both deformed and a natural fool, but he fit in splendedly with Italian high society. Twice, he was sent to cheer up the Duke when the latter took sick, and was so successful making him forget his illnesses that the Duke didn't want to give him up, and a courtier had to fetch him away. His talents included parody, especially delivering mock sermons as an amusement. Letters mention: "The venerable father, Bernardino Matello..." and that: ""His Majesty, Il Matello, is very well and is expecting to say High Mass..."

But Bernardino's – and many natural fool's – mainstay was writing burlesque letters. Isabella d'Este wrote the King of Hungary thanking him for sending a letter written by the Queen's (*Matto de la Regina*) Fool:

"...a letter which had caused her much amusement and had proved to her the fool was of good quality and capable of giving much pleasure."

— *Ibid*

Princes regarded a compliment to their fools as a compliment to themselves, and took pride in possessing rare specimens of folly or deformity. They valued their services highly, and loaned and traded them among friends. When Isabella's eldest son Frederic wrote his mother for money in 1518, she reproached him for his prodigal spending and warned him he'd have to cut back. She would pay for his fool – but not his tutor! Women could be fools too. Isabella had at least two; a Giovanna Matta and Caterina Matta were in her service at one time or another.

Since natural fools couldn't be held responsible for their behavior, they were free to speak their minds to anyone without fear of reprisal. And they were often credited with special gifts of insight akin to the poet's divine madness. In 1544, the story was told in Germany of how:

"...a bonfire was being made of Lutheran writings, when a fool appeared on the scene and said, 'It is light labor to burn books, but difficult to expel that which is in the head and heart,' pointed to his head and heart, and went away. He was reported to have been a natural fool from his earliest years."

— *Ibid*

Compare this with the following story about St. Francis:

"Having to preach on a certain day before the pope and the cardinals... he totally forgot everything he had [rehearsed] to say... and then, having invoked the aid of the Spirit of the Lord, he began at once to move the hearts of these great men to compunction with such fluency of powerful and efficacious words, as plainly showed that NOT HE, BUT THE SPIRIT OF THE LORD, WAS SPEAKING... fearing reproof from no man, he preached the truth with great confidence."

— *Legenda Sancti Francisci*

In his own time, St. Francis was reputed to be able to project himself in space and see into the future:

> "So fully did he possess the spirit of prophecy, that he foretold things to come, and beheld the secrets of hearts, and knew things absent as if they were present, and showed himself in a marvellous manner to those that were far off.
>
> For at the time that the Christian hosts were besieging the city of Damietta, the holy man was there, not armed with the armor of this world, but with the weapons of faith. The day appointed for a battle having arrived, and the Christians preparing for the conflict, the servant of God, when he had heard of it, began to weep bitterly, and said to his companion, 'If these fight today, the Lord hath revealed to me that our Christians shall not prevail; but if I tell them so, I shall be accounted a madman.'"
>
> — *Ibid*

From examples like these, the identification of St. Francis with the madman, natural fool and court jester becomes more understandable.

Medieval Folly

THE VISCONTI-SFORZA FOOL (*right*) DIFFERS FROM THE FOOLS ON OTHER EARLY CARDS.

Dressed in rags and wearing seven feathers in his hair, he is portrayed carrying a club. This is a medieval representation for folly, as on Giotto's early fourteenth-century fresco in the

Cappella dell'Arena in Padua. Giotto's figure also wears a feather headdress and carries a club – but is dressed like a woman. Gertrude Moakly has suggested the figure represents Lent, who had one feather removed during each week of the Ash Wednesday to Easter celebration. Additionally, she cites depictions of March with feathers, dressed in rags, and associations of Lent with March.

Echoes in Ancestor

SINCE THE FOOL IS NOT PART OF TAROT'S STORY, ITS ICONOGRAPHY IS MORE difficult than for other cards. One must rely on indirect arguments like the ones I've used out so far. It would be a real boon if The Fool were depicted in Ancestor. And perhaps he is! That is to say, a Franciscan, probably St. Francis, *is* portrayed there. Appropriately enough, he is shown (*following page*) with the elect who will inherit the Millennium, preaching from the eternal gospel:

> "And I beheld, and lo a lamb stood upon mount Sion, and with him an hundred forty-four thousand, having his name, and the name of his Father, written on their foreheads. And I heard a voice from heaven, ... as the voice of harpers, harping on their harps....
>
> These follow the Lamb whithersoever he goeth. These were purchased from among men, the firstfruits to God and to the Lamb: And in their mouth there was found no lie; for they are without spot before the throne of God.
>
> And I SAW ANOTHER ANGEL FLYING THROUGH THE MIDST OF HEAVEN, HAVING THE ETERNAL GOSPEL, TO PREACH UNTO THEM THAT SIT UPON THE EARTH, and over every nation, and tribe, and tongue, and people: Saying with a loud voice: Fear the Lord, and give him honor, because the hour of his judgment is come; and adore ye him, that made heaven and earth, the sea, and the fountains of waters.
>
> – *Revelation* 14:1-7

(mons Sion)

ISOLATED FROM ITS CONTEXT (*opposite page*), ANCESTOR'S DEPICTION OF ST. FRANCIS (*top right*) IS REMINISCENT OF THE FOOL. HIS COWL FORESHADOWS THE HEADDRESS OF THE BUDAPEST (*above*) CARD AND EVEN THE FANCIFUL ONE ON THE TAROT OF MARSEILLES (*right*).

Given the transformations between Ancestor and early Tarot cards it's not inconceivable that a Franciscan monk could become Tarot's Fool.

The Excuse

MORE THAN THE COWL, THE MENDICANCY AND ITINERANT LIFESTYLE of early Franciscans parallel that of Tarot's Fool. In St. Francis case, the resemblance goes even deeper. His biography is full of incidents like:

> "...partly induced by the love of poverty, partly by the delight which he took in the exercise of works of mercy, HE GAVE HIS OWN CLOTHES TO THE ONE WHO SEEMED MOST DESTITUTE; AND PUTTING ON THE POOR MAN'S RAGS, he remained there all day amidst these poor people..."
>
> "If he sometimes met with some one who in exterior habit seemed poorer than himself, he would immediately reprove himself, and exert himself to do the like."
>
> – *Legenda Sancti Francisci*

Francis was always trading down. His habit is preserved as a relic at the Sacro Convento in Assisi. Even allowing for the ravages of time, it's difficult to imagine he encountered many (materially) worse off than himself. The story is well known that the Friars Minor girded their habits with a cord because Francis encountered a man poorer than he doing so.

In his life, like The Fool in the game of Tarot, St. Francis, "lost to every one, and substituted himself in place of every one of them." A mere coincidence?

Bibliography

St. Bonaventure, *The Life of St. Francis of Assisi: From the Legenda Sancti Francisci*, reprint: (Tan Books, 1988).

G. G. Coulton, "The Chronicle of Salimbene, Thirteenth-Century Italian Franciscan." In *St. Francis to Dante*, (London: David Nutt, 1906).

Gertrude Moakley, "Il Matto." In *The Tarot Cards Painted by Bonifacio Bembo for the Visconti-Sforza Family*, (New York Public Library, 1966).

Enid Welsford, "The Professional Buffon, & The Court-Fool of the Renaissance." In *The Fool: His Social and Literary History*, reprint: (Peter Smith, 1966).

Internet

Note: There's no need to type this yourself. Current links to these and future sites, as they become available, can be found at: http://tarot-cards.com

Assisi
http://listserv.american.edu/catholic/franciscan/tour/tour.html

St. Bonaventure
http://www.knight.org/advent/cathen/02648c.htm

Civilization of the Renaissance in Italy: Ridicule and Wit
http://www.idbsu.edu/courses/hy309/docs/burckhardt/2-3.html

Dante
http://www.knight.org/advent/cathen/04628a.htm

Digital Dante: Home
http://www.ilt.columbia.edu/projects/dante/index.html

St. Francis of Assisi
http://www.knight.org/advent/cathen/06221a.htm

Brother Juniper in Assisi
http://ccel.wheaton.edu/u/ugolino/flowers/flow76.htm

Brother Leo
http://www.knight.org/advent/cathen/09173a.htm
Little Flowers of St. Francis of Assisi
http://ccel.wheaton.edu/u/ugolino/flowers/flow.htm
Little Flowers of St. Francis of Assisi
http://www.knight.org/advent/cathen/06078b.htm
Mystical Stigmata
http://www.knight.org/advent/cathen/14294b.htm
Salimbene on Frederick II, 13th Century
http://www.fordham.edu/halsall/source/salimbene1.html
Thomas of Celano: *First and Second Lives of St. Francis*
http://www.fordham.edu/halsall/source/stfran-lives.html

Chapter Sixteen

Loose Ends

I PROMISED EARLIER TO SAY MORE ABOUT ANCESTOR, AND HOW IT WAS FOUND. Now's the time. Most of the conclusions I've presented here were formulated long before I saw a single picture. I thought a common story was enough to explain Tarot's iconography then. Nevertheless, just to be thorough, I felt obligated to make an effort to look for picture evidence too. The problem was how. What I was looking for, if it existed at all, was likely to be buried somewhere in a museum collection – a veritable needle in a haystack.

As part of my research, I'd subscribed to a few Internet mailing lists, including one for medieval art history. One day, a cross-posting from another list appeared there, saying that an on-line version of The Index of Christian Art was available for a limited time, which by then was almost up. Nevertheless, there were a few days to go, and I decided to check it out.

The Index is a database of religious scenes described by keywords which you can search to locate images containing keyword objects. Looking up angel, for instance, leads to a vast number of pictures of angels created in seventeen different media.

When I tried it out, I got an encouraging number of matches but nothing conclusive. Unfortunately only a small part of the Index had been computerized. The rest was still on 3 x 5 cards, of which there are only four sets in Europe and North America. That was the bad news. The good news was that one set was at UCLA, only 45 minutes drive from my home! It would be criminal not to give it a try. So I called up and made an appointment to visit.

When I saw the Index for myself, I began to appreciate the magnitude of the problem before me. The keywords alone were stored in standard library card files which took up an entire wall of a 75-foot room. And there were 200,000 photos on 5 x 8 cards which hadn't been available on-line. I signed in and the librarian in charge explained the system and advised it might be a very slow process.

Luckily, it wasn't. After I got the hang of it, I found the photos, unlike the keywords, were grouped by manuscript. Since I wanted to see *Revelation* pictures, I had only to look up a subject occurring in most Apocalypses (illustrated *Revelation* books) and use it to find the manuscripts I was interested in. It's like using *Galaxy* to locate all the Astronomy books in the library. Once you've found the right book, you don't have to search again for *Star, Moon, Planet*, etc. They're somewhere in the volume you've found. The UCLA Index was letting me browse the shelves of dozens of major European libraries and museums.

Although I'd had trouble finding parking and arrived late, I managed to search six Apocalypses, and over 400 pictures in the few hours before the library closed. But nothing clicked. The Index stopped at the fifteenth century. Perhaps too early for what I was seeking? Or, maybe there was nothing to find? To speed my search, I'd restricted myself to the last century covered by the Index, but by quitting time there were still a few manuscripts I hadn't seen. I made another appointment to see them too, although the situation was beginning to look hopeless.

When I arrived home a message on my answering machine said some inter-library loans I'd requested had come it. Two of the books were on Apocalypses – which I'd just spent all afternoon looking at. I expected them to be full of pictures, but one had none at all. It was also fairly short, so I gave it quick scan when I picked it up the next day.

Anglo-Norman Apocalypses

READING THERE, I LEARNED THAT PICTURES DEPICTING EVENTS FROM *Revelation* are some of the oldest in Christian art. Mosaics depicting Christ with the four living creatures of the Tetramorph decorated the Basilica of St. Peter, and similar scenes adorned the church of St. John in Ravenna, in the mid-fifth century.

If you've seen any Apocalypse pictures, they were most likely from Beatus manuscripts. They make attractive book illustrations because they're done in a colorful, flat style that's reminiscent of primitive art. These manuscripts come mostly from tenth-century Spain. Beatus was the author of a *Revelation* commentary which the pictures illustrate, hence the name.

I'd found quite a few Apocalypses from the thirteenth and fourteenth centuries too. These are the so-called Anglo-Norman Apocalypses from England and France. Typically, they contain 80 or 90 hand-painted scenes and were first produced in the 1230's, possibly in response to Joachim of Fiore's prediction of Christ's Second coming in 1260.

Most Anglo-Norman Apocalypses follow one of two basic plans. The first is written in Latin and illustrates Berengaudus' *Apocalypse Commentary*. The complete commentary runs to 1,000 pages, so Apocalypses compromise by presenting verses from *Revelation* with an illustration and a few explanitory sentences from Berengaudus, in modular fashion. The technical term for the latter is a gloss, and is often found in medieval texts. The most famous gloss was the *Glossa ordinaria* of the entire Bible compiled by Anselm of Laon, France. The second type of Anglo-Norman manuscript illustrates an anonymous French prose translation of the *Glossa ordinaria*. The two glosses differ in their interpretations. Berengaudus takes the passage:

> "And the kings of the earth, and the princes, and tribunes, and the rich, and the strong, and every bondman, and every freeman, hid themselves in the dens and in the rocks of mountains."
>
> – *Revelation* 6:15

– as a reference to the rejection of the Jews, and the summoning of Romans Catholics to Christianity. The French gloss interprets the same verse as saints being severed from a society corrupted by Antichrist. Needless to say, the interpretations are illustrated very differently.

In general, Berengaudus' approach represented an older, more conservative view, popular in the monasteries, while the French prose gloss transformed *Revelation* into short, moralistic sermons, avoiding any historical or prophetic aspects. After a while the two styles intermixed, so in addition to the original forms, there are also Latin and French texts without a gloss, French texts with a Berengaudus gloss, and Latin texts with a French metrical translation, etc.

Although some Anglo-Norman Apocalypses reached Germany in the fourteenth century, they're unknown in Italy. That was why I wasn't finding anything at UCLA. Apparently I'd seen about all there was to see – except for one item. The book I was reading mentioned a handful of Apocalypses based on the commentary of Alexander the Minorite, or Alexander Laicus. These were described as being so far off the beaten track their illustrations even depicted popes and emperors! Two manuscripts were listed, one at Cambridge and another at Prague.

Alexander Laicus' Commentary

THAT I HAD TO SEE! SO THE FIRST THING I DID WHEN I VISITED UCLA again was to look up the Cambridge manuscript. It was from the thirteenth century and labeled Alexander Laicus, not Apocalypse, so I'd missed it before. Looking at some very dark photos I immediately spotted precursors of the Pope, Emperor, Lovers, Death, Tower, Star, and Sun cards.

Excited, and thanking my lucky stars I'd hadn't quit after the first day, I ordered copies of the pictures and resumed the search I'd left off before. The very next item on my list was from Prague and labeled Alexander Laicus in the Index – the other manuscript! If I hadn't had trouble with parking, I would have found it on my first visit. These pictures were even better than the

Cambridge ones. On the illustration where I'd found only Death before, Strength now also stood out clearly. And the Prague manuscript's Tower's illustration was much more revealing. In fact, this manuscript is what I've called Ancestor.

There are several other Alexander Laicus manuscripts. The illustrations I've seen from them suggest they're more like the Cambridge manuscript and are completely painted. Ancestor, of course only has line drawings and was probably left unfinished. And its text is replete with abbreviations – cryptic symbols, superscripts, arcs and slashes, as if scrawled by an impatient hand. Actually, this is more typical of medieval manuscripts than the flawlessly executed examples of medieval calligraphy reproduced on the pages of coffee-table books.

IMPORTANT PASSAGES (*below*) ARE HIGHLIGHTED BY POINTING FINGERS DRAWN IN BY READERS WHILE THEY READ.

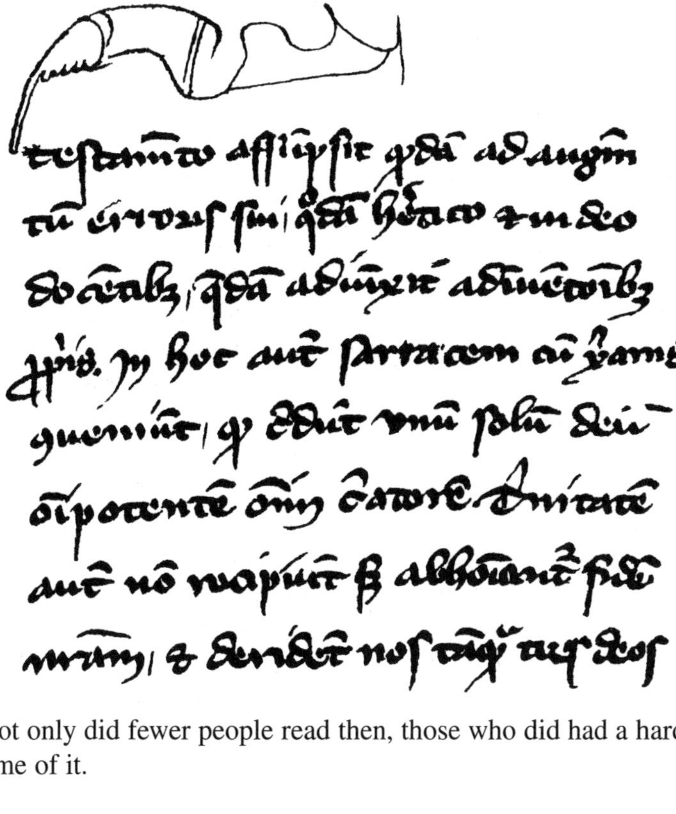

Not only did fewer people read then, those who did had a harder time of it.

Although now at Prague, Ancestor comes from Avignon, then the seat of the Papacy. It is bound together with the letters and papers of Cardinal Lucas de Flisco or Fieschi, who died there in 1336. As a part of the Prague Library's jubilee anniversary, it was reproduced by lithography and published as a book in 1873. Copies are not hard to find.

Little is known about its author Alexander Laicus other than what he himself tells us. In some manuscripts he's described as, "Alexander of the Order of Friars Minor."[1] In others he's, "a layperson (*laicus*) of no holy order, versed in nothing but the liberal arts..."[2] Other evidence places him in German Saxony, writing in the 1240's. Whether or not he was a member of their order, he had strong Franciscan sympathies. At the end of his commentary, St. Francis and St. Dominic are praised as the founders and upholders, after Christ, of the new Jerusalem. According to Alexander, the hopes of the world lie in the mendicants who will save mankind by the purity of their doctrine and sanctity of their example.

THIS IS ILLUSTRATED IN ONE OF THE FINAL SCENES OF ANCESTOR (*opposite page*) WHERE THE ELECT, DRESSED IN MENDICANTS' HABITS, ARE SHOWN WITH CHRIST (THE LAMB) AND THE WATERS AND TREES OF LIFE IN THE NEW JERUSALEM. THE HANDS AT THE TOP OF THE ILLUSTRATION ARE MEDIEVAL SYMBOLS FOR GOD THE FATHER.

Like Joachim of Fiore, Alexander adopted a historical approach for his commentary. And he used Joachim's concords occasionally, as in Chapter Four: "Of the concords between the reign of David and the reign of Jesus Christ his son [i.e. descendant]." Likewise he quotes from Joachim of Fiore's spurious commentary *On Jeremiah*, and identifies Frederick II as force working against the Church.

But mostly, Alexander presents a painfully slow retelling of world history up to the reign of Frederick II Hohenstaufen in his own time. I say slow, because by Chapter 20 (of 22) he's still on the second crusade and hopelessly out-of-sync with other Apocalypse commentaries. Thus, as I mentioned before, the people he identifies, have no significance for Tarot.

For Alexander, the Moslems and Persians were *Revelation's* beasts and dragons, and there would be a struggle between the Papacy and the Empire. But cooperation between the universal Church and the universal state against their common enemies, exemplified by emperors Constantine, Justinian, Charlemagne and Lothar III, would at last restore peace to the Church.

Thus, while his details are wrong, the general thrust of Alexander's commentary is in accord with Spiritual ideas. It's likely his Apocalypse circulated within the Franciscan cannon, and was avaiable either as the direct model for Tarot cards, or an "intermediate" from which they were later derived.

Legacy From the Middle Ages

SEVENTEEN OF TAROT'S TWENTY-TWO MAJOR ARCANA CARDS (bulleted below) have antecedents in Ancestor. This is far too many to be mere coincidence.

Card	Meaning
The Magician	Appearance versus Reality
• The Popess	Church
• The Pope	Angelic Pope
• The Empress	Empire
• The Emperor	Third Frederick
• Temperance	Purification of the earth
• The Lovers	Triumph over evil
The Chariot	Last World Emperor
• Strength	Daniel
The Wheel of Fortune	Ezechiel
• The Hermit	St. John / *Revelation*
The Hanged Man	Martyrs and Heroes
• Death	Sinners will perish
• The Devil	Followers of Satan
• The Tower	Great Earthquake
• The Star	Stars falling to earth
The Moon	Full Moon like blood
• The Sun	Sun black as a sackcloth
• Judgement	Resurrection
• Justice	Archangel Michael
• The World	New Jerusalem
• The Fool	St. Francis of Assisi

The conclusion is inescapable that Tarot is about the last times, that *Revelation* furnished its metaphors, and Ancestor its imagery. To help you recollect how this all came to pass, I've constructed the following summary timeline:

before 1100: St. Augustine dominates biblical exegesis. His doctrines discourage the literal interpretation of *Revelation* and deny there will be any Millennium for the Saints.

1190-1210: Joachim of Fiore introduces a "scientific" alternative to St. Augustine's interpretation which makes *Revelation* the key to history and the future struggles of the Church. He teaches that Antichrist's coming is imminent and will bring to fruition an age of the Holy Spirit presided over by two orders of monks.

St. Francis and the Friars Minor bring apostolic poverty and evangelical preaching into the bosom of the Church. The mendicant orders grow rapidly and render valuable services to the popes.

1240-1250: Frederick II Hohenstaufen wages war on northern Italy and the papacy. He becomes "one of many Antichrists" in the anonymous *On Jeremiah* prophecy, and the inspiration for the Third Frederick in future ones.

Influenced by Joachim and the Franciscans, Alexander Laicus writes a commentary on *Revelation* which is illustrated in some Apocalypses.

1280-1300: Poverty and "poor use" become a major issue dividing the Franciscan order. In the eyes of conservative Spirituals, Pope Celestine V becomes the model for a future Angelic pope who will embrace poverty.

Petrus Johannis Olivi's *Popular Commentary on the Apocalypse* explicitly writes the St. Francis (as the angel of the Sixth Seal) and the Friars Minor into Joachim's scenario of the future struggles of the Church.

1320-30: Pope John XXII condemns the Spirituals and launches an Inquisition against their followers from the Third Order in southern France. Beguines and fraticelli denounce him as a heretic and false pope.

Ancestor, an Apocalypse illustrating Alexander Laicus's commentary, is created for a cardinal in Avignon. It becomes part of the Franciscan cannon and copies reach northern Italy and Germany over the next 50 years.

1350-65: John of Rupescissa combines Joachim's, Olivi's, Arnold of Villanova's, and his own prophecies into a pro-French last times scenario which is widely read.

1375-85: The Great Schism of the Catholic Church splits the papacy between several claimants. Speculation about Antichrist and the last times is renewed in Telesphorus of Cosenza's popularization of John of Rupescissa's ideas.

A Second Charlemagne Prophecy about a French Last World Emperor appears in public records for the first time in France. It becomes the most widely disseminated prophecy for the next two centuries.

John of Rheinfelden sees "moral lessons" in the playing cards just introduced into Europe from the Islamic world.

1415-25: Cardmaking becomes a profession, and cards become affordable, even for common people. Playing cards is a popular pastime for all social classes.

Karnöffel, a German card game, introduces Emperor, Pope, Devil, etc., trumps with complicated, possibly religiously motivated rules, into card play.

Poverty and prophecy pervade popular sermons in Italy, Spain, and France. Illustrations portraying the pope as Antichrist are carried in the streets in Prague. Stories about religion and the last times are bestsellers in popular block-books printed in Germany and the Low Countries.

A New Card Game

AT THIS POINT ALL THE PREREQUISITES FOR TAROT ARE IN PLACE. WHETHER Ancestor was then used as a direct model for playing cards, or for placards carried in the streets, memory aids, etc., which in turn became Tarot cards is impossible to say. The essential point is that Tarot's story and images existed long before the game itself. No one sat down and dreamed them up after deciding upon the rules of play. They're just too complicated.

Something similar happens in nature all the time. If you investigate how land animal's lungs or insect's wings developed, you'll find they didn't begin with that "in mind." Rather, they once were something else, the lung a swim bladder and wings temperature regulators, and rapidly transitioned to their present function when the right opportunity presented itself. That's nature's way of getting from there to here with the least amount of effort. Like evolution, culture is a series of gradual steps built on what's gone before. Why shouldn't similar principles apply?

Thus, I'm in agreement with the premise of the chance hypothesis:

> "It was necessary to choose, for the picture cards, a series of very definite subjects, that could be easily distinguished, and with each of which could be associated a name that could be used to refer to the card."

but not its conclusion:

> "...they were precisely the sort of subjects which any fifteenth-century Italian, faced with the problem of devising a sequence of twenty-one picture cards, would have been likely to select."

In fact, Tarot cards present a strong *a priori* argument against this hypothesis. Twenty-two trumps are so many. Why wouldn't a number closer to thirteen, as in modern trump games, have sufficed? There would be less to remember and play would still be challenging. On the other hand, if 22 were already familiar for some reason, then reducing their number would make it hard to remember which ones were left out. It was best to "let sleeping dogs lie." In this way, old meanings were grandfathered in to the new idea of trumps, and people found that they knew practically everything required to play an interesting and novel game.

The possibility that Tarot is an Italian response to the German game of Karnöffel, substituting its own version of the last times scenario and 22 trumps for their German equivalents, can't be ignored. Early Tarot cards certainly show many German influences. But the number of simultaneous discoveries is legion. The seminal ideas might have just "been in the air" given the tenor of the times. It seems unlikely we'll ever know.

Where was Tarot invented? Definitely Italy, for several reasons. Consider The Hanged Man. His torture-punishment was unique to northern Italy at the time Tarot cards were first created. In the same vein, Tarot's Last World Emperor is the French one, popular in France and Italy, but not Germany – the other likely candidate for its place of origin. The Fool, too, shows a reverence for St. Francis consistent with popular sentiment in France and Italy. These clues point to Italy, inasmuch as France was decades behind her in embracing Tarot. Finally, of course, the earliest written records of Tarot come from northern Italy.

Who invented the Tarot card game? As opposed to the iconography of the cards. Most likely card makers who saw in popular religion an opportunity to create and sell new products to their regular customers. This solves the distribution problem, which otherwise would have to rely on the prestige of nobles and their courts. But an economic motivation may have been secondary.

The Brethren of the Common Life in Zwolle, the Netherlands, were a religious group whose members divided their time between teaching, meditation, and making and selling block-books. The latter were seen as useful tools for spreading God's word. A similar group in northern Italy might have introduced Tarot for analogous reasons. Block-book printing and card manufacture use the same technology and skills.

Despite its religious message, I think it's unlikely the official Church had anything to do with Tarot. This was precisely the kind of scandalous, over-zealous activity the Church was trying to get under control, and which would increasingly plague it until the Protestant Reformation presented even greater challenges. The religious message is another reason why I don't think Tarot was created in noble's courts. It certainly wasn't in their interest to promote spiritual over temporal power. And the ideals of the *Romance of the Rose* (*Roman De La Rose*) and Boccaccio's *Decameron* were more agreeable to sophisticated tastes then.

Eventually, nobles and their courts did pick up on the new card game everyone was playing, probably not long after is creation, because it was their business to know everything that was going on. And card makers would certainly have sought them out as customers for a new product. Thus it's easy to see how they might get credit for Tarot's invention.

Continuing the timeline further, we find:

1440-60: *Triumphi*, the original name for Tarot cards, are mentioned in account books of northern Italian nobles.

The Viscontis are replaced by the Sforzas in Milan.

Inquisition records mention fraticelli for the last time.

1520-30: French King Francis I, a Visconti heir, captures and then loses Milan. He brings Italian art and culture back to France and allies himself with the d'Estes of Ferrara.

Surviving early Tarot decks date from this time.

circa 1630: The Tarot of Marseilles deck is created. It supplants all other decks by the eighteenth century.

1770-1785: Court de Gébelin rediscovers Tarot and proclaims its Egyptian origin. His writings initiate the scientific and occult study of Tarot cards.

Alleitte invents the fortune-teller's spread, and, influenced by de Gébelin, revises his game of Ettiella to become Tarot.

circa 1810: Empress Josephine Bonaparte's interest in fortune-telling spreads to French high-society, forever linking Tarot and the occult in the popular imagination.

The First Tarot Decks

AFTER 1800 THE HISTORY OF TAROT IS WELL KNOWN, SO I'VE ENDED the timeline there. If you're interested, Kaplan's coverage in the *Encyclopedia of Tarot* is especially thorough. However, the last few entries in the timeline require some comment.

If, as I conjecture, the earliest surviving decks date from Francis I's time, and not earlier as currently believed, there's a question of what the first Tarot decks really looked like. On the earliest surviving cards, only traces of medieval and religious iconography remain. Was this always the case? Or did earlier cards look more like Ancestor?

The Renaissance made a conscious break with its medieval past. In fact, "Middle Ages" is their pejorative term for the backward period between the brilliance of classical antiquity and their own enlightened age. In scholarship, they threw away much of the hard-won knowledge of the classics gleaned from the medieval Islamic world, and sought it anew in Greek originals. And in art, they invented new conventions and techniques for capturing reality with *chiaroscuro* and perspective. In the process, many medieval symbols fell victim to their passion for portraying of the world as it appeared. Or were replaced by more prestigious models from classical antiquity.

So it's not without interest to wonder what cards from 1520-40 might have in common with those of 1420-40. Especially when there's reason to believe the original motivation for Tarot's iconography was completely forgotten a century or so after its invention. A long, angry poem by Flavio Alberto Lollio titled *Invective Against the Tarocco Card Game* (*Invettiva contra il Giuoco del Taroco*) published in Venice in 1550 concludes:

"He showed well he had little to do,
And was assuredly a big shit-brain,
The one who invented such nonsense;
I think he must have been a painter
Common, out-of-work, and penniless,
Who, to earn his bread, began making
This gibberish for children.

What else do The Trifle [Magician] and Fool say,
If not that he was a deceiver and a cardsharp?
What do the others mean, The Popess,
The Chariot, The Traitor, The Wheel, The Hunchback;
Strength, The Star, The Sun, The Moon,
And Death, Hell [The Devil], and all the rest
Of this bizarre merry-go-round,
If not that he was a daydreamer,
Full of smoke, caprice and idle tales?
And it's true from the one who empties
    the wine flask [Temperance],
He clearly demonstrates he was a drunkard;
And what a fantastic and bizarre name
Tarocco, without any entomology,
Making evident to everyone that fantasies
Have spoiled and ruined his brain."[3]

If the artists who manufactured them had as little understanding of their subject as the author of this poem, it's not surprising why so many contrary and inconsistent symbols turn up on Tarot cards.

On the other hand, the iconography of the Tarot of Marseilles deck suggests Tarot's meaning was still known at a later date than the poem. The Marseilles deck is probably a direct descendant of the New Haven one; the agreement between many of their cards is spectacular. Where differences arise, they're usually additions. The Marseilles Lovers card adds a priest to the New Haven scene, for instance. Its Moon card adds two dogs, The Star card a bird, and The Tower may add a lightning bolt. These are just the kinds of changes expected when one deck is derived from another.

On the other hand, the Marseilles Chariot card is closed, while the New Haven one is open at the sides, as can be inferred from the little feet at the top of the surviving card fragment. But this might merely reflect a style change in chariots, like the priest on the Lovers card.

The important point is that the Marseilles additions are either modernizations or bring the deck's meaning into closer agreement with Ancestor, so the newest of decks agrees best with their oldest source. (The Marseilles World card may be the most striking instance of this, but since its New Haven counterpart has not survived, it's impossible to say for sure.) This suggests to me that the Tarot of Marseilles revisions were made by someone familiar with the original purpose and meaning of Tarot. Someone outside of Italy, after 1600. For the fact is indisputable, that whatever the circumstances, the Tarot of Marseilles deck was created a master of symbolism. Its imagery echoes *Revelation's* text in a one-for-one correspondence down to the tiniest detail.

Popular Culture

WRITING THE HISTORY OF POPULAR CULTURE IS ALMOST AN IMPOSSIBILITY. Ideas of great men are preserved in their writings or chronicles of their deeds, but who speaks for the rest of us? Until a century ago history was exclusively about nations, laws and wars. Everyday matters were only captured accidentally in the course of more important pursuits.

So today, we find ourselves repeating strange rituals we can scarcely comprehend, let alone trace to their origins. For, by a strange perversity, customs that once made perfect sense are broken down into half-digested fragments and carelessly reassembled by later generations – turning them inside out in the process. Who would guess that today's dunce began his career as the great Franciscan Scholastic, Duns Scotus, who confounded his age by proving the doctrines of the Christian faith are beliefs (*credibilia*), to be accepted on the authority of the Scriptures and the Church, but which cannot be demonstrated by reason?

And once a good story gets started, momentum can literally carry it along for centuries; from Nero to Antichrist to Frederick II and his descendants – 1500 years – in the case of Tarot's Emperor. Or, long dormant, it may unexpectedly pop up again when a Shakespeare hybridizes John Ball with Jack Cade to "kill all the lawyers," and schoolchildren invoke Ball's name to slay their imaginary enemies.

The process continues to this day. One might think that the Apostle John and the *Book of Revelation* would be safe from tampering, but a visit to a neighborhood bookstore turned up a title claiming that *Revelation* reveals the seven levels of spiritual evolution to the children of the Age of Aquarius – melding eastern wisdom with Christian dogma in the best syncretic tradition of New Age literature. By the way, the illustrations are excellent!

In a religious bookstore, I found the Last World Emperor is still alive too. Two booklets from there predicted scourges for mankind, the purification of the world, and, after much suffering, a golden age for the Church brought about by a Great French Monarch. The Angelic Pastor or Shepherd also received passing mention, and a "third ruler of Aquila" [Third Frederick] had become a future president of the United States! But other than new identifications for the players, no creative additions had been made to the stories since the fifteenth century.

Interestingly enough, the first book appeared shortly after World War II, and is eerily prophetic about the European Theater of that conflict. The second appeared fourteen years later. What a world of difference this makes! The later author faces troubling questions: "What will the United States and the Soviet Union be doing while all this is going on? What is the role of democracy and communism in a prophecy about world monarchy? Why does the Angelic Pastor merit holiness for his strictness in rejecting Church reform?" At this rate, it seems unlikely the genera will last much longer. But who can tell?

Can There Be Any Doubt?

TAROT HAS BEEN DRIVEN BY THE SAME FORCES, ESPECIALLY IN THE LAST CENTURY – and the rate of change is increasing. Hardly anyone plays this oldest of card games, at a time when more Tarot decks are sold than ever before. The Marseilles deck, which in de Gébelin's day was synonymous with Tarot, now competes with hundreds of more exotic offerings, many provided with elaborate pedigrees proving they're the true article. Indeed, today, Tarot decks can be organized around almost any theme or iconography, and practitioners seem to be unaware of its history prior to the era of the Golden Dawn.

I expect that even after reading this book some of you still believe they're right, claiming perhaps, that de Gébelin was correct and the cards are Egyptian. But I've reproduced virtually all of the hard evidence he presents in support of that hypothesis here. The rest of what he has to say simply expands on its details and ramifications. Others will choose to remain with the chance hypothesis. Here again, I've tried to present, much of what its proponents have to say for it. So far, no camp has managed to find the crucial evidence which proves its own hypothesis correct and refutes all others. Until now.

Unlike many writers on Tarot, I haven't hedged my conclusions. I've used authentic historical and religious documents and images to establish unique meanings for each card, and held steadfast to them. The ensemble hangs together, and recounts (albeit obliquly) one of the greatest stories of all time. It accounts for all three canonical orderings of Tarot decks. And after adding a few missing cards, you could actually play a game or tell a fortune with cards made from the pictures I've shown in support of my thesis. Can other explanations of Tarot say the same?

Timothy Betts, Ph.D April, 1998

Bibliography

Bernard Bischoff, "Latin Handwriting in the Middle Ages, & Supplement." In *Latin Paleography: Antiquity and the Middle Ages*, (Cambridge UP, 1990).

David Burr, "Mendicant Readings of te Apocalypse." In *The Apocalypse in the Middle Ages*, R. K. Emmerson, B. McGinn, eds., (Cornell UP, 1992).

_____,"Respectable Apocalyptic." In *Olivi's Peaceable Kingdom: A Reading of the Apocalypse Commentary*, (U. Penn Pr., 1993).

Adriano Cappelli, *Dizionario di Abbreviature Latine ed Italiane, Sesta Edizione*, (Milan: Ulrico Hoepli, 1995).

Edward Connor, *Prophecy Today*, (Tan Books, 1956).

Michael Dummett, "The Order of the Tarot Trumps: Appendix." In *The Game of Tarot from Ferrara to Salt Lake City*, (Gerald Duckworth & Co., 1980), chap 20.

Yves Dupont, *Catholic Prophecy: The Coming Chastisement,* (Tan Books, 1970).

R. Freyhan, "Joachism and the English Apocalypse." In Journal of the Warburg and Courtauld Institutes, 18, 1955, pp 211-44.

Antonius Frind ed., *Scriptum Super Apocalypsim Cum Imaginibus,* (Prague, 1873).

J. P. Gilson, "Friar Alexander and His Historical Interpretation of the Apocalypse." In *Collectanea Franciscana*, ii. 20, pp 20-36.

Stephen Jay Gould, "Not Necessarily a Wing." In *Bully for Brontosarus: Reflections in Natural History*, (Norton & Co., 1991).

Montague Rhodes James, *The Apocalypse in Art*, (London, 1931).

P. K. Klein, D. Kinney, J. Williams, Y. Christie, S. Lewis, and M. Camille in "Part II: The Apocalypse in Medieval Art." In *The Apocalypse in the Middle Ages*, R. K. Emmerson, B. McGinn, eds., (Cornell UP, 1992).

Peter Lorie, "Lincoln College MS illustrations." In *Revelation: St. John the Divine's Prophesies for the Apocalypse and Beyond*, (Simon & Schuster, 1994).
Leo F. Stelten, *Dictionary of Ecclesiastical Latin*, (Hendrickson Pub., 1995).
Frederick Van Der Meer, "Queen Elanore's Apocalypse." In *Apocalypse: Visions from the Book of Revelation in Western Art*, (Alpine Fine Arts, 1978), chap X.

Internet

Note: There's no need to type this yourself. Current links to these and future sites, as they become available, can be found at: http://tarot-cards.com

Anselm of Laon
http://www.knight.org/advent/cathen/01550b.htm
Glossa Ordinaria: Beginning of the Book of Daniel
http://ccat.sas.upenn.edu/rs/eam/daniel.html
Ecclesiastical Latin
http://www.knight.org/advent/cathen/09019a.htm
Index of Christian Art
http://index2.Princeton.Edu:4001/ALEPH/
Illustrated Manuscripts
http://www.knight.org/advent/cathen/09620a.htm
Manuscripts
http://www.knight.org/advent/cathen/09614b.htm
John Duns Scotus
http://www.knight.org/advent/cathen/05194a.htm

Translations

1. Alexander de ordine fratrum Minorum.

2. laicus nullius sacri ordinis nullaque liberali arte instructus.

3. Ei mostró ben d'hauer poca facenda
Et esser certo vn bel cacapensieri
Colui, che fu inuentor di simil baia:
Creder si dè, ch'ei fussi di pintore
Ignobil, scioperate, e senza soldi,
Che per buscarsi il pan si, mise a fare
Cotali filostroccole da putti.

Che vuol dir altro il Bagatella, e'l Matto,
Se non ch'ei fusse vn ciurmatore, e vn barro?
Che significar altro la Papessa,
Il Carro, il Traditor, la Ruota, il Gobbo;
La Fortezza, la Stella, il Sol, la Luna,
E la Morte, e l'Inferno; e tutto il resto
Di questa bizaria girando l'esca,
Se non che questi hauea il capo suentato,
Pien di fumo, Pancucchi, e Fanfalucche?
Et che sia ver, colei che versa i fiaschi,
Ci mostra chiar ch'ei fusse vn ebbriaco;
E quel nome fantastico, e bizarro
Di Tarocco, senz éthimologia,
Fa palese à ciascun, che i ghiribizzi
Gli hauesser guasto, e zorpiato il ceruello.

Index

The organization of this book is convenient for learning, but once understood, other arrangements of the material make equal sense. Thus, for instance, even though an entire chapter is devoted to Tarot's story, important references to it occur throughout the book. The index makes it easy to follow these threads. You may want to only study a particular card or deck or just look at their illustrations. Used in this way, the index becomes a mini-concordance for important themes.

A few word about strategy. Some terms like **Franciscan** capture only part of a concept; to find all relevant comments you should investigate: **Franciscan**, **Friars Minor**, **Spirituals**, **mendicants**, and perhaps **monks**. All of these, under the right circumstances, may refer to Franciscans. Other terms like **sermon** collect multiple concepts. No two sermons mentioned here are alike, they both endorse and opposing playing-cards, for example. But **sermon** illuminates the variety of subjects preached in the Middle Ages so well that it seemed counter-productive to further divide it into sub-categories. After you're moderately familiar with the material, you should be able to gauge the scope of each term in the index.

Lastly, pages containing illustrations and important tables are boldfaced. A single illustrated page typically produces several boldfaced terms. The Tarot of Marseilles Justice card illustration, for example, results in boldfaced **Marseilles** and **Justice** entries.

This book in Internet friendly...

Internet URLs are included in a special section of every chapter. In addition, the companion website:

http://tarot-cards.com

(don't forget the hyphen) maintains current links to all sites listed, so you don't have to waste your time typing and you'll always be able to find them.

And, you can consult, and download if you wish, your own copy of the Internet Psychic Advisor describeded in the book – free!